Also by Jerry Ellis:

Walking the Trail
Bareback!

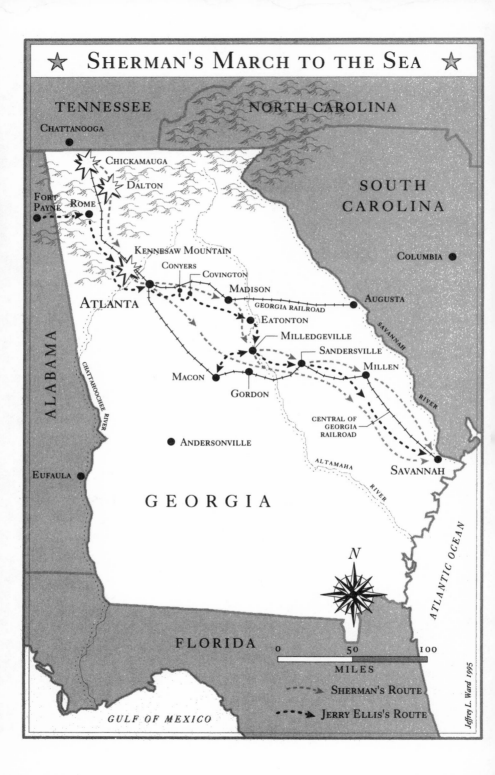

★ SHERMAN'S MARCH TO THE SEA ★

TENNESSEE

CHATTANOOGA

NORTH CAROLINA

CHICKAMAUGA

DALTON

FORT PAYNE

ROME

SOUTH CAROLINA

COLUMBIA

KENNESAW MOUNTAIN

CONYERS

COVINGTON

MADISON

ATLANTA

GEORGIA RAILROAD

AUGUSTA

EATONTON

MILLEDGEVILLE

SANDERSVILLE

MILLEN

MACON

GORDON

CENTRAL OF GEORGIA RAILROAD

ALABAMA

CHATTAHOOCHEE RIVER

ANDERSONVILLE

ALTAMAHA

SAVANNAH

EUFAULA

GEORGIA

RIVER

ATLANTIC OCEAN

N

FLORIDA

0   50   100

MILES

GULF OF MEXICO

SHERMAN'S ROUTE

JERRY ELLIS'S ROUTE

Jeffrey L. Ward 1995

Marching
Through Georgia

My Walk along
Sherman's Route

Jerry Ellis

with a new preface and epilogue

The University of Georgia Press
Athens & London

For Debi Anne

Published in 2002 by the University of Georgia Press
Athens, Georgia 30602
© 1995 by Jerry Ellis
Preface and Epilogue © 2002 by Jerry Ellis
All rights reserved
Printed and bound by Thomson-Shore

The paper in this book meets the guidelines for
permanence and durability of the Committee on
Production Guidelines for Book Longevity of the
Council on Library Resources.

Printed in the United States of America
02   03   04   05   06   P   5   4   3   2   1

Library of Congress Cataloging-in-Publication Data

Ellis, Jerry
Marching through Georgia : my walk along
Sherman's route / Jerry Ellis.
p.   cm.
Originally published: New York : Delacorte Press. 1995.
With new preface. Includes bibliographical references and index.
ISBN 0-8203-2425-6 (pbk. : alk. paper)
1. Georgia—Description and travel. 2. Sherman's March to the Sea.
3. Ellis, Jerry—Journeys—Georgia.   I. Title.
F291.2.E43 2002
973.7'378—dc21   2002069584

British Library Cataloging-in-Publication Data available

The original hardcover version of this text
was published in 1995 by Delacorte Press.

Preface

It's November 21, 2001, the day before Thanksgiving. It's been eight years since I walked the route of Sherman's March to the Sea from Atlanta to Savannah and seven years since *Marching Through Georgia* was first published. More has happened in American history since then than many of us care to remember. Indeed, the cliché is both profound and true: We are forever in the aftermath of the Twin Towers bombing in New York City on September 11 of this year. As General Sherman said about the Civil War, "War is hell." We now find ourselves engaged in a War on Terrorism. Like the Civil War, this current war has forced Americans to turn inward. What's at our core? What are our values? What are we willing to sacrifice to preserve our beliefs? What makes us distinct and holds us together as a nation in the midst of war's horror and tragedy?

A driving force in walking the route of Sherman's March to the Sea was to investigate these very questions as they pertain to Southerners and how we have evolved since the Civil War. While this book is interwoven with documented history and quotes from Civil War diaries, it also relies upon the stories of Georgians I met along the way to supply the living history, which addresses the depth of these questions. These stories are noses rough with warts as well hearts graced with love. None is short on passion, that sacred spark that thrived in the Civil War as brightly as today.

One of my great-grandfathers was a Rebel, wounded in the Battle of Atlanta when Sherman invaded that city. My other Southern great-grandfather died wearing a Union uniform. I do not judge the rightness or wrongness of the Civil War but approach it with respect, humanity, and—I hope—a strong dose of Southern humor. Didn't someone once say it's better to laugh than to cry?

Since I walked across Georgia, the Confederate flag has been removed in many places throughout the South, and just last month the Civil War Museum in Chattanooga closed its doors. Some shout that these changes are crucial steps toward greater American civility. Others mourn that America is becoming homogenized, that the New South—one we should all hope is free of racism and prejudice—is losing a part of its soul to the vacuum cleaner of political correctness. I trust that *Marching Through Georgia* inspires a candid look at the complexity of human nature and arouses the better parts of Southern and American hearts, roots of the same national tree, which has weathered more than one historic storm.

Acknowledgments

A man can dream that he walks alone. But he sometimes leans on the kind strangers he meets along the way. From the most tender place in my heart I thank all of you who helped me as I marched to the sea. Without your hellos and warm faces my Dixie trek would not have found the same magic.

I also must thank all the fans who wrote to me after they read *Walking the Trail* and *Bareback!* It was the excitement and humanity in those letters that made me feel that what I do as a writer reaches beyond my own needs.

Trish Todd, my editor and a fellow Southerner, deserves a band to march to her office and play "Dixie" for all her hard and enthusiastic work on my manuscript. Susan Ginsburg, my agent, has earned a star in the heavens for all her guidance over the years on my three books.

Thanks to my mother and my two sisters, Nita and Sandra, for all their support. It is, after all, a man's family who knows the valley he crosses before he even attempts to climb the mountain.

I must also thank Chris Grim, at my publisher, for his repeated encouragement. In fact, I thank everyone at Delacorte Press for all of their behind-the-scenes help. Without the book reps, publicists, and marketing folks a manuscript would be just a ship looking for water.

To my entire hometown of Fort Payne, Alabama, I salute all your support; I'd especially like to thank Marjorie Ferguson, Charlsie Shipp, Roland Walls, Don Lowery and Vince Dinardi.

My chiropractor, Dr. John Evans, gets a special note for helping keep my body in shape after all my long walks.

And you, dear reader, perhaps most of all earned a place in my heart. Without you, I would be but another man on that ship without water. Thank you for letting me into your life for a little while.

Author's Note

This book is based on my experiences walking the route of General Sherman's March to the Sea, although the names and other details of certain individuals have been changed.

Chapter One

The first time I heard of General William T. Sherman I was five years old. Daddy and I had stopped at a house to ask a farmer if we could fish in his lake and fry our catch on the spot.

"Yeah," he said, spitting tobacco juice over a hound curled up on the front porch. "But be right careful of your cook fire. That sage field and those pines yonder are as dry as hay. If they catch a spark, my whole place will blaze up quicker than Sherman burned Atlanta to the ground."

"Who's Sherman?" I asked Daddy, thinking it strange that I hadn't heard about the fire in Atlanta. My uncle had returned from there a few days before, after delivering a truckload of watermelons and corn, and he hadn't said anything about a fire, nor had the news I heard on the radio the night before, after *The Lone Ranger* and *Gangbusters*.

"Boy," said the old man, spitting tobacco juice over the dog again and onto the dirt yard swept clean. "You're old enough to catch a fish and you don't know General Sherman of the Union Army?"

"I start to school next year," I said, feeling that I wasn't very smart and hoping that this old man wouldn't be my teacher.

"He was a Yankee devil," said the old man, banging the tip of his wooden cane on the porch. "He came down here with a million men from the North and set our people on fire. When the wind's just right I can still smell 'em cooking in the kind of fire you can't put out. Just like the one in the middle of the sun or in a man and woman when they're crazy for each other. You know why he did it, boy?"

I was becoming afraid. The old man's voice was getting louder with each word and his hands were trembling. The cane pounded the floor again and the hound crawled under the porch. I wished the old man would join him so Daddy and I could walk away.

"He set the South on fire because we refused to lick the boots of Northern politicians!" he shouted. "We got minds of our own and we can rule ourselves!"

When the old man turned to spit again, I pulled on Daddy's pants pocket. I whispered that I wanted to go fishing.

"That fire didn't lead the colored people from their darkness as Lincoln said it would either!" yelled the old man. "They are cursed and the Bible itself says so. You read the Bible, boy?"

"No, sir," I said, pulling again on Daddy's pants. "I can't read anything yet."

"I'll be sure to close the gate to keep your cows in," Daddy said as his hand took mine to lead me from this old man, who wasn't anything like most elders I met. They were usually gentle and kind.

"Ain't worried about those damned cows," said the old man. "You teach that boy some history."

Daddy motioned for me to follow him, and I ran up ahead a few steps. When we got to the fence near the lake, I looked back to make certain the old man wasn't hot on our trail and beating the ground with his cane. The only other man I had seen that mad was a preacher in a sweat-soaked shirt. He swung his hands all about in the air, as if fighting a wasp that only he could see, as he shouted that the devil was coming down the road that very second to grab us by the throat and drag us to the fires of hell—unless we changed the way we were living right then and there. His threats only confused me because I thought it was the way I climbed trees, threw rocks, or jumped ditches that had gotten me into so much trouble. If I had to stop all of this to avoid hell I just knew I was already a goner.

I was as relieved to hear that we would not be going back to that church and that preacher as I was to look back from the lake and see no sign of the old man with the cane.

By sundown Daddy and I had caught three catfish, and we built a fire to cook them. I had always been awed by the power and beauty of flames, but that night I stood several feet away from the heat. I kept seeing Sherman in the flames with horns sticking from his head. I was afraid that he would spit fire onto my jeans or skin and I would become a fire like him. I wouldn't be able to put out the flames even if I jumped into the lake.

My older sister, Sandra, once told me that if I felt the presence of the Devil I could also find an angel who had come to help, if I'd just open my eyes wide enough to see the truth. I wanted to believe that as I looked at Sherman in the fire and hoped that one of the lightning bugs, flickering yellow in the Alabama night, was my angel. But hard as I tried, I couldn't find an angel's wings or halo, and Sherman's fiery horns got bigger with each piece of wood Daddy threw into the flames.

"Why are you standing over there?" Daddy asked. "Smoke getting in your eyes?"

I dug deep to find courage.

"No," I said. "I see Sherman in there. He has long horns sticking from his head and he wants to set me on fire."

Daddy told me that Sherman had been dead a long time and had turned to dust. He tried to explain about the War Between the States and how both my great-grandpas and many of my other relatives had fought bloody battles to protect the woods and creeks where I now played. I thought that was nice of them, especially since they didn't even know me.

"Sherman is buried and can't hurt you," said Daddy, handing me a plate with a fried catfish. "Do you understand now?"

"Yes," I said as Daddy poured ketchup on my fish.

But I sat on a log away from the fire. I could still see that old man pounding his cane against the porch, and horns rising in the flames. Then, when the wind shifted, it was not fish in the air that I smelled, but the flesh and bones of Southerners popping and crackling in boiling lard in a big black skillet.

* * *

When Daddy was three years old his mother died, and that same summer his house burned to the ground, leaving him and his nine brothers and sisters with nowhere to live but in the barn with their mule. Our own house was set afire by a bolt of lightning just two weeks after I learned about Sherman from the old man. I was sure that the devil-Sherman had somehow set this fire just as he had burned Daddy's home to ashes. We had no barn to turn to, and I feared that we'd have nowhere to live at all. But Daddy climbed into the attic with a bucket of water and threw it onto the fire. He put out the flames, but then he slipped on the wet boards, fell through the ceiling, and crashed into the piano and onto the floor. As Mother, my two sisters, and I helped him to his feet, I wondered when Sherman would strike yet again.

I was born and raised in Alabama, where my roots go back for hundreds of years: Daddy's grandmother was Cherokee, original owner of the Deep South. My non-Indian blood arrived in Dixie in 1740 and you don't get much more Southern than that. I'm part oak, lightning bug, rattlesnake, crow, snapping turtle, gentleman, and dirt—just whether it's the kind that you grow gardenias in is up to you to decide. I'll say this much plain and clear: *I love the South*. I'd die for it because it's the most sacred place in the world for me—*it's home*. Now, I haven't always felt this way about Dixie. No, sir, when I was a teenager I couldn't wait to get out of here. At the age of seventeen I ran away to New York City, thumbing the whole way. I stayed two weeks with my sister who lived there and I had a blast. I loved seeing all those exotic strangers speaking in tongues new to me. They treated me kindly, and not a single one of those Yankees had horns. Leastways, none that I could see.

   That New York trip give me hitchhiking fever and by the age of twenty-six I had thumbed enough miles all across America to circle the globe five times. I lived in several major U.S. cities, including Chicago, San Francisco, Denver, and New Orleans, and those I met often called me "Reb" or "Alabama." I didn't mind that they didn't let me forget where I came from, and most spoke in tones of affection. Those who had hatred in their hearts and saw the South as an open sore, I endured. Well, for the most part anyway.

I am now forty-five and have a deep need to better understand what it is to be a Southerner, because my father, who I loved more than anyone on earth, fell dead in our garden last summer while planting peas. He was my best friend, and I admired him. I loved him with all of my heart. In my eyes, he embodied the South.

No one in Daddy's family had gone to college. In fact, my great-great-grandmother couldn't even write her own name. Only last week I went down to the courthouse to check on some Civil War records, when I discovered that the oldest land deed on file there—1840—belonged to her and her husband. He could write his name, but her humble X stirred my heart. I think now might be a good time to confess a bit more about why that X moves me the way it does.

It's been said many times that Southerners have a legacy of feeling a bit inferior since we lost the Civil War. I don't doubt that. My childhood fears of Sherman were still-audible echoes of that war. The pain from old war wounds is still alive in Southern memory, and no wound is deeper than the one inflicted by Sherman's March to the Sea. Along a path 60 miles wide and nearly 300 miles long, from Atlanta to Savannah, 62,000 Union soldiers burned and plundered much of what stood in their way. Crush the South's determination and pride, the general reasoned, and it would fall to its knees; every individual in his path would feel stripped of dignity and honor. The Rebels would lose the will to fight, and the Confederacy would crumble, making a national hero of Sherman.

I also believe that, as a result, many of us Southerners have a great need to make something of ourselves. Our ancestors were poor and uneducated, but most importantly, they were defeated. I think this is especially true for us Southerners who are part Native American, because that race, like African Americans, has been defeated twice. My father, in fact, never showed any pride at all in being part Cherokee till after I became the first person in modern history to walk 900 miles along the Trail of Tears. I realize that I may sound a bit egotistical here, but frankly the idea for the journey came more from a need to prove something to myself and honor my ancestors than it came from courage or nobility.

My father was a living link with the past, but he also saw the future. "The South is changing," he would tell me. "Get yourself an education so you don't have to be a carpenter like me and your grandpa and your great-grandpa. You don't want to have to saw and hammer while standing in mud and cold wind, like I do, to make a living. Do something where you can use your mind and don't be afraid to take a chance if it's something you believe in. And have fun with it or you'll get old before your time."

He was pleased when I graduated from the University of Alabama and decided to become a writer, though no one in all our generations in the South had done such a thing. Daddy could read and write, but putting words on paper frightened him. Still, it didn't stop him from believing in me as a writer.

"I don't know how you do it," he sometimes said. "But one day your writing will pay off. As long as you work hard at it, you'll have a roof over your head and food to eat here with your mother and me."

I was honored that Daddy believed in me at a time when it seemed that the world didn't. The happiest day of my life was when Susan Ginsburg, my agent, phoned from New York to tell me that she had just sold my first book, and I got to tell Daddy the news and see the pride on his face. He gauged success by money and, at last, his only son's departure from the carpenters' tradition had paid off. That I could now make good on the loans he had granted me didn't hurt matters too much either. He was so embarrassed that the wonderful news from Susan had brought tears to his eyes, as well as mine, that he turned away so I couldn't see his face. But I simply put my arms around him anyway.

"Thanks for believing in me all these years," I said.

"Ah, hell," he said, not fooling me for a second about the great joy he felt inside.

When Daddy died, I wondered where I'd get the strength to go on. His faith in me had been my inspiration. He'd pushed me into the future. He'd shown me how to walk my own path, a path that led me all over the country, but somehow he must have known that that path would eventually lead me back home. He never showed me much of what he was feeling, and I confess I used to go to some lengths to get the closeness I craved. Sometimes I'd sneak up behind him at the barn where he thought he could be all alone with the birds and the towering pines. Daddy had hidden over a dozen bottles of wine he made from blackberries and muscadines in the hayloft, because that's how he hid wine from his father when he was a boy. Southerners, as they grow old, love to live as much in memories as the present. There at the barn he made up songs and sang them as he cracked walnuts on a big rock and ate them:

> Birds can't fly to the moon
> Rabbits don't sing to loons
> Fish don't bite at noon
> People don't really need spoons

Okay, he was no musical genius, and frankly, he couldn't carry a tune in a bucket. But every time I heard him making up a song it gave me a lift because I knew he was feeling carefree.

I needed to find a way to get that close to Daddy again. I couldn't spy on him, but maybe I could walk his path to honor him. And there is no path that would lead me closer to Daddy, closer to the heart of the South he embodied, and closer to my own future and the future of my native land than the path of Sherman's March.

I found myself wondering about its impact. What stories about the Civil War have been passed from generation to generation to those who live along that once-fiery route? What commonly held traditions hold Southerners together, and what traditions are changing? It seemed to me that if I could walk the path of the South's deepest wound, I could walk through the past and into the future. Then, I could move on.

I wish I were carefree enough right now to sing a playful song, but my proposed march is not without problems.

Chapter Two

I must face two primary problems before I march to the sea. First, there is the matter of my lover, Debi. I'm crazy about her, trust her, and have more fun with her than anyone I've ever known. We met two years ago at a publishing seminar in Denver where I spoke about my first book, *Walking the Trail*, which concerns my 900-mile walk along the Cherokee Trail of Tears. When I finished my speech, a young woman came up to me and said she wanted to give me a hug. I melted with her embrace. That evening we had dinner and went to my friend's house, where I was staying. I had trouble walking because only days before I had completed a 2,000-mile trek along the Pony Express Trail to do research for my second book, *Bareback!* It had been a rough trip both emotionally and physically.

"Sit on the couch," she said.

I did. She sat on the floor and removed my shoes and socks.

"Now close your eyes," she told me, "and don't open them till I say so."

In the darkness I heard her walk from the room, but her scent lingered, and I floated about in some exotic garden of anticipation. I have always liked to be titillated and enticed by the sensual and I hoped that she was preparing to lead my bare feet down a path they had never explored.

"What are you doing?" I called out.

"I'm almost ready," came her voice from the back of the house. "Don't open your eyes yet."

I couldn't control my fantasy and began to envision her long, slender body naked. Then I heard her footsteps approach and felt her sit beside me on the floor. She rolled my jeans up to my knees and her fingers were warm and strong as they lifted my feet and placed them into a pan of warm, soapy water.

"You can open them now," she whispered.

I did so and beheld the most beautiful woman in the world. She bathed my sore feet and rubbed them. She still wore her clothes, but there was a nakedness in her face, her heart, that I had rarely ever seen in other women. It made me want to be free of any pretense or walls that might get in the way of knowing *all* of her.

"No one ever did this for me before," I said.

"My first time to do it," she said.

Months later, after we had seen each other many more times, she moved from her home in Tacoma, Washington, to Alabama to live with me in the north wing of my parents' house, which sits in the woods in the valley between Lookout and Sand mountains. Save for the death of Daddy, these past two years with Debi have been the happiest times of my life. In fact, I have come to believe so much in romance and love since meeting her that I thought my third book should address the great love stories of history. I wanted to travel around the globe with Debi to visit the most famous lovers' sites and write about the adventures and the lovers we met along the way. I'll not pretend here. We're both intrigued and excited by sex and all its passion as part of love, and I had hoped to gather some of the juiciest erotic confessions ever made by lovers as we wandered across America and Europe and back home again. That Debi shares my urgent need to travel and experience life is one of the qualities I find irresistible about her.

But our plans to travel around the world together evaporated when Daddy died. I felt I must march across Georgia and explore my questions about being a Southerner or I would never be at peace with the passing of my father. And without that peace I couldn't offer Debi the quality of love she deserved.

*   *   *

"I want to go with you," Debi says as we crawl into bed after I tell her of my plan to follow Sherman to the sea. A whippoorwill calls from the April darkness, and the cool mountain air drifts through the open window.

"It's something I have to do alone," I say, easing my arms around her as I cuddle next to her naked back and long legs.

"Why alone?" she says, turning to face me.

The whippoorwill continues to call out as moonlight shines through the window onto her face and breasts, her nipples big and tender. I ease my fingers into the hair behind her ear and kiss the tiny beauty mark on her left cheek.

"I'm afraid you might get hurt," I say. "It's nearly three hundred miles across Georgia, and the sun will be pure hell. There will be chiggers, ticks, and snakes. We both know how scared you are of snakes. The South has its share of lunatics too. People will be more open to me if I'm alone, and if something bad happened to you on the hike I could never forgive myself."

"I'm more afraid of not being with you," she says, lowering her face into the pillow.

I run my fingers under her chin and gently lift her head so I can see her lips in the moonlight.

"I'll phone and write to you often," I tell her.

"That doesn't make my fear go away."

"What's the fear?"

"It isn't easy to talk about," she says.

I start to pull her into my arms, but she stiffens.

"I don't want you to be afraid," I say. "Please try to talk to me and understand that this isn't easy for me either."

"I'm afraid you'll be killed on this trip."

"Killed?"

"Just a moment ago, when I put my face in the pillow," she says, "I saw you walking down the road with your backpack on and somebody pointed a gun from a car window and shot you. You rolled down this bank into tall grass and couldn't get up."

"It's only an anxiety fantasy, your mind's way of dealing with emotion," I say, not totally believing myself.

"Maybe. Maybe not. I've had other intuitions that came true."

"I can't deny that, but . . . Debi, despite all the logical reasons I have for why I must do this walk alone, I must tell you there's something about it that's pulling me that I can't explain. As much as you understand me you may think it a bit strange when I tell you that I sense my father's spirit wants me to make this trek. Twice now I've had a dream in which I see Daddy standing in a cornfield. He's looking right at me and pointing at something. When I turn to see what he's pointing at, I wake up. It's like he's trying to reach me from the other world, and I've got to see what he's trying to show me. I've got to get to the bottom of this mystery."

Debi liked Daddy, and I hope telling her about this puzzling dream will help her better grasp my need to make this journey.

"I can see how the dream of your father calls to you," says Debi, sitting up in bed. "And I can't blame you for wanting to follow your heart. Most people won't or can't do that, and it's one of the strengths about you I find so compelling. But there's so much about you being a Southerner and why it's so important to you that I simply don't understand."

"Like what?"

"Maybe it's because I grew up in the Northwest," she says, "and my family moved around a lot, but I don't understand your obsession with living where you were born and raised. It's as if the land and its trees and creeks were as alive as a human being and that person has a hold on you and won't let go. Nor do I understand your bond with your mother or your near obsession with the past. These things are woven together as tightly as a weaver could ever make a basket. I'm not so certain that basket always holds our best interests at heart."

"Take away those things, however, and the man you fell in love with would vanish."

"I realize that," she says, "and that's why I *try* to understand. I certainly realize things are more complex than I thought they were when I first came to the South two years ago. Before then I thought of the Confederacy as being a bit like Nazi Germany. I saw it as a country of cruel slaveholders who fought for the right to own blacks. When we went to New Orleans, and I saw that statue of General Lee, I couldn't believe it at first. I didn't realize the South's heroes were Civil War soldiers."

"And do you still see the South the way you did two years ago?" I ask her.

"Of course not," she says. "You know I don't because I've gotten to know people here. There are more layers to Southerners than I first thought. But there's still so much about you being a Southerner that I simply don't get."

"Just as you have enriched my whole life," I say, "you now give a vital and deeper meaning to why I must make the journey with Sherman."

"What do you mean?" Her hand reaches for mine.

"On my walk I'm going to carry a copy of a diary that was written by Henry Hitchcock, who was Sherman's right-hand man on the March to the Sea. Hitchcock wrote the journal as he traveled across Georgia as a means of sharing that experience with his wife. I'll keep a daily journal as a means of sharing my experience with you and trying to shed light on who I am as a Southerner and what the South means to me. It'll be a kind of test to myself to see if I can be that open with my thoughts and feelings to better reach you, the most important person in my life."

"I haven't been totally open with you and what you're saying makes me feel I should be."

"What?" I say, her tone making me uneasy.

"I'm afraid you'll fall in love with somebody else," she says. "You fell in love when you walked the Trail of Tears and again when you retraced the Pony Express Trail."

"I had no one special in my life then," I say, kissing her fingers. "I have you now. I wouldn't do anything to chance losing you."

"You say that, but you're willing to make this journey without me and that risks our love. I know I'm much younger than you and maybe I'm too dependent on you for my identity, but for the past two years I've been thinking so much in terms of *us* that it isn't easy to change all at once."

"The walk will only take a few weeks," I say. "And then we'll be together again."

"I know how passionate and romantic you are, and I crave that, but how can you be sure you won't sleep with other women as you go day after day without sex?"

"In all honesty," I say, "I guess that will be another test put before me."

"Make me a promise?"

"I'll try."

"If you do sleep with someone else, will you put that in your journal as well?"

"I'll admit my lusts as well as my love," I say.

I have never loved or been in love as much as I am with Debi, and I feel at this very moment the only way I can fully answer such an intimate question is by touch itself. I move my fingers once again through the hair behind her ear and gently try to guide her toward me. At first she resists. But then, when I kiss her eyes, I feel her shoulders relax, and she sinks into my embrace. My arms now wrap around her and hers do the same with me. How reassuring it is to feel our bodies pressed together as if we are one in spirit. Her breasts against my chest, however, get me to thinking more of flesh than spirit and I can't help but pull back from her a few inches to allow my hand to find her nipples. We both begin to breathe harder as those nipples grow firm in my fingers and her hand slides up my thigh to find the right spot. From the first time we kissed two years ago I have not been able to get enough of her lips and tongue, and this is especially true now as my mouth, warm and wet, pulls from hers to inch down her neck to her nipples. I suck on one and then the other till the smell of her sex and the sound of her moans make me feel just a bit crazy, and I turn her over onto her stomach and wrap my arms around her as I nibble on her ears and lick her neck till some ten or fifteen minutes later we lie at peace, wet with sweat that glows in the moonlight on our naked bodies. I blow on her face to cool the hot skin.

"I like your fan," she whispers as she falls asleep. I lie awake for over an hour, watching her breathe, thankful that she is in my life and that we talked openly tonight.

But when I awake at dawn, Debi isn't beside me. I crawl from bed to look out the window and find her packing her car. I slip into my robe and hurry outside.

"What are you doing?" I say.

"I awoke in the middle of the night," she says, "and couldn't get back to sleep. I want to be supportive, but I don't know if I can take you being away from me. I don't know if I'm that strong. I'm going to Washington while you do the walk."

"I'll fly out to see you as soon as I get back home from Georgia," I say, taking her into my arms.

"I don't know, darling. I just don't know if I can allow that or not."

She gets into her car and I reach for her face.

"I love you," I say, my fingertips on her lips.

She opens her mouth just enough for my index finger to be licked by her tongue. Then she disappears down the road with part of my heart, our future now as uncertain as what awaits me as I walk across Georgia.

Chapter Three

With Debi's departure I feel as though I have more at risk than I've ever had in my whole life. Not only is my relationship with her in danger because of my proposed march to the sea, but I have taken on the task of baring my soul to one and all concerning what I find about my heritage as I walk from Atlanta to Savannah. Do I really have the guts to write what I think and feel along the way? Is Debi's pillow vision the product of her anxiety, or did she really foresee some great danger awaiting me? Is this dream I'm having about Daddy simply conflicting emotion, or is he really trying to reach me from the Spirit World to show me something? Sherman and his soldiers made the march in November, when it was cool and ideal for walking. I can't do the hike then because I'm obligated to be on a promotional tour for my second book, *Bareback!* I'll be walking across Georgia in the heart of summer, and while I like to think I'm in good physical shape, people half my age have been known to suffer heat strokes while carrying heavy packs like the one I'll have strapped to my back. The Yanks made the trek in one month and I, too, am determined to make it in that short a time.

If you recall that I said I had two primary problems to address before my march, and that I've only thus far looked at the first one, Debi, then you're a good counter and have one helluva memory. The second problem that faces me is, in some ways, deeper and more difficult than the first one.

But before I can discuss that second problem and leave for Atlanta to begin my walk I feel an important need to plant the garden, something I always did with my father. The tradition always brought us closer, as it did him to his father and his father before him. Then, when the first beans and corn began to sprout, we'd walk between the rows and test our modesty.

Must be the way I placed the seeds, I'd say, failing the earthly trial.

No, I covered them with soil just the right depth, he'd say as he gladly joined me in failure.

Alone in the garden now, preparing the soil to be planted, I find it haunting that Daddy isn't here with me. There, on the plot of ground beneath the giant poplar, is where he fell with his heart attack. It wasn't until he was pronounced dead in the emergency room that my family and I learned from his doctor that Daddy had been told over two years earlier that he had a bad valve in his heart. He refused to have it operated on and kept it a secret from us so we wouldn't worry. That's a Southerner for you—too proud for his own good sometimes.

There in the soil where he fell is also where I had buried several owls I found killed by cars on the highway. I placed them there to nourish the earth and believed that they might live on in the corn and pumpkins that usually grow there. But now, every time an owl—a *witch*, says Cherokee lore—hoots in the night, I do not see a table graced with boiled corn or pumpkin pie. Rather, I behold my father falling to his knees.

> Birds can't fly to the moon
> Rabbits don't sing to loons
> Fish don't bite at noon
> People don't really need spoons

For the past few weeks I've been readying myself for my march to the sea. Each day after working in the garden I lift weights and go for a long walk back in the woods along trails Debi has cleared on the two hundred acres my father bought back in the fifties, before real estate in the area shot through the roof. One of these trails leads to the Courting Tree, which grew in the shape of a bench before reaching skyward. Debi and I have carved our names in a heart on this oak. Just fifty yards from there the trail passes a salt lick that we set in the soil for our deer. Then the trail leads to our retreat cabin, which we have named Tanager after a bird that looks much like a cardinal and migrates each year from the rain forests of Guatemala. That's a tanager calling out up there now among the leaves of the hickory. It loves fruit, and I slice an apple or banana for it every two or three days and place it on a board I've nailed to a dead tree. I hope its whistle doesn't lose any of its beauty while I'm away in Georgia and can't give it food.

Just beyond the bird feeder is the cabin. Eight years ago, it began as a giant tree house my father and I built with my nephew who was visiting from Colorado. It blossomed the next year when I added a ground floor with a fireplace, and the flames within it light a room filled with Indian artifacts, folk art, and unusual roots I've found dried and twisted in the shapes of birds and animals.

On the mantel sit faded photographs of my ancestors who fought in the Civil War. For those who have ever dared to question the open-mindedness of an Alabama man, they have only to eyeball the picture of my great-great-uncle Panter. He fought for the Confederacy the first year and then sided with the Union the next year. Dedicated to fairness on all sides, he decided the third year to say to hell with the war altogether and went back home to fight with his wife. My great-grandpa Ellis, pictured to his right, lived within a stone's throw of my great-great-uncle Panter, but was not as willing to stretch his mind. He joined the Union Cavalry with pride, though he may have had second thoughts as his Alabama Confederate neighbors pelted him with rocks when he came home on leave.

My great-grandpa Croft, on the other hand, was a single-minded Alabama Rebel who preferred death to dishonor. One of our Croft cousins "owned" over one hundred slaves at the beginning of the Civil War, but Grandpa Croft himself was a dirt farmer living on Sand Mountain. He was shot in the neck by a Yank at Noonday Creek, Georgia. His brother, also a Johnny Reb, had his right elbow blown off in the Battle of Atlanta when my old buddy Sherman and his men invaded that city. That wound in Grandpa Croft's neck left him partially paralyzed and his head often shook out of control. Some said the shaking wasn't from the injury at all though. It was his enduring response to his daughter marrying an Ellis and bearing his children.

To the right of the mantel where my grandpas' pictures sit —I've followed the gentlemen's code in keeping them as far apart as possible—is a doorway under construction, leading to a huge new room that Debi and I recently started. The fourteen-foot-high ceiling is strengthened by four exposed red oak logs, which I cut back in the woods near the deer lick. We're making the cabin bigger so we can live here instead of just using it as a retreat. But if she doesn't forgive me for taking this walk without her, this addition will become the skeleton of a lifelong dream—to live with the one I love in harmony on this sacred hill.

My proposed march becomes more real when the seeds begin to sprout in the garden. With them up and strong I can leave the plants to the care of my mother. We don't save much money by raising our own vegetables, but this garden feeds us something that no can or grocery store offers. Our pantry shelves are full of vegetables that my mother, my father, and I have raised and preserved for the winters. Sometimes when we'd open the door to get some green beans or corn we'd find ourselves calling out as we stood in the pantry doorway.

"Look at all this food," I'd say.

"Sure is pretty," Daddy would say, "the way your mother placed it in those mason jars."

"I didn't do a very good job with the tomatoes," Mother would say.

"They all get a blue ribbon from me," I'd say.

"Don't know how they could look any better," Daddy would say.

And there in the pantry doorway the three of us would sometimes find ourselves, as surely as if we'd been a little lost, and we'd celebrate our homecoming again and again.

"Good to see you."

"Good to see you too."

"I've never seen ya'll look better."

As a young officer Sherman had been stationed throughout the South—Charleston, Marietta (near Atlanta), New Orleans —and understood much about the hearts and minds of my ancestors and their agricultural ties. To raid Georgia's homes and smokehouses for food for the March to the Sea would do far more than fill Union bellies. It would hit Southerners where it hurt the most, in their bond with the earth, the very meaning of their lives. Cut a wing from an eagle and it cannot fly. Saw a leg from a horse and it cannot gallop.

Sherman himself was no stranger to being in a crippled position, and he grasped what it does to a man's spirit. He had failed at banking and real estate in the 1850s in San Francisco and New York. Each of his failures was a nightmare come true, because Sherman's father had died as a financial failure and Sherman feared the same destiny.

Born in 1820, in Lancaster, Ohio, William Tecumseh Sherman was the son of a judge of the State Supreme Court. Sherman's father died when he was nine years old, and the boy was left to the care of a wealthy neighbor, Thomas Ewing. Ewing got Sherman into West Point, which he graduated from in 1840, sixth in his class, though his many demerits almost got him kicked out. Following thirteen years in the army, and his stints in banking and real estate, Sherman married Ewing's daughter, Ellen, and became superintendent of the Louisiana State Seminary of Learning and Military Academy. When the Civil War broke out he had five children and was working as the president of a St. Louis streetcar company for forty dollars a month. Ditching the desk job, Sherman hightailed it to the White House and took President Lincoln off guard when he refused a commission as brigadier general.

"I want to *win* my stars," said Sherman. "Not have them tied to the bootstraps of a politician."

Entering the War Between the States as a colonel of the regular infantry, Sherman was more than ready to prove himself in battle. When he had served in the army earlier, his superior officers, much to Sherman's disgust and frustration, denied him the opportunity to fight in the Seminole War and the Mexican War. He resented being a paper pusher, but the lack of combat duty plus Ellen's constant insistence that he leave the military and get a civilian job to care for their growing family finally drove Sherman to abandon his true love, the army. Now at the age of forty-one—many men were already dead by that age in the 1860s—Sherman had a second chance to fulfill a lifetime dream of becoming a famed fighting soldier. He could redeem himself from his earlier failures, escape that routine desk job at the streetcar company, return to his first love, and help save the Union all in one clean sweep. That he could do all this and direct the biggest fire in American history to boot was no small feat. Why, the very thought of it inspires me. Anybody got a match?

Chapter Four

The day before I leave for Atlanta I'm starting to load my backpack when I get a phone call from Raymond. He's my cousin, but I always think of him as an uncle because he's almost seventy. A Southern tradition that's dying, and I'm not so sure that's good, is that older folks—whether or not you are truly kin to them—are called Aunt or Uncle So-and-so as a way of showing respect.

"Is something wrong?" I say, hearing an urgency in Raymond's voice even though he simply asked how I'm doing.

"I can't talk about it on the phone," he says. "Could you come out and see me?"

"Yes," I say, puzzled as to what's bothering him. "I'll be right out."

The sun is setting as I crawl into my car to head for Sand Mountain, where Raymond lives, some five miles away. I could take the paved Smith Gap road and save time getting there, but I prefer to follow the old dirt wagon trail called Wooten Gap. It meanders past a cliff, its rock wall housing a small cave called Hole in the Rock. Some say it's where an Alabama girl made love to a Union soldier and her daddy caught them. He heard their passionate moans coming from the small, dark room where they had made a bed of pine needles. The father, a moonshiner, killed the Yank with a butcher knife and threw his body down a well by a log cabin that rotted away long before I was ever born. An older boy who lived near me—his hand was so fast that he could catch a fly in midair and throw it onto a web so we could watch the spider come from its hole and eat it—said the soldier's spirit lived in the bottom of that well and if I drank from it the phantom would go up my nose like smoke and chew part of my brain. Then I'd have to be put in a cage for the rest of life because all I could do was howl like the northern wind. He claimed that happened to a girl years ago and her father sold her to a carnival that traveled to Chicago where people paid to see her.

I had a picture of her in that cage, the boy told me. But Daddy traded it to a man in Mississippi for my .22 rifle.

When the dirt road curves around the cliff at the top of Sand Mountain I stop my car, because this spot offers a great view of Lookout Mountain to the east and the valley in between, where my little hometown of Fort Payne stands. It was a Cherokee village before my ancestors were moved to Oklahoma on the Trail of Tears in 1838. It gets its current name from the fort that was built to imprison the Indians for a month prior to the dreaded removal. We're a community of almost fourteen thousand and the main livelihood is farming and making socks. Yep, we're one of those textile towns you hear about. If you're wondering where you've heard the name Fort Payne, Alabama, before, it's probably because the musical group Alabama was born and raised and still lives here. It's also the town where Sequoya lived when he began developing the Cherokee alphabet. Did you realize that he is the only known man in history to develop an alphabet on his own, and that it's the *only* alphabet to be developed in the past five thousand years anywhere on earth?

My hometown has changed a great deal since I was a boy growing up in the fifties and sixties, and one of my most haunting memories relates to the Civil War. In the center of town is Union Park, where a twenty-foot-tall stone Confederate soldier stands holding a musket. It seemed that almost everybody I met was my cousin and I asked Daddy if that soldier was a cousin too.

Yes, he said, his name is Johnny and if you look at him long enough he'll come alive.

Every time we went to town I wanted to sit in the park and stare at Johnny till he opened his eyes and gave me a ride on his shoulder. I wanted him to carry me to the home of Sparky, a black dwarf who was Fort Payne's self-appointed street cleaner. I was spellbound by Sparky because he was the only adult I knew who was my height when I was five years old and he was the friendliest person I had ever met. He wore baggy, faded blue overalls with brass buttons, and every time I spotted him sweeping the sidewalk he would place his broom against his trash can, take off his old hat, and bow.

There he is, Sparky would call out. There's my friend Jerry.

I had never had a man bow to me before and he was the only black person I knew. His skin fascinated me and I'd sometimes rub his hand to see if the blackness would come off on my fingers.

Don't rub too hard, Sparky would always say, or it might get my magic to working and turn me into a dozen black snakes. Then I'd have to sleep all night before I could become a man again and clean these streets. Do you have a nickel for old Sparky today so I can buy me a nice, cold Coca-Cola?

When he asked that, and he always asked that, I'd turn to Daddy for help. Sometimes he'd give Sparky a nickel and sometimes he wouldn't. Anyway, I somehow got it into my head that when Sparky went to bed at night he became those twelve black snakes he spoke of when I rubbed his rare skin. I wanted to see him work that magic.

"Can I come to your home?" I asked him one day after Daddy gave him a nickel and he raised a cold bottle of Coke to his sweaty black face.

"I wish you could," he said. "Oh, I wish you could. But I live on the other side of a creek too deep for you to cross and there's no bridge."

"But how do *you* get home each day?" I asked him.

"I can step across the creek," he said, "because I was born on the other side. But if you weren't born there, you can't learn how to do the right step to cross."

In my private dreams I decided that if I could get my twenty-foot-tall cousin to come alive from stone, then he could carry me across that deep creek to behold Sparky at night when he turned into all those snakes.

I was a grown man when Sparky died, and to this day I can't drink a Coke or eye a stone Confederate soldier without feeling a sense of wonder and a need to cross that creek to see where Sparky still lives in my mind.

Sparky lived in Douglas, the black community on the south side of the tracks in Fort Payne. Even when I was a teenager in the sixties it was rare to find a black living outside that part of town. A billboard greeted you when you entered town from Highway 35 and said THE KKK WELCOMES YOU TO FORT PAYNE. One night somebody threw paint over the hooded Klansmen pictured on the sign and it dripped to the ground, causing the Klansmen to look as if they were melting.

That billboard is now long gone, as are the COLORED and WHITE rest rooms and drinking fountains I saw growing up. Blacks now live throughout town and work side by side with whites in Wal-Mart and Kmart and most any other store you care to name. I'm not pretending that there aren't still elements of racism here in my hometown. From time to time I hear "nigger" this and "nigger" that, but the slur is, thank goodness, not tossed around like it once was. And, frankly, I used to think that Sparky's name was Nigger Sparky, because that's all I heard him called when I was a child. When I called him that to his face one day, he gave me an odd look and he did not bow as usual. I had no idea what was wrong. When Daddy and I walked on down the street and left Sparky drinking his cold Coke, Daddy told me never to call Sparky "Nigger" because it hurt his feelings. That bothered me because the last thing I wanted to do was hurt somebody I liked so much.

But on the whole I'm proud of Fort Payne and its people. We're a pretty good bunch of folks, trying to join the modern world, though I can't do much bragging on its greed, violence, and drugs. My hometown's historical society honors the past; it has saved the old train depot and turned it into a museum. I'm pleased that it sells copies of my books in what was the depot's waiting room and that a striking painting of Sparky hangs on the wall. I never dreamed we'd end up in the same room, as if—at last—we both crossed that deep creek together.

If it's starting to sound like the postcard I'm creating of my hometown is just a bit too pretty, don't judge too quickly one way or the other. I have a story concerning myself and the blacks in Fort Payne that will thrill some of you and sicken others. As a writer and a human being I have challenged myself to see if I can truly bare my Southern soul for this march to the sea, but this story—let's call it "The Confession"—must wait till you know me better, for trust takes a little time in this day and age, doesn't it? Perhaps by the time I've walked halfway across Georgia you and I will be comfortable enough with each other for me to face this memory.

Concerned about what's bothering Raymond, I drive on along the dirt road beneath the cliff and leave the valley of Fort Payne behind, Lookout Mountain towering to the east. But two miles from Raymond's house I stop the car again on another dirt road to overlook the site of the house where Daddy grew up. Do you recall that I said his home burned when he was a child and his whole family then had to live in their barn? Well, they built another house atop the same stone foundation that held the first one. But last summer, the same summer Daddy died, that house burned to the ground, apparently the result of arson. Its charred remains now stare me in the face and make me sad. This site is what us Southerners call "the old home place." It's a kind of altar because it's always the oldest known site where a man's ancestors lived. It is a true Southerner's obligation to keep that old home place alive as long as possible by recounting stories about it that have been passed down from generation to generation.

I'm thinking Raymond and I might tell the Weasel Story from the old home place when I move on down the road toward Raymond's house, which sits in the middle of a peach and apple orchard.

Raymond, toothless, sits on the front porch eating a glass of corn bread and buttermilk. His handsome face holds the same urgency his voice did when he phoned me.

Chapter Five

Even before I get out of the car I feel my heart try to protect itself from Raymond. For years now he's been a gauge for me to know where I am inside. If I'm afraid of what I'm feeling or trying to deny it, I view him as a whining old man caught up in sentimentality. But if I'm strong and in touch with myself, I see him as a man of courage who isn't frightened by his feelings and refuses to put on a mask and pass time with small talk like much of the world does.

"Watching those fruit trees grow?" I say as I come from my car.

"Get out, Jerry," says Raymond. "Get out and make yourself at home. How's your mother?"

To ask another how his family is, and especially his parents, is expected as soon as possible upon greeting another Southerner. To not do so shows both poor manners and disrespect. The Southerners—and I'm mainly talking about those of us with roots going back for many generations—who live in big cities and don't ask about family are sadly caught in Dixie Denial.

"As long as Mother stays busy she's fine," I say. "She's got the garden to take care of now. How's Ruth?"

"Her leg still hurts," says Raymond. "But I got the best wife on Sand Mountain. Ain't seen the thing yet she can't walk into after rolling up her sleeves."

I shake his hand and place my fingers upon his back as if to encourage the greeting to flow into his aging and thinning body. He suffers from emphysema and wears no shoes over his swollen feet. A brown paper bag stuffed with newspapers rests on the porch to the right of his rocking chair. He takes his last bite of corn bread and buttermilk and places the glass and spoon by the bag. Then he clears his throat and spits into the newspapers as if in contempt of the stories printed there.

I see now that the urgency about him is more serious than I first thought; it borders on desperation. I want to get to the heart of his problem right away, but every Southerner has to take his own time to tell what's on his mind.

"I would've been out a few minutes earlier," I say, "but I stopped at the old home place."

"If the law ever finds out who put a match to it," he says, "I hope they lock him in a room with a bushel basket of rattle-snakes and copperheads. Nature knows something about justice."

"It made me feel mighty heavy inside to look at the ashes," I say. "But I got to feeling better when I thought of the weasel Daddy had when he was a boy and living there."

"I played with that weasel myself," says Raymond, responding as another Southerner should to a kin's story about the old home place. "Red [my father's nickname] told you about the time that weasel hid in the wall?"

"Yes, he and his brothers and sisters did everything but sing songs to try to get him out of there. Daddy got afraid he'd stay in there till he died, so he went down to the creek and caught a perch, tied it on a string, and dropped it through a hole in the wall to the weasel. Then he pulled it out and the weasel followed till Daddy grabbed him."

"I been feeling like that weasel in the wall," says Raymond. "That's why I phoned you."

"I don't understand."

"I feel trapped inside the walls of this old body," he says, "and there ain't no fish shiny enough on the end of a string to pull me out into life. I got a feeling I'll die while you're away on your walk across Georgia and I—"

"What?"

"I wanted you to hear in person that I care about you and

what you're doing. I'll be thinking of you every step of the way till I—"

"I'll be thinking of you, too," I say, seeing in his eyes the very real fear that he'll die this summer. It dawns upon me, too, that I'm especially sensitive to people his age because Daddy's death has made me realize that a unique generation of Southerners is fading away. With their deaths, what is the New South becoming?

"Others may see a need to hide their affection for their kinfolks," he says, "but I've never seen any sense in putting in a dark room what you could hang on a line in broad daylight. Course, there's plenty of folks don't see it that way, but then they don't work these fingers or scratch this old dry skin either. Maybe I think too much, Jerry, but ever since I retired from grading those county roads I been remembering trees I climbed that have since been cut down and burned up like they were only old ragged clothes. You and me and all of Alabama know I never had no money nor any land except for these few acres here, but I've never felt poor as long as people came to see me. You've made me a rich man this evening by coming out here, and your daddy was good to do the same before he left us."

"You make me a rich man, too, by telling me what you're feeling," I say, following one of the South's oldest traditions that one kinfolk must honor the other by responding with equal praise. This custom is, in part, a result of us losing the Civil War. The Yanks may have put us down, but we can build each other up. We can show a little pride in our mutual identity as Southerners.

Raymond's eyes begin to water and, frankly, I don't want him to get more emotional, because it makes me sad.

"You're not going to die anytime soon," I say. "Hell, you're too ugly to die. If we buried you, the ground itself would spit you right back out just to make us look at you some more."

I see a faint grin appear on his lips, and I don't want to lose it. I bait my line with my own kind of fish and toss it toward him.

"Yeah, I say, you, Daddy, and me had us some good times

back when we bird hunted together. I still grin when I remember old Blue. You ever think about him anymore?"

Raymond looks up at the moon for a moment and I would swear he's catching a whiff of that fish. Then he lowers his head and eyes me, and I can see he's having second thoughts about staying trapped inside his own walls.

"Do I ever think of Blue? Why, son, that bird dog was smarter than most people who went to college. And run? He could run faster than the devil from the holy word. I once saw him catch a copperhead by the tail and sling its head into an oak so fast, that snake thought a bolt of lightning had delivered him to the promised land. He could dance on two hind legs like a fool doing the fox-trot. Of course, I had to help hold him up a little, but he wasn't so proud he couldn't accept it and keep his head high at the same time. And if I started to sing, he'd join in just so I wouldn't sound so bad and shame myself in front of company."

It's been true for years that the longer Raymond goes without spitting into his paper bag the better he's feeling, and it's been over twenty minutes since he splattered yesterday's news. I not only savor hearing him get right with himself and the world as he spins his tales, but I enjoy seeing across the orchard and down into the hollow where his son Paul, my age, has a home. He, like most folks around here, works down in the valley in one of Fort Payne's many sock mills. A light shines now in Paul's little house as an owl begins to hoot. Its eerie sound drifts through the dusk to where, farther down into the hollow, another light shines through the pines from the house where Raymond's twin brother lives. Funny, I came out to comfort Raymond, and it's me that ends up receiving the night's gifts. I am part of a clan on a mountain. A man about to undergo a journey can never have too much assurance that he is connected to family as surely as the roots of a tree can split a rock to get to water.

The moon is bright over Sand Mountain as I leave Raymond and head home. I go to my room and stuff my camping equipment into the same backpack I wore when I walked the Trail of Tears. In addition to my tent, canteen, cooking gear, journal, and camera, I now place a copy of *Marching with Sherman* in there as well. It's the diary Henry Hitchcock wrote so he could share the March to the Sea with his wife. A lawyer from St. Louis, Hitchcock had the job of answering a flood of letters and telegrams that were up to General Sherman's neck.

Just tell them something sweet, Sherman told Major Hitchcock. All molasses and honey.

As I walk from Atlanta to Savannah down the very path they followed, I think it'll be a hoot to compare and contrast what Hitchcock found in 1864 to what I find in 1993. I just hope some of my Southern comrades don't spot me reading it while I'm stretched out under a shade tree and take me for a Yankee spy.

When I finish loading my backpack I walk up to the garden where the moon shines down on my brass CS—Confederate States—belt buckle as well as tender new rows of corn, beans, potatoes, beets, squash, tomatoes, and okra. Leaning in the fork of an apple tree is a straight limb from a chestnut tree that Daddy cut last year and placed there for me. It's over five feet long and almost as big around as my wrist. I had planned to carve it into a bow, but it will now become my staff as I make my way across Georgia. I seek no harm nor plan to give any, but should someone dare to push me too far I'll show him just how fast a walking stick can become a mule's hind leg.

This is the first time I've held the tree limb since the day Daddy cut it, and I'm surprised and pleased at just how light it has become after drying out. The smooth, tight bark feels a bit like skin and it's easy to imagine that it could turn itself into a mighty snake for a holy man.

Under the pear tree is a chair facing the garden and two old pipes stick from either side of the wire seat. Daddy used to sit here in the evenings and smoke as he savored the peaceful feeling that came from being satisfied with his work. I now sit in that chair with the staff across my legs and lift one of the pipes to my nose. I can smell Daddy in the charred tobacco. Following Cherokee tradition, I light a match, put the flame to the old tobacco and puff, letting the smoke carry to heaven my prayer for his soul in the Other World and mine as I trek across Georgia.

As I walk from the pear tree and down the path toward my mother's house, I use the staff for the first time and I can already tell that we're going to be good friends. It is solid and strong, something to lean on when the going gets rough. I need some strength right now, for when I enter the house it's time to deal with the second primary problem my march is causing.

Chapter Six

"Do you like my staff?" I ask Mother when I enter the house. "Daddy had cut it for me to make a bow."

I hold it out and she takes it as if to touch Daddy one more time. Her lips tighten and I fear she feels more than she wants, but seconds later, as she lifts the stick this way and that, her face begins to relax.

"It will serve you well," she says. "Mean dogs don't like big sticks."

I like seeing her hands around the staff that will be my companion on the journey. They're the same two hands that helped Daddy and me build this home more than thirty years ago. We had the lumber cut from the trees here on our land, and in today's world of prefabricated houses we feel as though the very beams of this house are parts of ourselves, extensions of our bones. Sawing and hammering, we poured our sweat into it as if our lives depended on it, and in a way they did. For as long as I can remember I heard Mother and Daddy say we'd one day build a place and own it and have a garden and flowers with birds singing in all the trees. That may sound a little corny to some people, but that's okay. Our building this house brought us closer together, and there's nothing more important than making a dream come true with those one cherishes.

Mother grew up on Sand Mountain only a mile from Daddy's old home place. Her family was even bigger than Daddy's. She had eleven brothers and sisters. Her father owned a gristmill and was a stone mason. They were as poor as

Daddy's people and she and her sisters washed the family's clothes in a spring a half mile from their home. They cooked on a wood stove and made quilts and clothes out of feed and flour sacks. Plumbing and electricity were out of the question.

We were never poor in spirit, I've heard Mother say more than once about her family.

Since Daddy died, however, I have seen Mother grope for her spirit, and that is the source of the second problem my march to the sea is causing. I take the staff from her now and place it in the corner, against the fireplace.

"Could we sit and talk for a little while?" I say. "There's a couple of things I'd like for you to know before I leave in the morning for Atlanta."

She nods, and I take a chair across from her, at the dining room table her father made from rough lumber from their old home place more than eighty years ago. It's the same table Mother made bread on when she was a child learning to cook alongside her own mother. When I was a child I heard the story more than once about how Mother's daddy walked over three hundred miles from Shady Valley, Tennessee, to Fort Payne, Alabama, to begin a new life for himself and his wife. As you may have already gathered, Southerners shape their lives by the stories that are passed down to them by their ancestors. Mother's daddy was a walker and now so am I. He also wrote poems, but to claim that I, too, am a poet might be trying to sell the whole hog as a bundle of silk. There is no question in my mind, however, that a poet lives in Mother's soul. As I look at her now, seated before me, I see the person who has always been there for me with unconditional love. From the time I was seventeen and ran away to New York she has had to cope with my restless and hungry spirit. I came and went so many times across America, and back home again, that I created a trail through the woods to Interstate 59. Daddy was more stoic about my wandering, perhaps because a part of him wanted to be on the open road with me, but Mother was always afraid that something horrible would happen to me out there. She lay awake countless nights with only prayers and the songs of crickets to comfort her. Then, when I walked from Oklahoma to Alabama along the Trail of Tears, she had her nights of crickets and prayers again. After my two-thousand-mile journey along the Pony Express Trail you can almost make a sure bet that those song-singing bugs as well as God Himself are starting to get just a bit weary from Mother keeping them awake at night. Well, you're a grown man, you might say to me. It's your business what you do, not your mother's. I can't argue with your logic. But here in the South there is and always has been a special bond between mother and son. He idealizes her, and she does the same with him. I'm not claiming it's right or healthy, but it's as real as taxes and death. And it's that bond with Mother that now compels me to talk with her about my march to the sea.

"When I went to see Raymond this evening," I begin, "he asked how you were doing."

"How was he?" Mother says.

"When I first got there he was dragging," I say. "He said he feared he would die this summer while I was away. But you know how he is. After we talked awhile he got out of himself by recalling that old bird dog he used to have. But what I really wanted to get to was him asking about you. I told him you were doing pretty good as long as you stayed busy."

"There's plenty to do," she says. "I'll need to stick those green beans before long or those vines will be halfway up Sand Mountain before you know it."

"I don't want you to get too hot up there working in the garden while I'm gone," I say. "Early morning or late evening will be cooler. And don't you worry about me walking in that Georgia sun. In fact, this is getting down to what I've got on my mind. I realize all the worry I've put you through over the years with my travels, and I don't think I've ever really just sat down and thanked you like I'm trying to do now. With Daddy gone my trip to Savannah may be the hardest one you've ever had to endure. But it's for him in great part that I'm making this walk. I had that dream about him again last night. He was walking through this cornfield like before, and his hand kept waving for me to follow, and then he pointed that just up ahead there was something I must see. I was telling Debi about it before she left so that she might better understand my need to make this trip without her. Maybe it's just emotions for Daddy and still trying to deal with his passing, but I got this gut feeling that I'll see what he's pointing at in that cornfield if I make this journey with an open heart. Do you understand?"

"I understand that I love you," she says. "I understand that there's nothing I can say or do to stop you, and I guess that's all I need to understand right now."

I get up from my chair and put my arms around her. I feel her breathing, and each breath seems like my own, just as it once was long ago when she and Daddy lay in bed and held each other and I grew inside her while they perhaps wondered who and what their second child might become.

I go to bed that night with a sense of warmth and well-being. But the next morning, the day I'm to leave for Atlanta, I wake and expect to find Debi there beside me. I want to cuddle up next to her naked body and lick her back till she wakes with a gentle moan. But as I come more fully awake I discover only wrinkled sheets where once we made love while doves cooed beyond the bedroom window.

I get dressed and go to the kitchen, where Mother is mixing flour and buttermilk to make biscuits. I pour myself a cup of coffee as we say good morning and she rolls the dough with a wooden pin.

"How'd you rest?" she says.

"Better than I will sleeping on the hard Georgia ground." I wink. "How about yourself?"

"Better than I would have if we hadn't talked last night," she says, cutting out biscuits from the flattened dough with one end of a Vienna sausage can—the same one she's used for over thirty years.

I hear a car arrive. I go to the window to see my younger sister, Nita, and her three-year-old daughter, Logan. Following Southern tradition, Nita was named after a friend of the family, the landlady where Mother and Daddy lived in South Carolina when my older sister, Sandra, was born. Sandra's youngest son, Jessie, was named after my father. This naming business is one way Southerners show respect and honor for those they love. It also helps keep the dead alive.

"You don't look like much of a Rebel to me, standing there with a cup of coffee in your hand," says Nita as she and Logan enter the house.

"Don't go to judging the Confederacy," I say. "For all you know I might have a whole regiment hiding in the bottom of this cup."

"Well," she says, eyeing my stained shirt, "don't spill any more soldiers on yourself. We can't afford to lose any men."

Ever since Nita and I were children we have played together as if that were life's greatest meaning. One of her favorite games was for us to run together across the massive, golden sagebrush field behind the woods where we lived.

Catch me! she would call out when she got tired. Then it was my job to open my arms as she pretended to float in slow motion toward the earth. In just the nick of time I always saved her from the hard ground.

Like me, back in the seventies, she roamed America to seek her own adventure and truth. She longed for a lover who could feel life's magic with her. But so often after meeting a new man she was left feeling blue. I recall one night when we lived together in San Francisco I awoke to find her sitting up in bed in the darkness in the next room as she sang out the window to the heavens "The Moon's a Harsh Mistress," written by Jimmy Webb. It made me sad that I couldn't once again catch her as she floated toward the hard ground on the rebound of a romance. Only days later we hit the road to thumb back home to Alabama, planning to stop over in Aspen, Colorado, to visit some friends. We got stuck on the outskirts of Las Vegas, and night and cold closed in on us. We didn't have enough money to spare for a motel room and the situation looked hopeless.

"This sucks," I said. "I wish we were home."

"I can take part of us there," she said. "Don't get discouraged."

She reached into her pack, pulled out a harmonica, and began to play "Dixie," doing a fancy jig right there on the side of the road as if we were back once again in that magical golden sagebrush field, pretending to blow in the Alabama wind. Minutes later, as if her music had conjured it, a van full of hippies gave us a ride all the way to Colorado. The heater didn't work, however, and Nita gathered her blanket around us as we cuddled across the starry desert to the snow-capped Rockies. She had, at last, returned the favor in the sagebrush field, catching me before I hit the ground.

You may wonder why I'm telling you this story, but I do so, in great part, because I care so much about my relationship with Nita. I'm glad to say that her longing for the right man was fulfilled several years ago. Her husband, from Virginia, is at work right now at Fort Payne's huge bakery. He and Nita moved back to our hometown from Atlanta when Logan, their only child, was born. Nita was already forty when she became pregnant, and she refused to have any tests to see if her baby would be normal, because she said she'd care for it just the same no matter what. But Logan is healthy and bright, and Mother is as crazy about Logan as Nita and her husband, Clay, are. By the way, when Clay sleeps with his great-uncle's Confederate blanket, he dreams that he's a soldier in the Civil War. It comforts me a bit that Logan will help keep Mother from worrying about me on the walk.

When the four of us sit down to eat breakfast, Mother puts the ho-cake on my plate. What, you're not familiar with ho-cake? Made from dough scraps left after the biscuits are cut, it's patted out by hand to become the biggest biscuit of the lot. Whoever gets the ho-cake is considered special, and today that's me because I'm Georgia-bound. There's no telling just how many young Rebels ate ho-cakes for the last time on the day they went to fight the Yanks. I'm reaching for the gravy to pour over my prize biscuit, when Logan holds out her hands as if to part the Red Sea.

"Make the circle, Mama," she says.

Then Nita, Mother, Logan, and I hold hands to create a ring around the table. How very small Logan's hand is in my left one, while Mother's hand is warm and wrinkled in my right.

I'm in the very middle, holding on to both the New and Old South.

"Thank you for this food," says Logan. "Happy we're together."

Then we lower our hands and she begins to clap as if it's the duty of even the youngest Southerner to applaud his or her own attempt to reach the heavenly powers that be. Why, for all I know she may become one of those arm-waving, tent-shouting evangelists when she gets older. I don't make this remark totally out of the blue, because my older sister, Sandra, is in show business herself. She lives in Hollywood. If I could show you her picture right now you might very well recognize her. The past two years she has appeared in several feature films and TV movies. I can't say that I love one sister more than the other, but Sandra has little interest in living back here in Alabama. She does, however, come home from time to time to recharge her batteries and be reminded by the trees where she played as a child that all that glitters isn't gold. Frankly though, I think she suffers a little from Dixie Denial. The last time she was home and I got her to give a Rebel yell the folks in the next county couldn't hear her. I blame it on Hollywood.

When we finish breakfast, I load my pack and staff into the trunk of a rented car, which I'll leave with an agency in Atlanta. It's almost hard to believe that I'm once again about to leap into the world and see what will happen. I won't deny a kind of lust for excitement and intrigue starting to swell within me. So much of my life has centered around hitting the open road that I'm a bit like a dog conditioned for his mouth to water the very moment he sees a piece of meat. I hope my trek is prime beef instead of ragged rat bones.

Another die-hard Southern custom is for folks to walk a friend all the way to his car to tell him good-bye. Then, however, just to show how interested you are, you must keep talking and asking questions to prevent the departure as long as possible. When all else fails and it seems that the departee is finally going to drive away, you must place your hand on the car fender or even grab the window to hold him back. If you're not from the South—and I'll try not to hold that against you—

you may think I'm putting you on about this tradition, but it's a hard-core fact. Us Rebels follow this practice because we think company is the best thing that was ever invented. Once the traveler is free to leave, it's crucial that his host tell him to come back sometime. *Ya'll come!* is enough. If you're not invited back, your host has amnesia or you did something to offend him and he is gracefully letting you know what a low-down, sorry son of a bitch he thinks you are. If this happens, you may have done one or more of three things. First, you didn't brag enough on how good the meal was. Second, you didn't listen to all the host's stories as though they were the first and only stories you'd heard in your life. Third, you didn't tell the host enough tall tales to keep him entertained and he feels like you suckered him out of a free meal. I take no pride in telling you these things about us Southerners, but somebody's got to do it. Okay, so I'm getting a bit goofy right now, but it's because I'm a little nervous about leaving home. Yes, I said I was excited about the trek and I am, but at this stage of a journey I often go through a kind of transformation—a bit like a snake shedding its skin before it slides into a new hole to explore another world.

"Be careful out there, Reb," says Nita, taking her hand from my car window once I start the motor. "Don't let 'em take you prisoner."

"Not if I can help it," I say.

"Just come back," says Mother. "That's all I ask. Just come back home."

"Bring *me* a gift," shouts Logan as she waves from Nita's arms. "A bear or a monkey."

I move down the driveway and stop at the road to make sure no cars or trucks zoom my way. I don't see any, but a large, near-extinct woodpecker—an Indian hen, Southerners call it—flies overhead and makes his loud clucking sound. I know this rare bird, for he lives at Tanager and Debi has named him Clyde, just as she has named the blue-tailed lizard there Lizzie, the chameleon Camille, and the frog that lives under the front yard stump Freddie. My God, I've got far more going on inside me than I fully realized, because when

Clyde calls out again I think for a second that Debi is in the front seat of the car with me. I can see already that this march with Sherman across Georgia is going to be anything but a simple stroll through the park.

Chapter Seven

Home disappears behind me as I drive down the road and already I feel another part of myself coming more awake. It's that part of the mind, soul, and body itself that retreats from the world when I stay at home, away from the thrills, vices, dares, games, lusts, intrigues, and varieties that, honestly, I sometimes crave observing if not downright sinking my teeth into. I don't mind telling you this, because anybody who's had half a thought or daydream knows the power and seduction of so-called civilization. I'll even go a step further and admit that Debi was right about my passion and romance sometimes being almost more than I can contain. She's been gone now for over two weeks and my whole body is starting to ache, not only for tender touch but for wild sex. I have been a weight lifter and body builder for thirty years and it seems to me that one of the finest gifts the Great Spirit has blessed man with is his ability to release his deepest passion and poetry through his flesh. I'm not saying this to make you uncomfortable, but if it does, you might be wise to abandon the journey now, for I feel already that my steps will take us further in this direction.

I still don't feel comfortable enough, however, to even begin to tell you about "The Confession," and this is especially true now that I am aiming the car up Lookout Mountain, overlooking my little hometown of Fort Payne, located fifty miles south of Chattanooga or one hundred miles north of Birmingham. This feeling, in part, is because this is the same Lookout Mountain that Martin Luther King, Jr., spoke of in his "I Have a Dream" speech when he cried out for freedom and equality for all mankind. Yes, I realize you're still puzzled as to what I'm driving at, but I will make "The Confession" crystal clear before my feet reach Savannah.

It's only 140 miles from my home to Atlanta and when Route 27 leads me into Rome, Georgia—some 50 miles from Fort Payne—I stop at a café to have a cup of coffee and dig into Hitchcock's diary. It was in a field near here that Hitchcock met Sherman for the first time. Though a graduate of West Point like the general himself, Hitchcock had never been in a battle and was in awe of Sherman—nicknamed "Cump" from his boyhood—from the moment he laid eyes on him:

> My "chief" occupies a position and has already done things which certainly invest more than ordinary interest; and he impresses me as a man of power more than any man I remember. Not general intellectual power, not Websterian, but the sort of power which a flash of lightning suggests,—as clear, as intense, and as rapid. Yet with all his vigor, his Atlanta campaign showed, as his conversation and dispatches do, abundant caution and the most careful forethought. Without any signs of arrogance, he has complete confidence in himself. . . .

Sipping my cup of coffee over Hitchcock's journal, I see Hitchcock's eyes, wide with wonder, as they follow every move Sherman makes. The general, on the other hand, has his determined eyes set only on the future. His dream to become a famed fighting soldier is coming true and he is obsessed with capturing Atlanta.

Then I envision Sherman and 100,000 Union soldiers closing in on Atlanta after a bloody battle at Kennesaw Mountain some 20 miles to the northwest. There Sherman lost 2,500 men in less than an hour. But a week later he had outflanked the Rebels and pushed his way toward Atlanta again, showing no mercy to his men. To the quartermaster, who doubted that he could handle the pace, Sherman made it clear: *"If you don't have my army supplied, and keep it supplied, we'll eat your mules up, sir, eat your mules up!"* And to the engineer who wanted four days to rebuild a burned bridge Sherman offered a little advice: *"Sir, I give you forty-eight hours or a position in the front ranks."*

When the general finally took Atlanta on September 2, 1864, he had lost 31,000 men. The Confederacy mourned the lives of 35,000, despite the leadership of General John Hood. Hood had survived having twelve horses shot from under him, the laming of a leg at Chickamauga, and the loss of the use of an arm at Gettysburg. He now rode into battle strapped to his saddle.

Sherman's capture of Atlanta was a great victory because the city was a main source of Confederate war supplies, including clothes, weapons, wagons, and ammunition. They were manufactured here and reached the Rebels all across the Confederacy via the trains roaring from the city's stations. As for the food that fed the Rebs it was mostly grown here in Georgia, but that, according to Sherman's plan, would soon come to an end.

When Sherman presented his plan to march to the sea to General Grant, however, he was brushed aside. To push into enemy territory without knowing what forces waited there and cut themselves off from railroad supply lines and telegraph communication, as Sherman proposed, was reckless if not plain stupid. Sherman argued that he knew the Georgia countryside better than most of the Rebs, because he had explored it back in the 1840s when he pushed into Florida to seek the Seminoles. In fact, it was through them that he first experienced the devastating power of fire on civilians. He had seen entire villages ablaze.

President Lincoln, needing a feather in his political hat for the approaching election, was thrilled over the capture of Atlanta and persuaded Grant to go along with Sherman's plan to march to the sea. If he captured Savannah all three of them could do some fancy crowing.

November 15, 1864, was to be the day the official burning of Atlanta began, to kick off the March to the Sea. Days earlier, however, some Union soldiers got drunk and began the arson party on their own. Flames from the city's wooden buildings towered hundreds of feet into the night air, as if the soldiers sought to cook the moon itself. The light from the fire was so bright that those camped a mile away could read and write letters by it. Others sang and danced in a wild frenzy inspired by the fact that Dixie was finally getting a strong dose of the medicine it had long deserved. While the Atlanta Hotel, slave markets, theaters, dry-goods stores, fire stations, and jails burned like the pit of hell, the horrible smells of burning horses, cows, feather beds, leather, and pine drifted up Yanks' noses. A band even played, its light show perhaps the rarest in American history. Bricks were thrown through plate glass windows, and new clothes were dragged into the streets and sold for pennies. It was a looter's dream come true, and that night Major Henry Hitchcock wrote this in his diary:

> First bursts of smoke, dense, black volumes, then tongues of flame, then huge waves of fire roll up into the sky: Presently the skeletons of great warehouses stand out in relief against . . . sheets of roaring, blazing, furious flames . . . as one fire sinks, another rises . . . lurid, angry, dreadful to look upon.

I close Hitchcock's journal, exit the Rome café, and get back into my rented car, heading for Atlanta. When the city's skyscrapers loom before me in the great distance, I feel an increased mixture of excitement and anxiety because the city marks the spot where I will abandon my armor, this car I'm in, and make myself vulnerable to the world. It's natural for me to feel this way and I've gone through it many times before as I was about to embark on other journeys. I actually thrive on the sensation because it creates a kind of rush, an inner thrill and knowledge that I'm breaking through a barrier behind which most people live. Did you realize that Southerners who live in little towns and rural areas usually find it frightening to visit a big city like Atlanta? This is even more true about the New South than the Old South, because people are so bombarded with the six o'clock news and its endless reports of people being shot or stabbed to death in big cities. I can't deny that

I'm also disturbed by these images and that it'll take a couple of days on the road without being attacked by a stranger before I feel, a step at a time, that my new territory is safe. After all, I'm used to walking among trees and birds. I have yet to see a news report in which a woodpecker, crow, dove, or hummingbird has killed a man. Then, too, Debi's fear that something horrible will happen to me on this march has me a bit concerned. I'll also confess that I've had some trouble sleeping the past few nights. One of those nights I crawled out of bed and stuck *Gone With the Wind* into the VCR. I hadn't seen it in years and stayed awake till dawn watching Atlanta burn to the ground and Scarlett swear that she'd never go hungry again. The Civil War followed me to bed that morning; my dreams were filled with Tara, Union soldiers, and cannon fire.

Gone With the Wind is on my mind again when I arrive in downtown Atlanta and drive through a thunderstorm to park in front of the old home where Margaret Mitchell wrote the Pulitzer prize-winning novel. Translated into twenty-nine languages, it's second in sales only to the Bible. I've come here now to look at the place because of the woman who lived inside it.

The three-story house is falling apart and it looks out of place next to the modern skyscrapers towering over it, as if the New South wants to choke the Old South to death. A plastic canopy has been pulled over the roof to protect it from the weather. The plastic flaps in the wind and makes me think of a rain bonnet on the head of an aging Southern lady.

I'm still imagining that lady when a yellow cab parks behind me. Its back door opens and two figures with an umbrella hurry toward the crumbling house, its plastic canopy yet flapping in the gusting wind. Wiping the fog from my window to get a better look, I discover a Japanese couple shivering under their umbrella by the house's iron fire escape. He readies a camera while she holds up a copy of *Gone With the Wind* written in Japanese.

I can't control my curiosity and hop from the rented car. The rain has let up some, but the wind blows my face wet by the time I run to the Japanese couple.

"You've read *Gone With the Wind*?" I say, hoping they speak English.

"Oh, yes, very good," says the man, water dripping down his nose.

"I read *two* times," says the woman.

"Movie *four* times," says the man. "Last month we have *Gone With Wind* party in our home. I dress like Clark Gable—"

"Oh, he good-looking," says the woman, breaking into the silliest giggle I've ever heard. Then he starts to giggle along with her. "I wear hoopskirt," she adds, her face blushing as if she's remembering something very private about that night.

"You take our picture?" says the man, trying to regain his composure.

"Sure," I say, taking the camera.

When I snap the shutter it starts to rain harder and we run back to our cars. Their cabdriver, working a match from one corner of his mouth to the other, opens the back door for them. As they hop inside with their book and camera their giggles begin again. The cabdriver, having shut their door, looks at me as he stops the wooden, red-and-white-tipped match in the corner of his mouth.

"When they get that Gone With the Wind theme park built south of the city," he says, "we'll have more wanna-be Southerners than we can shake a stick at. But I don't care what their fantasies are as long as they pay their fares—*and tip*."

He jumps into his yellow cab and the Japanese couple wave as the car disappears down the rainy street. Before I drive away I turn to the old Margaret Mitchell home again. Sherman's men may have started a fire that could be seen for miles, but she lit a flame that still circles the globe. Why does some part of me fear that someone will put a match to this old house?

Chapter Eight

Inman Park is a lovely old Atlanta neighborhood some ten minutes southeast of downtown, and by the time I drive there the rain has stopped. The clouds are parting and the sun proves once again that a glowing day can lift a man. I inch along Edgewood Avenue seeking the address of a bed-and-breakfast in one of the houses built here after the great fire. When I find it, I feel lucky to have made reservations for the next two nights. It has an iron gate and a wide, long front porch with rocking chairs. What a contrast to the little home, my green nylon pup tent, I'll sleep in part of the time as I march to Savannah.

It's not only the grandness of the old home that pleases me but the wooded ravine that runs alongside it. I even hear a dove cooing somewhere down there as I get out of the car, and it makes me feel a touch of Tanager. It's so peaceful here that it's almost hard to believe I stand in what was once the heart of a battlefield, Yanks and Rebs alike getting their arms and legs blown off. In fact, down there in that gorge, the Springvale Park Ravine, is where the Confederate soldiers re-formed their lines as Sherman and his men closed in on Atlanta on July 22, 1864. I wish I knew the exact spot where my great-uncle Croft got his elbow shot off by a Yank.

I walk down into the ravine and the world of today vanishes. The smell of earth and damp leaves fills the air, and wisteria vines, blooming purple, climb through the trees as if seeking just the right branch to befriend with fleeting beauty. Some ten feet up in a massive oak someone long ago carved JIM

LOVES KATIE, the words now fading. Running along the exposed roots of the tree is a spring-fed stream only a foot wide, where Rebels placed their lips for one last drink. I can almost hear them talking as they pour black powder into their muskets, their feet bare and bleeding.

"You having fun yet, Johnny?" says one, poking his ramrod down his barrel.

"Fun?" says another. "Son, I ain't had so much fun since I saw a blue-tailed lizard run up a fat woman's skirt in church. She jumped and hollered like the Holy Ghost Itself took her to bed."

"I can't talk against Jesus myself. I done been baptized in a creek back home. I promised Mama I'd see her in heaven if I got killed by one of these Yankee bullets. Every letter she tells me how much she's praying for my soul. Ain't you scared of catching a minié ball and going to hell?"

"*Going?* Son, look around you. We're the coal and shovels."

The Confederate soldiers vanish into the spring's trickling as I climb from the gorge. I take my backpack and staff from the car and enter the bed-and-breakfast. I'm the only guest here tonight and my attic room overlooks the ravine. When I wake in the middle of the night, I find moonlight soft and silver on the tops of the trees growing from the gorge. For all I know, the person who long ago carved JIM LOVES KATIE in the oak is also awake, perhaps stroking the other's hair or feeling the emptiness of what once was. This makes me think of the Courting Tree where Debi and I have carved our names at Tanager. I'd like to have her beside me just now, as she is when we sometimes wake after we've had enough rest and dreams to help heal us from anything the day may have thrown against us. It's then that we can talk about each other's more discreet beauties, needs, and thoughts that we may have overlooked during the rush of the day.

That's one of the things I'm missing the most about her right now, the conversations we have. We're not afraid to tell each other our fears, fantasies, or silliest thoughts—and how often can a person truly do that with another? If you think it sounds like I worship the ground Debi walks on, you're right.

A Southern male is taught from birth not only to respect his mother as if she were the greatest gift on earth, but to treat the other woman in his life as if she were the owner of the moon. You may be thinking that you've seen some Southern men who had the manners of a pig around women, treating them as if they were property and nothing else. Well, I have on rare occasions seen that too. I don't condone it, but I understand it. These poor men act that way because they have so little control of their own lives that they want others to think they can control their wives or lovers.

A bus passes by and my bed shakes just a bit as if the house's ancient timbers have learned when to give to avoid breaking. This makes me think of the old Margaret Mitchell home I saw earlier today with its bonnet on. A sign out front was seeking donations to save the place where one of the greatest love stories of all time had been written. Intrigued to learn more about Margaret Mitchell and the birthplace of *Gone With the Wind*, I decide that tomorrow I'll visit the foundation that had put up the sign.

At The Margaret Mitchell House, Inc. I view a video that includes interviews with people who knew the author. I'm captivated by the man with only one eye, Boyd Lewis, who was the last person to live in the Mitchell house. Not only does his black patch call to the pirate within me, but he speaks with the passion of the seven seas. Also, it's a very Southern trait to be drawn to people who look as though something dramatic has happened to them. How did he lose that one eye? This tradition was strengthened during the Civil War, because so many thousands of Rebels returned home missing ears, eyes, jaws, hands, arms, feet, legs, and minds. All their friends and kinfolks had to know what happened in the greatest detail, thus fortifying the Southerner's role as a storyteller.

Hoping to meet Boyd, I phone him and am pleased that he agrees to see me for lunch at Manuel's Tavern. When I hang up the pay phone I decide to leave my rented car parked and walk to the restaurant even though I'm not yet adjusted to being around so many people after living among birds and trees. I hope my mingling with folks will help free me from being too on guard.

It's a beautiful spring day and this part of Atlanta, Five Points—near the B&B I'm staying in—offers cafés, bars, a theater, camping store, bookstore, and a New Age shop. The streets are jumping with people. Well, okay, one couple isn't exactly leaping; their bodies are stretched out on the sidewalk as if ready for the Lost and Found. They're either passed out or doing some kind of Zen exercise that has sent their psyches swirling through the hole in the ozone. Fifty feet from them a black man is strumming a guitar, and an upside-down hat at his feet holds quarters, dimes, nickels, and three one-dollar bills. When I drop some change into his hat, a girl in a red tank top, with a tiny yellow dragon tattooed on her shoulder, hurries from a bench to ask me for a quarter. She appears to be around nineteen years old, and that tank top is so tight on her that her big, braless breasts look like they're ready to pop through the material at any moment. A Southern gentleman, I will try to catch and return them at once should they do just that.

"Your dragon hungry?" I ask, referring to the change she seeks.

She offers a seductive grin, sticking her hand into the back pocket of her faded, tight shorts, cut from old jeans. Her long legs are muscular and tanned, and bare flesh peeks through the now-fashionable holes in the shorts. What a contrast those trendy holes are to the ones my mother tried to keep patched in our clothes to show we had some pride in ourselves. However, I was part of the sixties crowd and some of its fashions, so I'm not knocking this young lady's fix on threads. Who am I to say love beads have anything over holes in short shorts? In fact, I find the suggestive openings far more interesting. Each hole is a tiny stage and every move she makes is an erotic show.

"Not really," she says. "But he likes for me to smoke with him sometimes. Cigarettes aren't cheap."

I pull a buck from my pocket and her eyes light up.

"It's yours," I say. "But could I sit with you and your friends for a few minutes and talk?"

"Talk?" she says, eyeing the money in my hand. "Talk about what?"

"How you feel about the South," I say. "Where we've come since the Civil War and where we're going."

"Why do you care?" she says. "People your age don't usually want to know what my generation thinks about anything."

"I'm a writer," I tell her. "I'm curious about what everybody thinks. I assure you, I'm trying to get over this condition, but it's taking a while."

Judging by the new gleam in her eyes, she decides that I'm not all bad.

"My friends call me Dragon Woman," she says, taking the dollar bill from my hand. "Come on over and I'll introduce you to the gang."

Two nearby cops give me a suspicious eye as I follow Dragon Woman to a bench under a small tree.

"Those cops ever bother the street people?" I ask.

"No," she says, waving at them. "They're cool. It's those two guys over there we have to watch out for."

She points at two skinheads leaning against a wall outside an Indian restaurant. They wear big black boots, black jeans, and black T-shirts. Their heads look like they've just rolled through Marine boot camp. If they've had a good laugh lately, I can't tell.

When we arrive at the bench under the tree, Dragon Woman introduces me to her friends, Sandy and Cyclone. Sandy is white and in her early twenties with a bird in flight tattooed over her right breast; gold bracelets dangle from each wrist. She sits on the sidewalk while Cyclone, a black man in his twenties, sits on the bench behind her and braids her long hair. It's apparent that he lifts weights because his arms are so muscular. A single ivory earring hangs from his right ear.

"How'd you get the name Cyclone?" I ask.

"Gave it to myself, man," he says, continuing to braid Sandy's long hair. "Same way Dragon Woman got hers. This is the beginning of the Age of Aquarius and you make things

happen by what you believe and envision. I see myself as a
cyclone, strong, determined—"

"Full of hot air." Sandy winks as she scratches the flesh
where the bird in flight is tattooed over her chest.

"Oh, girl," says Cyclone. "You're always eating out of my
bowl with your bare hands."

"You're too serious," says Sandy, reaching back to rub his
leg as he keeps braiding her hair.

"Life is serious," says Cyclone. "I want our child to grow up
realizing that."

"You have a kid?" I ask.

"On the way," says Sandy. "We just found out last week."

"We'll have to find a bigger apartment when she has the
baby," says Dragon Woman.

"The three of you live together?" I say, and Dragon Woman
nods. "Did you know each other in high school?"

"No," says Dragon Woman. "We all met on the street. Well,
around the corner at Fellini's, a pizza place."

"Last year, man," says Cyclone. "We put all our change
together to buy a pizza. By the time we finished eating it we
knew that pizza had brought us together for a reason."

"I grew up in a little town in south Georgia," says Dragon
Woman. "It was so boring that I felt like I was dying. I mean,
the most exciting event there was snapping green beans. I
thumbed a ride with a truck driver to Atlanta last March and
been here ever since. I don't always bum money. I usually
have a job cooking in a restaurant, but it had a fire last week
and I'm out of work till the kitchen is rebuilt. I don't mind.
It's fun to hang out sometimes."

"I ran away to New York from Alabama when I was seventeen," I say. "But I missed home and went back. Ever since,
though, I've been coming and going. It helps me find a bal-
ance between nature and the world."

"I'm never going back home," says Dragon Woman.

"Don't you miss your family?" I say.

"I never knew my daddy—"

"Didn't know mine either," says Cyclone.

This news about their fathers makes me feel sympathy for

these people. I can't imagine what going through life without
a caring father does to a person.

"I phone Mama from time to time," Dragon Woman continues. "She comes to Atlanta sometimes and we eat together.
Yeah, if I get to thinking about her I miss her. She always tells
me I can come back home anytime I want, that she was young
once herself and that she understands. But I'm not sure she
really does. So much has changed since she was my age."

"She don't like me," says Cyclone, now braiding the last
few strands of Sandy's hair.

"He's right," says Dragon Woman. "Mama has a hard time
with me living in the same apartment as a black man. I haven't
told her yet about Sandy's baby. She'll have a hissy fit when I
break the news to her."

"You'd be smart to just not tell her," says Sandy. "No sense
in hurting her feelings any more than they have been already."

"Did you run away to Atlanta too?" I ask.

"Oh, no," says Sandy. "I grew up in the city. My folks are
old hippies and don't have any trouble with my lifestyle. Well,
not usually. They think my having a baby with Cyclone is a
mistake. Not that they're racists and won't accept him. They
just say the South isn't ready for mixed children. And you
know, they're right. But I refuse to live like others want me to,
and if they can't handle it that's their problem. Besides,
there's plenty of people in Atlanta who are beyond all that
racial stuff anyway."

"How do your folks feel about you being with a white
woman?" I ask Cyclone. "Are you from Atlanta?"

"I'm from Macon," says Cyclone. "Mama thinks I should
marry an African American, but she saw so much racism when
she was growing up that she has a heart too tender to be any
way but warm to Sandy and the baby. Besides, there's already
some white blood in my family. My great-great-grandmother
was a slave and had a baby by the overseer. They say they
made love in the smokehouse when the hams were curing and
that's why my eyes have this smoky look about them. All
kinds of crazy stories get passed down in families. They say

the overseer's wife found out about the affair and tried to kill
the baby with a pot of boiling lard, but her husband grabbed
her. She fell and burned her hand so bad she couldn't use
three of her fingers for the rest of her life. She always wore a
white glove to hide the scars. Mama has one of those gloves
that her mama passed on to her. Says she keeps it as a reminder of how close my great-great-grandmother came to being killed. Mama keeps it in a little cedar box in her closet and
I opened it one time when I was young. I put my fingers into
that glove and I swear I saw that white woman appear in the
closet with a pot of boiling lard. I threw that glove down and
ran out of the house and all the way down to the cotton field
where Mama was hoeing. If there's such a thing as a ghost, I'd
seen one. Man, I hadn't thought about that since I was a kid.
Why are you so interested in all this old stuff anyway? It's the
Age of Aquarius, the dawn of a new era. Look ahead to the
future. Don't look back, it'll only put a kink in your neck.
We're looking ahead. After the baby's born we're going to go
to Europe and travel so he can grow up with a world view. I'll
continue to make my leather goods and sell them and Sandy
can read palms like she does now."

"You read palms?" I ask Sandy.

"Yes," she says. "Want yours read? I won't charge you."

I give her my hand and I'm surprised at how warm her
fingers are. She turns my hand up, so she can see the palm,
and studies it. I must admit that I like the attention and that
I'm drawn to the idealism of these young people. They remind me a great deal of my generation back in the sixties,
when we felt that we could change the world, spread love, and
do away with small minds and racism. I hope their dreams of
traveling in Europe and having their child mature with an
open mind and world view come true. But by the time they
get to be my age I can't help but think that they, like myself,
will start to reflect on the past and how they are part of it. Or
am I simply out of touch with the nineties and there's no real
reason to look back—only ahead?

"You have a big heart," Sandy says as her fingertip traces a
line on my palm. "But that sometimes gets you into trouble.

You feel close to people quickly, and it's difficult for you to part from them. That's why you're a writer. It's your way of holding on to people, by writing about them."

"She's been blessed with the sixth sense, man," says Cyclone. "Don't she see right into you?"

"Yes," I say, a part of me wanting to rationalize that what she tells me is a kind of stock response to anybody with an artistic bent like myself. But what she says is also true about me and I decide to let go of my defenses.

"You're very much in love with someone right now," says Sandy. "But you're troubled about this because you're apart."

"You see that in my palm?"

"No," says Sandy. "I see *that* in your face. Your eyes."

"My friend here would like to have his palm read," comes a stranger's voice from above me.

I look up to see the two skinheads who were leaning against the wall outside the Indian restaurant.

"Ah, man," says Cyclone. "We've done this dance before with you guys. Now why don't you just go back to holding up your favorite wall."

"You're not very friendly for a man who preaches peace," says the first skinhead.

"You guys are creeps," says Dragon Woman. "Get lost."

I feel Sandy's fingers, still holding my hand, starting to tremble. Mine aren't as calm as a mountain either. It's obvious these skinheads are looking for trouble, and I'm not sure how far they'll push or how much Cyclone, or I, for that matter, will endure before retaliation seems appropriate.

"Well," says the second skinhead, taking the hand of the first one, "since this fortune-teller is all tied up, I guess I'll just have to read your palm myself. My, my, don't you have an interesting future. This line here shows you've got a long life ahead of you, while this line over here shows me you've got a lot of worthless niggers to deal with."

Cyclone bolts to his feet.

"Move, man," he shouts, "or I'll make you eat that damned palm."

Sandy jumps to her feet to stand between Cyclone and the

skinheads as the two cops hurry toward us. I'm relieved that
they show up because a mixture of fear and anger has been
building in me since the two skinheads arrived.

"What's the problem?" says the first cop.

"These assholes are looking for a fight," says Dragon
Woman.

"Now, Officer," says the first skinhead, "can I help it if they
don't like what we read in our palms? I do, after all, have
freedom of speech—don't I?"

"Yeah," says the second cop. "You also have the freedom to
get your ass on down the street, as in *now.*"

"We'll see you around," the first skinhead says to Cyclone.

Then he and his friend walk on down the sidewalk. The
cops follow them. If I needed a reminder that the South is yet
charged with the seeds of violence, I just got it. But looking at
Cyclone, Sandy, and Dragon Woman, I'm also reminded that
the New South is filled with idealism and hope.

I'd like to get to know these three young people better, but
it's been twenty minutes since I talked with Boyd and if I
don't leave now for Manuel's I'll be late.

"Thanks for letting me in for a while," I say. "You're fuel
for thought."

"Look ahead," says Cyclone. "The New Age is here."

He pulls Sandy into his arms and Dragon Woman winks at
me as I walk away, the song "Age of Aquarius" playing somewhere in the back of my mind among brain cells lucky enough
to have survived the sixties.

Chapter Nine

Walking up the street to meet Boyd, I spot the two skinheads circling the block. One taps the other's arm and motions for him to look my way. I wish I had my staff in my hand in case they try to give me a hard time. But before we cross paths I spot Manuel's and go inside.

The turn-of-the-century bar is ornately carved, and its huge mirror invites all to get a good look at themselves. I ask the bartender if he knows Boyd, who suggested this spot.

"He wears a black patch over his right eye," I say.

"We got a couple of those who come in here," he says. "Yours nicknamed Hawkeye?"

"I don't know," I say. "Yours work at a radio station?"

"No," says the bartender. "He doesn't have to work. He gets a big fat check from the government. He was wounded over in 'Nam. He don't talk much and it's hard to read a man with only one eye. It's like he's always got a secret whether he wants to or not."

A few minutes later Boyd enters through the back door and we wave at the same time. His patch brands him, and he recognizes me from my faded and sweat-stained trail hat, a crow feather sticking from the side and a rattlesnake rattler riding snug at the back of the band.

"When I was a kid," says Boyd after we take a booth and order lunch, "I used to play in Grant Park, running through the trenches that had been built to fortify Atlanta during the Civil War. One day I found one of the railroad spikes that

Sherman's men had pried loose when they wrecked the lines coming into town."

"So you grew up in Atlanta?"

"No, I was born in New Orleans," he says.

"I lived there eight years," I say, feeling a kinship as I look into his single eye, the black patch staring back . . . intriguing my own darkness.

"I'm afraid we left there before I was old enough to be corrupted by its unique ways," he adds. "We moved to Ohio and then I came here in 1969."

"That's when you moved into the Mitchell place?"

"No, I didn't do that till 1977," he says, lifting a glass of beer to his lips. "I had been renting a storefront I wanted to turn into a photographer's studio, but I was freelancing at the time and that's a hell of a way to make ends meet. I went to the landlords and said I didn't think I would be able to meet next month's rent. I asked if they had any work I could do to pay them, and they topped that. They needed somebody to stay at a house at the end of the street to keep out vagrants. I was warned that it was shabby, but the rent was free, so the next week I moved into 979 Crescent Avenue. It was behind what had been a Chinese restaurant called the House of Eng. Nine seventy-nine used to be called the Hippie House back in the seventies because a lot of longhairs lived there. Right off the Peachtree and Tenth Street strip, it had been notorious for years. Bohemians and artists lived there back in the fifties. This guy called Mother David lived there and opened Bottom of the Barrel, which was Atlanta's first coffeehouse. Anyway, he was painting naked women on the garret. This brought the cops to him and a citation to the old woman who owned the house. She threw up her hands at the whole mess and sold the place for around twenty-five thousand dollars. That's when it became the Hippie House and then was vacant for years till I moved in. I ended up living in the lower left-hand apartment, apartment one. It was small and dark and I had no idea about the historic significance of the place when I moved in. But at the first party I had, someone said, 'Hey, did you know this is where Margaret Mitchell lived?' I said, 'You're kidding.' 'No,'

he said, 'she lived somewhere in this building.' The next day I
went to the public library and dug into the Margaret Mitchell
files. I found a lot of newspaper clippings from the 1930s. It
had her biography and her address as 979 Crescent Avenue,
apartment one, which was exactly where I was living. I threw a
party to celebrate the news and a bunch of us had a séance
trying to reach the ghost of Margaret Mitchell. Damned if we
didn't begin to hear this awful noise in the wall and I just
knew any second the plaster would explode, with her jumping
to the floor. It turned out to be two rats who had migrated over
from the Chinese restaurant. They were fighting over the privilege of seeing who could drag a box of d-Con back into the
walls so they could eat it. But the remarkable thing about the
apartment, which Margaret Mitchell called the Dump because
it was small and dark, was that in the front room was this
beautiful little alcove that had beveled glass mirrors on three
sides. Leaded glass windows faced west on Tenth Street, so
when the sun set, red and gold rays came through the windows
to bounce off the mirrors onto the mahogany walls. It created a
sphere of light and pulled you into it. I later discovered this
was where Margaret Mitchell wrote *Gone With the Wind*. At one
time the manuscript had been used to help hold up a couch
that was missing a leg. I took pictures of the alcove and they're
going to be used to help restore it, if the old house is saved."

"Will it be saved?"

"They might be able to save the apartment, but as far as the
whole building it's taken so much rain with that big hole in
the roof, it's been there I think ten years, that the structural
beams would have to be replaced. You'd really be rebuilding
the place."

His single eye drifts away for the first time, as if finding
himself living back in 979 Crescent, apartment one. Sticking
the last of his corn bread into his mouth, he brings the eye
back to me. It's really starting to bug me that I don't know
what happened to the eye behind the black patch.

"The apartment never did have hot water," he says, "and it
was February when I moved in. The shower demanded the
jerk-and-scream method. I was the only one living there, and

it was a wild neighborhood with bathhouses and bars all around. Sirens went off like crazy. It was rumored that the mansion had been converted into an apartment building after the owner's daughter was killed there. One night when I threw another party some fifteen of us wandered upstairs to the room where the murder was said to have occurred. I had this hand from a department store mannequin and placed it on the center of the floor. We sat around it and lit some candles as we tried to move it with our minds. We wanted to summon the murdered girl's spirit or the ghost of Margaret Mitchell. We weren't feeling a lot of pain at the time so maybe some more rats would've been welcome. Five, ten, fifteen minutes we sat there trying to move this hand with our wills, and then I started to hum. The others joined me and the humming started to get louder and louder till we heard this big rattle coming from the side of the building. We all ran to the windows to see what the noise was, but the panes were boarded up. I finally found this slat and could see outside as the rattling got louder. Two bare asses were running up the iron fire escape. They'd been making love and our hums had scared the devil out of them."

Downing his third beer, Boyd grins as if he's most happy with himself for having such memories. He isn't as pleased, however, about the memory of losing his eye when I ask him what happened.

"I went through the windshield of a car," he says. "I wasn't the one driving."

Feeling as though I've rubbed Boyd the wrong way with my question and that he has no interest in telling me about what led up to the accident, I return to Margaret Mitchell.

"What do you think about the Gone With the Wind theme park coming to Atlanta?" I say.

"How can you create a plantation without making everybody feel as uncomfortable as hell?" he asks me. "It would have Negroes, and what African American with any kind of pride in self, heritage, and family would go down there and shuck and jive for a bunch of white tourists from Ohio? Atlanta has a peculiar history with blacks to begin with. Martin Luther

King, Jr., had his civil rights headquarters here, but this town was so satisfied with itself that he had to go abroad to Birmingham in the sixties to get things happening in the streets."

"During that time," I say, "I thumbed to New York to get out of the South and see what other parts of America were like. I was eighteen and felt mature to be old enough to enter a bar and be served whiskey legally. When the bartender asked where I was from I hesitated to tell him, because I thought he might look down on my state because of the racial trouble there. But when I said *Alabama*, he grabbed my hand and shook it. 'You sure know how to hang "niggers" down there,' he said. I told him I hadn't hung anybody and hadn't wanted to. He leaned over the bar and whispered, 'You don't have to keep it a secret from me. I know how you feel down there in the South.' Then he gave me a drink on the house. It was the first time in my life that I realized some people could see only stereotypes. That trip was also the first time I realized that my identity was as a Southerner. I looked around me everywhere I went in New York and I saw ethnic groups— Jews, Italians, Chinese, Germans, Irish, and so on, but I was a *Southerner*, a person from a nation called Dixie, and others recognized their own concept of it the moment I opened my mouth and they heard my accent."

"I'll drink to that," Boyd says, once a new glass of beer is set before him. "Now back to the Dump. Right outside the front door was this oak lion's head, beautifully carved. When I was there it was painted black and was kind of rubbed off. It had once been quite grand, but people had taken nicks out of it. To exit her apartment you had to make this tight turn in the stairs where the lion's head set, and your hand would always fall on it. You had to pet the lion to go outside. Well, in *Gone With the Wind* there's a scene in which Rhett builds Scarlett a fancy mansion on Peachtree Street during reconstruction. This is where he takes his ill-gotten gains from the Confederacy and buys land, and she has lumber mills going everywhere. But there's this scene in which Scarlett comes down the stairs and places her hand on a lion's head. Everything in *Gone With the Wind* is based on Margaret Mitchell's life."

"Any idea what became of the lion's head?"

"I lived there for nine months," he says, "and the moment I moved out workmen came in from the realtor and took out the three leaded glass windows in the alcove as well as the post where the lion's head had set all those years. They disappeared down the street in the back of a truck. One night a while later some men came at night and climbed ladders to chisel away at a set of gargoyles that faced Tenth Street. They ended up in a glass case in the Gone With the Wind museum [Road to Tara]. I know this for a fact because I went down there to see them. But even if they vanish and a meteorite crashes into the house, I have lots of photos of them with the Atlanta Historical Society. It's my little bit of immortality that might surface a hundred years from now. The same with the signals from FM radio, they shoot from the station and follow the earth's curve till they continue on into outer space. So if you've ever been on FM you're immortal. Someone way out there a hundred thousand years from now will tune you in."

I pay the bill as Boyd, downing his last beer, looks ready to throw one more party back at the Dump. Before the waiter brings my change Boyd hurries out the door so he'll be on time for work at the radio station where he's a classical music DJ. After all, a man can't afford to be late for immortality.

I leave the restaurant feeling that I, too, have now become part of 979 Crescent Avenue, apartment one. But with no FM station ready to broadcast my two cents' worth up to the gods, I walk back down the street as mortal as the gum I step in on the sidewalk. Yes, sir, this Sherman stuff is sticky business.

Chapter Ten

The next day, as I drive toward the Atlanta airport to drop off the rented car, I tune in the city's National Public Radio affiliate and lo and behold I hear Boyd introducing Tchaikovsky's "1812 Overture." I'm a bit envious, for not only is Boyd once again blasting his immortality to the heavens, he's getting to do it to music with cannon shots as loud and bold as those fired during the Battle of Atlanta. I don't envision soldiers fighting, however, as I turn the music up. Rather, I see a box with a picture of a smiling Quaker in a big black hat because that same music was used in a TV ad for cereal when I was growing up in Alabama. The commercial ended with a cannon firing puffed wheat. Oh, the battle scars of breakfast.

Finally getting rid of the rented car at the airport, I feel the trek taking a new turn. Now free of my armor, I have only people and experiences between me and Savannah. I believe in my abilities and what I've set out to do, but I won't deny that a tiny voice somewhere inside me is whispering, *But will you make it all the way across Georgia? How could you chance losing Debi over this trek? Does anyone really care what you think and feel about the South of today or yesterday?*

With the pack on my back, the staff in my hand, and my old sweat-stained trail hat covering my thinning hair, I board MARTA—Atlanta's rail system. The other passengers stare as if I just stepped into the modern world from the 1860s.

"Fly in from Australia?" asks a black woman dressed in a business suit. The diamond in her ring is so big, I wonder if she isn't taking a chance that someone might mug her on the street.

"No, I'm from Alabama."

"Oh . . ."

"Sorry to disappoint you."

"Not at all," she says. "That's as outback to me as Australia. I'm from Los Angeles. My goodness, that's a snake rattler in your hat."

"Yes," I say, "these are my trail clothes. I'm about to walk the route of Sherman's March to the Sea to collect stories about the South. What brings you here?"

"I'm a doctor," she says. "I'm speaking at a seminar in the morning."

"Are you nervous, or do you like speaking to groups?"

"I don't mind it. Mama used to make me and my sisters sing for company when they came for Sunday dinner. I never got very good at singing, but I got over being afraid to stand before strangers. The only problem with getting up before people now is that I expect dinner to come next. I blame Mama for every pound I gain."

"You sound real close," I say, having heard her voice become more tender at the mention of her mother.

"Mmmmm," she agrees. "She grew up in Georgia, but it's my first time here."

"Were your ancestors slaves?" I ask, hoping that she's not offended by my directness.

"They were," she sighs, "and I never let myself forget it. That's one of the things that helped me get through medical school. That, and I didn't want to be poor like my mama and daddy. You want to see something?"

I nod and she opens her purse to remove a set of keys. She hands them to me.

"Know what the key ring is made from?" she says.

"It's gold, isn't it?"

"It's gold plated," she says. "The ring itself is a link to the chain that held my great-great-grandfather when he was a slave. The keys it holds go to my convertible. A car isn't free-dom—that's something inside a person—but I love to put the top down and let my hair blow in the wind when I hit the freeway."

She breaks into a wonderful, carefree laugh, and takes the keys from me and drops them back into her purse.

"If I have time," she says, "I hope to visit some of Mama's cousins and see where Mama lived when she was a little girl. The house rotted down, but my aunt Sarah said the well is still there. Mama and she used to call it their wishing well. They didn't have enough money to spare pennies, so my grandmother told them if they'd draw pictures on pebbles with a safety pin and drop them into the well, that would work better than dropping coins because it was a wish made with their hearts and hands instead of money. You tell children all kinds of things to keep them busy."

"Yeah," I say, admiring her beauty and poise, "but I've got a hunch at least one of your mother's wishes came true."

"Excuse me?"

"You were born to her."

She almost blushes and her eyes take on a new light, or perhaps mine have just become clear enough to see what was already there. At the next MARTA stop I have to change trains and I tell her I hope she has a good stay in Atlanta.

"Be careful out there," she says, her voice becoming tense and making me just a touch uneasy.

"I will," I say, "and if you visit your mother's well wish me safely to Savannah."

She nods as I hurry from the car with the pack and staff, my brass CS belt buckle catching the morning's sun. Though part Cherokee, my skin color is light, and when the train disappears down the track toward Atlanta's great skyscrapers I find that I'm the only white person at the station. This wouldn't usually bother me, but two teenagers wear blue bandannas around their foreheads and I can't help but wonder if they're members of the Crips, a street gang. And if my imagination isn't working overtime, that's a pistol I spot under the shirt of the teenager in the Nike tennis shoes. No, I don't think most black kids are killers or even violent, but it would be equally stupid for me to forget that I had a lover who was shot on the streets of New Orleans fifteen years ago as she walked to the grocery store near Tulane University. The bullet hit her spine, and she'll be paralyzed from the waist down for the rest of her life. Following five more shootings of college girls on the street, the New Orleans police arrested two black kids. They admitted that they had to shoot a white person to get initiated into a gang. Just as that bullet is forever lodged in my friend's spine, that memory—the most horrible of my life—is forever stuck in my heart.

Hoping the train will soon arrive, I stand looking down the tracks. When the kid in the Nikes yawns and stretches, I see for certain that he does have a pistol stuck in his pants. His buddy looks over at me and our eyes lock for a moment, before I have enough common sense to look back down the tracks as if the train is my only business and what he does is his, as long as he doesn't confuse the two.

I'm relieved when, only seconds later, the train arrives. I make certain not to get on the same car as the pistol and place my pack on the seat next to me; my staff stands between my legs, a welcome friend from back home.

The train pulls from its stop and I drift back in time, envisioning the thousands of mighty wheels on the wagons that went with Sherman and his men when they started their March to the Sea. Atlanta lay smoldering behind them, smoke rising to the sky like a tombstone marking the dead, charred city. In fact, there were so many Union wagons—2,500—that they formed a line 25 miles long and were pulled by more than 25,000 horses and mules. It took a whole team of 8 horses to move each cannon, and 65 of the big guns rattled toward Savannah. While the marchers planned to forage for their food, they had one hell of a backup snack: 10,000 heads of cattle were herded between horses and mules, some of the soldiers riding the beef like rodeo clowns. In the midst of the grand madness Major Hitchcock rode horseback beside General Sherman, whose single spur jingled and jangled as he reined in his sometimes flighty stallion named Sam. Surrounding Sherman, and acting as his bodyguard, was the Alabama Cavalry to which my grandpa Ellis belonged till he made that generous and historic decision to go back home to fight with his wife and give someone else the opportunity to become a hero.

The train slows as we pull in to the next stop. I'm happy to see the two pistol packers get off. A black man with a leather briefcase gets on and sits in front of me and he's joined by an old black man in ragged clothes. Both of his shoes are untied and a red rose, short half its petals, sticks from his lapel. A can of Prince Albert smoking tobacco rides in the torn pocket of his ketchup-stained shirt. He's so tipsy that his shoulders bump against his fellow passenger as the train moves on.

"Rough rides," says the old man. "My whole life is rough rides."

He reeks of booze and the man seated next to him opens his briefcase and takes out a Bible. The drunk leans over the holy words.

"You a preacher?" he says.

"No," says the man. "Just trying to get right with myself."

"I gets right," says the drunk. "Then I gets wrong. Right in Chicago, wrong in Atlanta. Right and wrong and wrong and right. Sometimes they the same. Ain't that right?"

The man continues to stare into the Bible as the train takes a curve and we approach Oakland Cemetery. How odd it seems to me, because after lunch with Boyd yesterday I drove to that graveyard to see where Margaret Mitchell had been put to rest. Some magnolia leaves had fallen on her grave as though they, too, had had enough. I brushed them aside.

"Tombs," says the old drunk, eyeing the sea of graves. "Tombs, everywhere you look. Nobody knows what down there. Some say bodies. Some say ghosts. No way to know without digging 'em up. Ain't got time myself. You got time, Bible-reading man? You got time, white man?"

He looks into my eyes and I feel sorry for him.

"I'm tired," he says. "Need to rest."

My stop comes up and I lift my pack and staff to get off the train. The old man grabs my hand and squeezes it as if wanting me to help him up.

"You'll feel better when you sleep," I say.

The doors open and I start to get off, but he continues to grip my hand as if to let go will break a link and send him twirling down a dark, endless hole in the earth. Finally taking the plunge, he releases my hand and lowers his weary head toward the man with the Bible in his lap. I hurry to beat the closing doors.

The end of my staff bangs against the platform at the Decatur stop as the train shoots on down the tracks. A flight of stairs leads up to the ground level, and a gust of cold air hits my face as I slip into my pack.

When I reach the top of the stairs I find myself outside the old Decatur courthouse. This building touches a special spot inside me because it's where Nita and Clay got married, her days of loneliness buried.

Tree limbs blow in the morning wind over my head and only fifty feet in front of me stands a Confederate soldier. Carved from stone, he's a majestic giant looking like the brother of Johnny, my cousin, back home in Union Park. He seems to be here waiting for me, his heart not at all a rock.

"Well," I say after making certain that no one is around but me and him, "you about ready to make this march?"

With my staff in my right hand, I start walking down Ponce De Leon Avenue toward Stone Mountain twelve miles to the east. It's so good to hit the trail that I feel light despite my forty-pound pack. I don't even mind the cool spring wind gusting into my face.

When Sherman and his men made their way down this very route, the November cold snapped at cheeks and noses, but many of the soldiers didn't have to worry about it. As they marched they stayed warm from the flames of fence posts they set afire in front of homes and fields holding hogs and cattle. Much of the livestock, along with chickens and turkeys, didn't have to concern themselves with the cold either; Union bullets invited them into their traveling butcher shops.

Most of the soldiers had a hand in the foraging, but those who were officially assigned to do it were called "bummers." Inspired to the frenzy of a riot, soldiers swiped more than they could carry. Major Sam Merrill of the 70th Indiana wrote this about one evening's returning parade of looters:

> At the head of the procession . . . an ancient family carriage, drawn by a goat, a cow with a bell, and a jackass. Tied behind . . . a sheep and a calf, the vehicle loaded down with pump-kins, chickens, cabbages, guinea fowls, carrots, turkeys, on-ions, squashes, a shoat, sorghum, a looking glass, an Italian harp, sweetmeats, a peacock, a rocking chair, a gourd, a bass viol, sweet potatoes, a cradle, dried peaches, honey, a baby carriage, peach brandy and every other imaginable thing a lot of fool soldiers could take in their hands to bring away.

Some of the bummers stuck fine ladies' hats on their heads, the long plumes waving in the wind. This circus atmosphere was heightened by the pets the soldiers carried. Bun, a squir-rel, played on his owner's back while he chewed hardtack and flickered his bushy tail. Old Abe, a war eagle with a Wisconsin regiment, preferred to ride on the tip of a cannon. During the Battle of Atlanta he circled high in the sky till the smoke cleared and he could once again land in peace. Minerva, a screech owl, hooted at night while a pet bear stuffed himself on foraged meat. Dozens of dogs rode in saddles while their masters rubbed their heads and sang. Southerners peeked from windows praying the arson circus would spare their homes, while their barns, mills, and cotton gins went up in flames and the shadows flickered on the faces of the devilish entertainers.

The land is not afire today as I march toward Stone Moun-tain, but the wind has stopped and the sun is beating down. I've been walking two hours now and half that time back I pulled off my jacket. Sweat drips from my face and from time to time I catch a drop just right and blow it from the tip of my nose, an acrobat flipping to death on the red Georgia clay.

Modest homes line both sides of the road and I wave at people mowing their lawns or hoeing their young gardens. They wave back, their eyes investigating my pack and staff. An old man in a front porch rocking chair whittles on a piece of cedar, the shavings curling and piling up at his feet like some rare thread.

"Going far?" he calls out.

"Savannah," I say.

"*Savannah?*" He stops his knife halfway down the piece of cedar. "You'll burn up between here and there in this heat."

"I'll find a shade," I call back.

"I'd find me a car," he shouts, his knife returning to its business. "One with a good air conditioner."

"Where's your sense of adventure?"

"Three wives and eighty-two years behind me," he shouts.

I salute him as I walk on and leave the side of the road to start down railroad tracks. When Sherman's men did their good deeds for the Federal Government in Georgia they tore the iron rails from the tracks and burned the wooden ties. Once that fire got hot enough the stronger and more creative soldiers bent the rails around trees and poles to form *U* and *S* letters to show the Rebs that they could brand their asses in more ways than one. The rails that were simply twisted out of shape became known as Sherman's Neckties.

I leave the tracks when I reach Stone Mountain, one side of its bald granite dome carved with the colossal figures of General Robert E. Lee, Jefferson Davis, and General Stonewall Jackson atop horses. There's a park there where camping is allowed, but I choose a secluded spot under an oak and near a rock wall surrounding a Confederate cemetery to pitch my pup tent for the night.

These graves make me think of where Daddy is buried, on the side of a hill about a mile from our home. It faces Lookout Mountain and Wills Creek, which meanders past a thirty-foot-high Indian mound built hundreds of years ago. When I was a boy, it was a Southern tradition to take a dead person to his home and open the casket so all could see him one last time before he was placed in the earth. I recall seeing both my grandpas like that, in their homes where they once walked and talked like the rest of us. But now that tradition is dead, too, and the bodies are taken to funeral homes. A part of that tradition, however, lives on, and it's the practice of cooking food and taking it to the home of the deceased. It's a gesture to help lighten the burden of those in mourning, but it's also a sacrament. The food is the body and soul of the dead. Each third Sunday of May it's an old tradition for many of the folks in my area to have Decoration Day, a time to place flowers on the graves of those we cherish. This is followed by a meal at a family's old home place. I'll miss this year's Decoration Day because I left for this walk. But the day before I departed I took a single red rose to Daddy's grave. It made me feel good to see that the grass over it was thick and green. Days after he was lowered into the ground I sodded the grave with grass that grew along the edge of our garden. That's not an old Southern tradition—just a new one, one between Daddy and me.

I've only walked about fourteen miles today, but my feet hurt like hell. Removing my shoes and socks, I rub my precious toes and pour cool water over them from my canteen.

I crawl into my tent this afternoon to simply rest a bit, but fall asleep and awake to see that night has arrived. Exiting my little nylon home, I find the air cool and the moon and stars bright over the Confederate tombstones. Most of those buried here did not die in some glorious battle, but faded away—as most soldiers did, both North and South—in an unsung struggle with some disease for which science has since found a cure.

I decide not to build a campfire tonight because I suspect the cops patrolling the nearby road might investigate, and I'm fresh out of cake and coffee to entertain. When the Union soldiers camped, however, the night crackled and popped with thousands of campfires. Freed slaves, following them, danced and sang in African tongues and rattled bones to charge the heated and smoky night with music, celebrating what they believed to be a new dawn. Young black women, afire with this rebirth of hope, made love to some of the soldiers, their moans unshackled and their bodies wet with sweat. Thousands of the Yanks were only teenagers and they had never known such luxury and excitement as this March to the Sea afforded them. Many were veterans of Shiloh, Vicksburg, and

Chattanooga as well as Atlanta and the horror and hurt of war had, at last, been replaced by sweet heaven—no fighting, plenty of food, and a woman's warm arms.

But for every man who had a gal to hold him close there were a hundred who were lonely. They sat around their campfires to write letters to loved ones back home. This gets me to thinking about Debi and how far away she is, way out there in the state of Washington. When I crawl back into the tent to retire for the night, I snuggle against my backpack and pretend it's her. We're slow dancing in the backyard at Tanager under the big oak. She wears a silk dress and no panties. My fingers slide down her back to her hips. Wind chimes hang from a limb of the oak and a breeze makes them send a delicate song through the forest, our feet dancing to the tune. With each step Debi takes, my fingers feel the movement of her hips. Her arms are around my back and our bodies are as close as lips in a midnight kiss. The sound of the wind chimes is joined by the creaking of a wooden swing, which hangs from two chains dangling from a wooden beam stretched between two trees.

"Swing me," she whispers, and runs the tip of her tongue up my neck to my lips.

We slow dance over to the swing and the wind chimes continue to sing out in the Southern breeze as she leans back into the wooden seat. I stand before her and gently push the swing back and forth, a continuation of our dance as her legs now spread and I lift the silk dress up her long thighs past the private place where panties sometimes hide her secrets.

"Swing me higher," she whispers, wrapping her legs around me and pulling me into her as if the wind, the chimes, and our souls were one and the same, soaring through the forest on the moans of our flesh.

Chapter Eleven

My arms around the backpack, I fall into a sleep of erotic bliss with Debi. But I awake at dawn with the memory of another dream of my father. As before in this dream, I was walking between rows of tall corn, and Daddy loomed from the earth itself some thirty feet in front of me. He motioned that I must follow him. I did and hurried to catch up with him. When I was within an arm's length of him, he pointed up ahead. I stepped closer to see what he wanted me to behold, but then I awoke. What was this dream trying to tell me? What's Daddy trying to say? I stick my head from the tent's nylon door, expecting Daddy to be there to meet me. Instead I find only the tombstones of the Confederate cemetery, floating in early morning fog.

I break camp and push on down the road to the tiny town of Lithonia. It was here that Sherman saw the first homes on the March to the Sea go up in flames as his men wrecked the railroad, twisting the iron rails into Sherman's Neckties. And in the midst of the thousands of freed slaves, still singing as they danced toward Savannah, the general beheld a bummer marching with a ham stuck atop his bayonet.

On the outskirts of Lithonia I climb a granite hill to behold quaint old Southern homes, towering pines, and in the distance, the office buildings of Atlanta touching the sky. What a contrast this is to what Sherman's men saw when they stood where I am now.

"Atlanta is still burning!" one Yank shouted down to the general. "Enough smoke to choke the whole Confederacy!"

Pleased at the news, Sherman directed his arson circus toward their next victim, the town of Conyers, some twenty miles from Stone Mountain. I descend the granite hill and head that way, determined to get there before darkness falls.

Along the sun-baked way I run out of water and stop at a grocery store for three cold oranges. The clerk is from India.

"You're on a pilgrimage," he says, eyeing my staff.

"In a way," I say. "How'd you know?"

"It's written all over your face," he says. "A man cannot easily hide when he is driven by purpose."

The aroma of curry drifts from the back room through the store and I wonder what my grandpa Croft—accustomed to the smell of cooked turnip greens, pinto beans, corn bread, fried potatoes, and the occasional piece of beef—would think if he could rise from the grave and see this man who had come so far, from a country where a cow was never eaten or killed for fear it might be a relative, to start a new life in the Deep South. Me, I like his musical voice and warm eyes. The aroma of rare spices filling the store makes me want to explore his kitchen. I'm reminded, too, that in just the past five years in my hometown a Mexican restaurant has opened and is owned and operated by Mexicans. There's also a new Chinese café. The owner, from Taiwan, has given birth to a child since she moved here three years ago and many of the locals adore her as she wobbles about the tables while her mom cooks and waits on people. The child, named Jennifer, is learning both Chinese and English—with a Southern accent. It amuses me that she'll soon be saying "Ya'll come back now" to customers and then turning to speak to her mom in the language of wise old Confucius. But then again, wasn't it Confucius himself who said, When East meet West in New South, no better biscuit be baked. Well, okay, you might want to double-check that quote, but it goes something like that and no matter how you state it the South has started opening its arms wider to people from all around the world.

"What brought you to Georgia?" I ask the Indian, thinking he might shed a little light on my changing Dixie.

"I had friends here from India," he says, "and there are

many people in America who will not work for minimum wage as I am doing here in the store. They prefer to be on welfare and this is fine for me because I make three times more money here than I did in India. I have so much more to give my wife and children."

I admire his work ethic because I was raised to believe in it. And, frankly, it hits a raw nerve in me that some people, Yanks or Rebs, black or white, are too damned lazy to work. My heart goes out to those who have hit hard times, but those who simply suck money from taxpayers need a good swift kick in the ass. Or would that only give the person more reason to claim that he's a victim? You may recall that when we first met I said I believed many Southerners want to excel today because our ancestors were uneducated and poor. The flip side of that, it seems to me, is that some Southerners feel trapped. They reason that their forefathers didn't have anything, so why should they?

When I place money on the counter to pay for the three oranges, the Indian puts it back in my hand.

"Take the fruit as a gift for your pilgrimage," he says. "In India people sometimes wander their entire lives to gain enlightenment. Is that your kind of journey?"

"I hope I don't have to walk the rest of my life," I say, a bit amused. "I'm on my way to Savannah right now."

"Well," he says, "it's the distance the soul goes that matters, not the body. Do you know what is at the heart of your pilgrimage?"

"Yes," I say, being reminded that sometimes we discover more insight into ourselves when we least expect it. "At the core of my walk is the love of my father, the South where I grew up, and the woman in my life."

"Oh," he says with a laugh, "you have your hands full."

"Yes," I say, starting to laugh along with him. "It's a good thing I have two of them."

"Ah," he says. "You are laughing at yourself and this is a good sign for a pilgrim."

As I walk on down the road squeezing and sucking the cold juice from the oranges—Confederate General Stonewall Jackson had a habit of sucking lemons in battle—I feel as though my talking with the Indian has helped me complete the first important step in my transformation from woods-dweller to voyager. I haven't been attacked by anyone, my confidence is growing, and I've managed to start laughing at myself a bit. I also have a better grasp of what's at the naked core of my journey. Last, but not least, I've had my clothes soaked with sweat, which is a kind of baptism, humbling a man. It's difficult to deny my humanness with sweat dripping from my pants into my shoes and making them squeak like a child's rubber toy with every step I take.

But when I drag into Conyers this afternoon I've had all the humbling and squeaking I want for the day. As soon as possible I find a motel room with an air conditioner and fill the sink with crushed ice and water to soak my feet. When I strip from my sweat-soaked trail clothes, I discover that my thighs are covered with a heat rash. My red skin looks as though it has been scrubbed with coarse sandpaper. Oh, but how sweet to feel the cold air blowing against my body as I stick my feet into the ice water in hopes of taking the swelling from the little piggy that went to market as well as the one that stayed home. You know that I'm a humble Rebel pilgrim, but a stranger peeking through my window might see an Eskimo fisherman over the ice using his toes for bait.

A good night's rest allows me to crawl from the cozy bed eager to explore Conyers. The heat rash on my thighs has lessened and fresh clothes on my clean body put zip into my walk as I leave the motel.

I'm also grateful that the place on my right hip that was rubbed raw by the backpack belt is better. So are the blisters on my feet, which I popped with my pocket knife to release the water pressure. Some choice pieces of Dr. Scholl's moleskin between my toes come in handy as well. Okay, so I march a little funny as I head down the street because my feet are sore, but I'm my own general and I passed this morning's inspection.

Conyers is little more than a village, its downtown old and

charming while Interstate 20 roars with cars and trucks only a few blocks to the south. There the fast food joints—I bet you can name them as fast as you can name your parents—are already heating up the day's cooking oil to fry their way into our clogging hearts.

I forget the sound of the interstate and its distractions as I hike among houses built in the 1930s. On the porch of one of the houses sits a black woman drinking a bottle of Coke, and I can't help but see my magical friend Sparky in her face.

"How are you today?" I say, after seeing her eyes get big at the sight of my pack.

"Doing fine, mister. Is that pack heavy?"

"Not as heavy as it was yesterday afternoon when I drug into town from Stone Mountain."

"Whoooo-weeeeee!" Her eyes get bigger. "You walked all that way? Bet your feet hurt. My legs hurt today. Yesterday I weeded the corn at my mother's house, and squatting down like that puts rocks on my back. I'm not doing anything today but sitting and listening to the mockingbird. That's him now, hear him? You know he mocks other birds' songs and that's why they call him what they do. I never heard anything so pretty in my life. Well, except maybe the way my daddy played the fiddle. He's gone now, but I swear him and that mockingbird were a team. Daddy would play a little and whistle and then that bird would answer back. Some folks didn't care, but then some folks can't hear music in the wind either. Mostly white folks are that way. Oh, but not all. I didn't mean you, mister. Some blacks are just as hard of hearing."

"I love birds of all kinds," I tell her, feeling a connection to her story. "My grandpa also played the fiddle. When he did he sang sacred harp songs and they always made a chill run up my back."

"Lord, yeah," she says. "I know just what you're talking about. Mama and Daddy both sang gospel and sometimes I'd feel like sprouting wings and flying away when they hit certain notes."

"Can you whistle the song your daddy did?" I ask.

"I wish I could whistle," she says. "I can hear it as plain as day in my mind. But if I tried I might hurt that poor bird's head so much, he'd up and leave the whole county. Daddy was sick in bed a month before he died and I watched after him here at my place. He was too weak to whistle, let alone play his fiddle, and that bird never sounded so sad in the trees. He's his old self now. I don't know how but he got to singing better and better each month after Daddy was gone, just as I got better. What are you doing in Conyers with all that stuff on your back anyway?"

"I'm walking to Savannah to collect stories," I say. "I'm a writer."

"Oh"—her eyebrows go high—"you're a Johnny Apple-seed. But instead of planting you're gathering."

"I never thought of it that way," I say. "But maybe you're right. Would I be imposing if I sat on your porch for a little while?"

"No, no, indeed," she says, coming from her chair. "Get that heavy pack off your back and sit a spell. Here, you take this chair and relax."

"I don't want to take your chair," I say, thinking how mannered and very Southern she is to offer. It also dawns upon me that the first time I lived in California for a summer, when I was only eighteen years old, I was surprised to find myself feeling closer to some blacks than whites, because their ancestors came from Dixie. We had more in common than many of the whites who had no Southern connections.

"I'll get another chair from inside," she insists. "Now you go ahead and sit down."

I place my pack and staff on the steps and take her chair as she goes inside her house. How odd it is to feel her body heat rising from the chair bottom into my hips. It's as though her very spirit lingers in the wood and now joins mine. I'll tell you this, too, she's a real looker, this woman. Only a few years younger than me, she's well built and has a face that would stand out in any crowd. Her skin is closer to brown than black and I can also smell the perfume she's wearing. I don't know what it's called, but it entices me. Do you think I'm odd for feeling attracted to someone so quickly? I can't help it. I've

been this way for as long as I can remember. If I meet someone who opens up to me, and especially if I like her voice, I
start to feel close right away. There's one thing about this
situation, however, that makes me uncomfortable and a bit
ashamed. Being on her front porch makes me recall all too well
what happened the night of "The Confession" I've promised
to tell you. In all fairness, though, I don't think I'll mention
this again till I'm ready to tell you the whole story, because it's
painful for me and must be frustrating for you, since I'm being
so secretive about it.

"What's your name?" I ask when she returns with another
chair and sits several feet away.

"Linda," she says. "What's yours?"

I tell her my name and get a fresh whiff of her perfume
when a breeze stirs, shaking the limbs of the tree with the
mockingbird.

"How did your daddy train that bird to sing with him?" I
ask.

"No training to it," she says. "Daddy was just sitting out
here like we are one evening with his fiddle and when he
started playing that bird sang back. I think some people and
birds are just born with something needing to come out. I got
something in me, too, that wants to find daylight, but I just
don't know yet what it is. Sometimes I'm afraid I'll die still
not knowing what it is that wants out."

There's such an openness and innocence in her face just
now that I can't imagine anyone looking at her wouldn't see
beauty, and some sadness.

"How do you make a living?" I say.

"Today's my off day," she says. "Six days a week I care for
an elderly white woman who's bedridden. She's almost ninety
years old and I've known her since I was a little girl. Mama
kept house for her for over forty years. Her name's Willie.
Well, that's not her real name, but what we've always called
her. Her mind is going now and she likes for me to read her
children's stories. Her favorite is about a little boy who catches
a caterpillar and they become friends. When the little boy
plays his harmonica, the worm dances and other kids pay to

see it. Then the worm disappears and the boy is lonely. No one cares that he can play music. He's lost without that dancing worm. Then one day when he's about lost all hope he starts playing his harmonica and a butterfly comes to dance in the air over his head. I like it when friends get together again, don't you?"

"Yes," I say, melting at her childlike ways. "I like to see people feel whole."

"So many don't," she says. "I got a nephew I helped raise since he was a baby and he's all broken into pieces right now himself. I'd give anything to help get him back together. He won't admit it, but I'm pretty sure he's doing drugs and selling them. I went to Atlanta last week to see him and he was driving a new car. Only twenty years old and driving a new car. I've never had a new car. Anyway, I tried to talk to him about all this but he wouldn't listen, told me I was a fool for not getting a piece of the action myself. He carries a beeper so his customers can phone him. He thinks it's cool every time it sounds off. When I was his age, I thought it was cool to carry a transistor radio. He thinks any black who works a regular job is an Uncle Tom."

"Have you ever felt that way?"

"No," she says. "Mama and Daddy brought me up to be honest and not afraid to work. It's just some of these younger people who feel like the world owes them something. Well, not just the young people either. I got a friend my age in Savannah who's joined this group to petition the government to try to get money because their ancestors were slaves."

"Do you agree with that?"

"I don't blame them if they can get some money that way," she says. "I'm not saying I wouldn't take it myself if somebody dropped it in my lap. But I'm sure not going to cause a stink over it. 'Let sleeping dogs lie' is what Daddy used to always say."

"I would like to have met your father," I say, "and heard him play that fiddle."

"You mean that, don't you?"

"Yes," I say. "Getting to know you some has made me all

the more curious about him. Do you look like he did or more like your mother?"

"I'll let you tell me," she says.

She disappears into the house and soon returns with a fiddle case. She hands it to me and taped to the cover is a picture of a black couple.

"That's Mama and Daddy when they were young," she says.

"You look like both of them," I say, as a Southerner must respond when put in such a position, because to say someone favors one parent over another in a photograph is a sin in Dixie. "But," I add, "I think you got your daddy's eyes."

"I like to think so," she says, almost blushing. "Daddy used to play his fiddle for Mama when they first courted. She told him she could see the gates to heaven when he did. Daddy asked her what they looked like and she said they looked just like his arms. You want to open the case and see the fiddle?"

I open the case and the fiddle seems to wait inside for me to take it out and lift it overhead so that the mockingbird might once again behold a dear friend. Then, when I dare to run my fingertips over the tight strings, notes fly into the air as if they know just where that bird awaits them. My trance is interrupted by the sound of the phone ringing just beyond the screen door, speckled with tiny balls of cotton stopping up holes to keep out mosquitoes and flies.

"That'll be my sister, Flora," she says. "She calls every day about this time to tell me her man problems. Hers ain't right in the head. He drinks too much and drives too fast and ever since that Rodney King beating she lives in horror that the same thing will happen to him. I better run and answer her."

"Good talking to you," I say.

"You're leaving?" she says, disappointment in her voice.

"I got a feeling your sister needs to talk for a while," I say. "I don't want you to feel rushed."

"There's always some big talk down at the feed store," says Linda, pointing at a building a block away. "Why don't you visit there and come back here later and we can talk some more?"

"I'd like that," I tell her, and her face lights up.

When she hurries into the house with the fiddle, the phone soon stops ringing and I hear her voice. It fades with the song of the mockingbird as I walk away with the pack once again on my back, the staff in my hand.

Chapter Twelve

I walk toward a weathered wooden building on the railroad tracks. A sign says HOLMES SEED AND FEED, BUILT 1870. Dozens of young tomato and pepper plants grow from small plastic cups on a table outside against the west wall. Stepping closer, I smell sweet feed like the type horses are sometimes fed.

A door big enough to drive a pickup truck through is open on the south wall and I set my pack on the ground to enter. But I'm stopped by a man coming down the sidewalk. In his seventies, he wears a hat decorated with fishing lures, hooks dangling like a fancy, shiny trotline wrapped around his head. Southerners are the most nosy people in the world and he's no exception. Before he even asks my name he wants to know what I'm up to, and I get to the point.

"I got a stick about the size of yours," he says. "I use it when I wade down creeks to fish for bass. Mine's made out of a piece of bamboo I cut down in the Florida swamps. Me and my wife took our grandkids to Disney World in Orlando. My wife and the kids liked that Mickey Mouse, but I thought Goofy was a little more with it. Your stick heavy?"

"See for yourself," I say, handing him the staff.

"Hey, this is a humdinger," he says, "light as a feather. What kind of wood?"

"Chestnut."

"It's stronger than my bamboo. Mine's got a split started up the side. I got a pretty little pocketknife I'll trade you for this walking stick."

Southerners are notorious for wanting to trade, which is a

tradition that has been handed down to us from our ancestors, who did it when money was scarce and trading was both a necessity and a sport.

"My daddy cut it for me," I say. "I couldn't part with it. Besides, I already got a good knife."

"Yeah," he says, "but you don't have a knife like this sucker. Just take a look. That won't show no disrespect to your daddy."

He digs into his pocket and pulls out a yellow-handled knife. He gives it to me and I spot three lines cut in the handle.

"What are—"

"I thought those notches would get you. What do you figure they're for?"

"I don't know," I say, thinking that it's an unwritten law in the South that everything—especially anything to be traded—must have a story. Trading and storytelling, there's Dixie for you.

"Guess," he says.

"I have no idea," I say. "The three times you cut loose in life?"

"No, no," he says, "I've done that more than these handles can hold. They're the times I won the County Buck Dancing Contest back up in Gum Holler, Tennessee. That's where I'm from."

My cousin Doodle Bug, back in Fort Payne, used to be considered the best buck dancer in our parts. A logger, he wasn't afraid to dance solo and swing his arms and legs as if he just swallowed a pint of white lightning and the only way to handle its mean punch was to shake it all about.

"I'm not sure I believe you," I say, amused. "Why would you trade something that special for a stick from a total stranger?"

"You don't like my buck dancing knife?"

"It's a good one, but . . ."

A whole new look comes over his face as if I've hurt his deepest feelings.

"I thought maybe if I had that walking stick of yours I'd

somehow be part of all this. I'm too old to hoof it to Savannah myself. My right knee is weak. I fell out of a honey tree when I was a boy and it's come back to get me."

"You're already part of this walk," I say, the old man melting my heart. "Why don't you take your knife and cut a notch in my staff. That way you'll be with me and I can show people your mark."

"I'll do it," he says, opening his blade and forcing the sharp edge into the chestnut. "I appreciate it, hear?"

I nod and he hands me back my staff. He hurries into the seed and feed store ahead of me, his fishing lures jingling and jangling from his hat. And, if I'm not mistaken, his walk now has a cocky little bounce.

"Say, Ernest, this Alabama man's walking old Sherman's route to the sea," he says. "Ask him where he got that notch in his stick."

"No need to," says Ernest. "Me and L.J. heard your big mouth clear in here."

"That's right," says L.J., a black man in his early thirties. "Me and Ernest think you should go with him. He can borrow that wheelbarrel back there by the hay and push you in it all the way across Georgia."

"I got an umbrella you can hold over your head," says Ernest. "Wouldn't want the sun to melt you."

"Don't pay any attention to these two," says the old man, whose name is Henry Walden. He turns to Ernest. "Now, give me a bag of fertilizer before I whip both of you."

Henry bounces from the feed and seed store with his bag of fertilizer and I discover that Ernest Thornton is the owner of the business. L.J. has worked for him for the past ten years. The old building, big as a barn, has lightbulbs dangling from the ceiling on wires five feet long and they're spaced apart about every ten feet. Stretched between two of them is a massive spiderweb with its owner spinning zigzags in the center. I learned as a child not to let such a spider count my teeth or he'd write the number in his web and I'd die the next day. In very lucky cases the spider would take a liking to a person and

spare his life. But all his teeth would fall out by the age of
forty and he'd have to live on corn bread and buttermilk. Is
that what happened to my cousin Raymond, back on Sand
Mountain?

The building was created as a place to make buggies; the
giant beams holding it together were taken from heart pine,
towering ancient trees that were all cut down in Georgia by
the time automobiles had taken over. The smell of hay now
joins that of sweet feed drifting up my nose, and almost any
kind of seed you need for your garden or field is here. I feel
very much at home, because I've always thought our barn loft,
where such smells were common, was one of the greatest
places on earth. Me and other kids would play hide-and-seek
in the hay or get into a corncob fight. Getting hit stung like
the devil, though, and frankly I preferred to stick three feathers in one end of the cob to turn it into what we called a corn
buzzard. Thrown high into the air, it would twirl as it floated
back to the ground. That was almost as much fun as tying a
four-foot piece of sewing thread to the hind leg of a june bug
and throwing it into the air. The beetle would then fly around
while I held the other end. Eventually the delicate enslaved
leg would give out, pulling from the bug to dangle at one end
of the thread. The june bug, shooting into the woods, didn't
seem to care that it was short a leg.

It feels mighty good to my own legs to sit on a block of hay in
the old buggy factory as Ernest takes care of customers. Some
need peas because they had bad luck with the first batch they
planted: a cold snap got them. Others swear that they planted
at the wrong time and that they should have observed the
almanac. It recommends planting different seeds in conjunc-
tion with phases of the moon.

"Lots of people prefer to get their seeds here instead of at
Kmart or Wal-Mart," says Ernest, "because we don't hide ours
in packages. People like to smell seeds and run their fingers
down into the binds so they can feel what they're getting into
before they shell out their hard-earned money. That same
power that pulls you to a stream or a mill where grain is

ground for bread is alive in here. I'm about to mix some mustard, kale, and turnip green seeds and fill that wash pot there with them. You just watch as people come in and see them. They won't be able to keep their hands out of there."

Ernest is right, for I spend the rest of the day with him and L.J., and those who drop in to buy this or that end up sliding their fingers down into the seeds, no bigger than the heads of pins, as if it's a pool of sensual delight. Each time a pair of hands goes in, the owner smiles as if he's getting away with something forbidden.

I'm sticking my own hands down into the wash pot of seeds when Ernest returns in his truck from the post office. Pulling my hands from the pot, I find a few of the tiny seeds have stuck under my fingernails.

"I saw a milk cow while I was gone," he says, coming from the truck. "It made me remember something from when I was only seven or eight that might interest you.

"My great-aunt said she hid her cow when Sherman came through. She tied it up in a ditch and covered it with pine and cedar branches. She was so scared, though, that she forgot to take the bell off and it got to ringing when the soldiers approached. She just knew they'd hear it and she'd lose her cow, but they made such a racket along with their wagons they could hardly hear themselves. That old bell was passed on with the story and used to hang over our mantel, but somebody outside the family did a little foraging on their own long before I left home. I'm not usually a vengeful person, but I hope every time it rings now that thief gets a briar in his bare behind."

His story reminds me that many Georgia families buried things of value, such as fine china and jewelry, in the woods to protect them from the Yanks. The few that were rich enough to own silver doorknobs left them where they were but painted them black to look like metal not worth stealing.

While Ernest is busy in the office I help L.J. load hay onto a truck and then we fill bags with lime. It's a very strong Southern tradition to help out like this. If you don't at least offer to pitch in, you're highly suspect as a worthless bag of bones and it's one of the greatest topics of gossip in Dixie—right in there with who the preacher's sleeping with besides his wife.

"I got five kids," says L.J., "and a good wife. But sometimes she ain't too big on cooking. She'd rather eat out, but that cost plenty. Yesterday I put on a big pot of butter beans. Mmmmm, they good. Them and some corn bread."

"That's part of what my parents were raised on," I say. "Both my mother and father had big families. That's about all they could afford."

"Sixteen in my family," says L.J. "Fourteen after two died."

"Fourteen? You had your own army."

"Me and four brothers had to sleep in the same bed. I stayed warm in the winter, but it was hot as an oven in the summer. I don't know why I always got stuck at the end of the bed by Leroy's feet. They were worse than a skunk. Me and Leroy got along real good though . . . most of the time. We were always challenging each other to this or that. Who could climb a tree the fastest or throw a rock the highest. One summer he dared me to jump off the barn. He did it first and then I did it. There was some hay down on the ground, so that helped, but I landed the wrong way and bit my tongue almost in two. We didn't have a car, so we had to get a taxi to take me to the doctor. Mama was out in the cotton patch when one of my sisters ran out to get her. She came running and I never saw her face like that before. I tried to explain but I couldn't talk with my tongue about to fall off and Leroy wasn't too big on talking either. He was done afraid he'd get the blame. The doctor couldn't sew my tongue, so he had to use two Popsicle sticks to tape my tongue. When we got back home Mama beat the living tar out of me and Leroy both. I never jumped off any more barns. Never was too big on eating Popsicles again either."

"How'd you feel about Leroy after that?" I ask.

"I felt just fine. He didn't make me do it. We were just kids trying to have a good time. I had more fun with Bobo."

"Bobo?"

"A pet hog. He weighed around eight hundred pounds and

had ears as big as an elephant. Me and Leroy used to ride him. He knew just what we wanted and as soon as we got on his back he'd take off. Every day after school he'd be waiting for us."

"He liked you a lot."

"I guess. He sure liked the candy we brought him. Old Mr. Jones lived across the cotton patch and he had a barn that always had five-gallon buckets of candy. Some were red and others were yellow. We never did know where he got that candy, but we'd steal a bunch and feed it to Bobo. He'd snort every time we gave him a piece. He was the sweetest pig in the state of Georgia. Then we ran into some trouble on the farm and had to move into town. We didn't have room for Bobo and Mama had to sell him for next to nothing. I thought my heart would never stop breaking. My city cousins in Atlanta made fun of me for missing him. But he wasn't just a big pet, he was my friend."

I like it here in the seed and feed store with L.J. and Ernest, but Linda keeps crossing my mind and I want to see her again. I slip into my pack and walk up the street to her house. The two chairs we sat in earlier today look as empty as my arms sometimes feel when I want to hold Debi and she isn't around. A Coke bottle, half filled, sits by the chair where Linda sat. I haven't forgotten how warm the chair was she insisted I sit in.

I climb onto the porch to knock on the door when I find a note fastened to the screen by a wooden clothespin. I unfold it and read:

Jerry,

I'm sorry I missed you. Me and my sister, Flora, have gone into Atlanta to look for her fool man. He ran off this morning with her checkbook. I hope mockingbirds all along your trip sing you some pretty songs. I'll remember the one we heard while we talked.

Warmly,
Linda

I take a pen from my pocket and write at the bottom of her note:

Linda,
Sorry I missed you, too, and thanks for the tip about the seed and feed store. I found some good apples there.

I stick the note back on the screen door and head down the street, when I hear the mockingbird begin to sing. For a fleeting moment I think I hear a fiddle among the treetops as well.

I'm a mile down the road with my brass Confederate States belt buckle leading me toward Covington when a car pulls up behind and honks. I assume that someone has stopped to offer me a ride, but I turn to find Henry at the wheel with his hat of fishing lures. A woman about his age sits beside him and her eyes sparkle as much as his do.

"I wanted my wife to meet you," says Henry.

"Hi, honey," she says, sticking a paper bag out the window. "We brought you a little something."

"Thanks," I say, seeing how proud Henry is of the lady in his life. "Is it true Henry was once a good dancer?"

"Oh, my, yes, honey. When he was young he could dance the hair off a bear. He could almost keep up with me."

"See," says Henry, eyeing my staff where he had cut his notch. "Didn't I tell you?"

"You be careful," says his wife. "Most of these country people out here are decent. But there's always one in a crowd who feels like he's been stepped on and wants to blame the first stranger he meets."

"I'll keep my eyes open," I say.

They back up into a dirt road and turn around to wave as they vanish back toward Conyers. The sun is setting when I take off my pack to sit on the grass by a cornfield. I open the paper bag to find two pieces of fried chicken, raw carrots, celery, and a slice of pecan pie.

I don't know if it's luck or fate or what, but sometimes in my life I feel as though I find magical spots on earth and Conyers has been one of them. Not only do I now have a tasty

if greasy dinner, but I'm not alone on the trek. I make the
journey with a buck dancer, a fiddle player, a mockingbird,
and an eight-hundred-pound hog named Bobo. No, I'll take a
rain check for jumping off a barn, thank you just the same.

Chapter Thirteen

When Sherman passed through Conyers he was happy to find recent copies of the Augusta newspaper. So far, according to the stories he read, the Rebels had not yet guessed that Savannah was his goal. Indeed, the March to the Sea was proving to be as smooth as the general's balding head. There had been no resistance from the Confederacy. Camps were already set up and dinner was waiting for Sherman at the end of the day when he slid to the ground from his horse, Sam. On this second day out even the weather was in the Union's favor. Finding the ground dry, Major Hitchcock abandoned his cot and wrote in his diary:

> . . . prefer bed of blankets on pine boughs. . . . Am somewhat tired from loss of sleep last night and march today. Cup of tea tonight very refreshing—better than coffee.

Sounds a bit like a commercial, doesn't it? *Yes, friends, the next time the old firebug urge pays you a visit, don't forget to take time out for Sherman's Tea. With or without milk, sugar, or lemon you can savor the wondrous beauty of towering infernos. Always smooth, always hardy, feel like a general with Sherman's Tea.*

I could go for any kind of tea or anything cool to drink just now as I approach Covington, my water gone and my feet rebelling with new blisters. I swear the sun has chosen me as a winner of its Who Can We Cook Today? Contest, and while it might appear that I'm walking alongside a county road I know that I'm really stuck in a giant oven turned to BROIL.

I'm wondering if the heat hasn't already sizzled my brain when I spot a rabbit lying on its back in the weeds. He seems to be waiting for someone to give him a helping hand. I slow down and then stop to get a better look. It's a toy. Some kid must've thrown the critter from a car. Or maybe he ran away of his own accord, kin to Brer Rabbit, whose birthplace is in Eatonton, which is part of my walk. Well, I hate not to be a Good Samaritan and give the little guy a hand, but can a big, rough Rebel like me afford to be caught with a toy rabbit? His eyes seem to watch me and one of his fluffy ears is bent just enough to make me feel that life has been too hard on him. I can't take it. I bend over and lift him. Now I've really done it, for he's so soft to the touch that I can't possibly leave him here.

Unzipping my pack, I easily find room for him among my belongings. It's as if a cozy home had been there for him the entire time and I had only thought it was a pack of clothes. Hmm, I wonder, are there other things in my life I'm not seeing with true shape and form? Well, that's what I get for meeting strangers in weeds.

I hike on into Covington, a name that may ring a bell with you because it's where the TV series *In the Heat of the Night* is filmed. The small town is built around a park, its magnolia trees shading yet another cousin—a fifteen-foot-tall stone Rebel. What grabs my eye the most, though, are the magnificent antebellum houses.

Wonder why Sherman spared some homes and destroyed others on the March to the Sea? Rumors abound. Some say he saved this house or that because a friend of a friend lived there, or he had a Southern lover who asked him to show mercy. But—and this is hard for a Rebel like myself to admit —the truth is that the general mostly burned only buildings such as mills, that pertained to slavery. Of course, if he and his men were attacked, Sherman was quick to take out his wrath on all structures that stood within sight. Then, too, at other times he had little if any control over his thousands of men— miles from him—who sometimes had fiery thoughts of their own.

Each house around this park in Covington is practically a replica of the mansion on the hill in my own hometown. My family and I lived in a sharecropper's three-room house and every time we passed the mansion on the hill with its massive and towering columns I wished I could go inside and see how rich people lived. Did the kids who lived there also play in barn lofts and tie sewing thread to june bugs to watch them fly, or did those with money get toys that us other kids had never dreamed of? I imagined that they bought rare and exotic items from catalogs that cost so much themselves that I might never see a single page. Still, I never tired of looking at my wish book, the Sears Roebuck catalog. Now, standing in the center of Covington, I gawk at these great houses and wish again that I could see what happens behind their closed doors. And that is exactly what I tell Don Davidson, owner of the corner bookstore, when he says:

"Is there anything I can do to help you?"

At first Don squints, as if I've got some nerve asking him to get me invited to spend the night in one of these fine old mansions. But then his eyes warm, filling with that spark of challenge that comes when a Southerner realizes that he's stuck his foot in his mouth. The only way to get it out and save his honor is to back up his words with action.

"Give me an hour," Don says, rubbing his chin as if that might inspire a vision.

When I return to the bookstore I find Don standing at the counter. I can't yet determine if he has his foot out of his mouth or not. That may just be his tongue pushing against his cheek.

"Any luck?" I say.

"Some," he says. "I phoned the Faulkners. . . ."

"He's a doctor," says Don's elderly assistant, placing new books on the shelf. "He's the only doctor I ever met with such a smile that he could tell you you were about to die and you'd feel it was a very happy thing to have in your life."

"I talked to his wife, Priscilla," Don continues, "and she did some networking for us. She phoned Sandy Moorehouse in Atlanta. The Burge Plantation has been in his family for several generations and his great-grandmother kept a diary of when Sherman and his men ransacked her place. I understand parts of the diary were quoted in that *Civil War* series on PBS. Anyway, Sandy and his wife are headed for the mountains of north Georgia tomorrow but will be happy to put you up at the plantation tonight, if you don't feel slighted by them having to leave early in the morning."

"Not in the least," I say. "I'd love to spend the night on the plantation and maybe get a look at his grandmother's diary. How do I get there?"

I'm even luckier because the Burge Plantation is right on my route to Eatonton. But it's almost ten miles away and I need to hurry to get there before darkness falls. I push on, my staff tapping the way.

When the Yanks marched down this very street I'm now following out of Covington, Sherman rode his horse along another path to avoid the freed slaves who waited on the road for him. Know why the general did that? He was tired of them grabbing and kissing his feet as they sang praises to the "massah" for releasing them from bondage. The sad truth is that Sherman didn't much care for African Americans or Native Americans. He believed in the "law of nature," a common philosophy at the time that said whites were superior to people of color.

The Yanks had fun in Covington by telling the blacks that Sherman was coming down the road any minute dressed in a hat from the American Revolution. When the unsuspecting Union soldier arrived wearing that hat, one he swiped from a nearby plantation, the slaves mobbed him with hugs.

"I'm not Sherman," the Yank cried out, trying to push through the sea of grabbing hands.

"Don't be modest, massah," the slaves called out. "You's a good man, praise God."

A few miles east of Covington I march across the bridge at Alcova River near where Sherman and his men camped on the farm of Judge Harris. The blazing Georgia sun cooks sweat on my face, but so far today my feet are free of blisters. The occasional car or truck that roars by and the telephone poles with their wires sagging remind me that I'm in the 1990s, but the march to the sea seduces me time and time again to tramp with the Union soldiers down the same route. Black smoke bellows in all directions from mills, cotton gins, barns, and homes being torched, while the constant rattle of wagons assaults human ears. Those 10,000 cattle, herded along for food, heighten the noise, and the smell of horse and mule shit is everywhere. War has little modesty and men's urine joins the bitter breeze to let those living downwind be assured that the arson circus is on its fiery way. Thousands of freed slaves follow and some of the pretty young black women have new Yankee sugar pies. They ride in wagons or on horses, dressed in fancy clothes and hats swiped from Dixie homes by the bummers.

No more picking cotton for me, giggles a woman with an ostrich feather sticking from her hat.

Not all of the black babies are so lucky, for a few have been placed on saddles only to fall off in creeks and drown. Others stick their frightened and confused heads from sacks swung over the backs of mules; their cries are lost in the noise of the soldiers' singing and joking. Gunshots signal the gathering of chickens and turkeys for the day's meal as well as the execution of any dogs in the army's path. This attempt by Sherman to make certain no dogs were used to track down runaway slaves was pushed to the limit. One Yank grabbed a poodle from a Georgia woman inside her house.

"Don't hurt him," she begged. "He's all I got left."

"I've been told to kill all bloodhounds," said the soldier.

"But he's only a lap pet."

"We can't take any chances," said the Yank. "He might grow into a bloodhound."

The dog whined under the arm of the soldier, who vanished into the sea of wagons, horses, mules, and slaves.

It isn't a dog but a snake on the side of the road that grabs my attention as I hike toward Eatonton. Seeing it brings me from the dirt-road past to the asphalt present. But as I walk closer toward it I discover that the snake isn't alive. Dead for days, it has been sunbaked in a curled position and looks like creatures I've seen sold in Mexican and Chinese markets for medicine. I stand over it now, the tip of my staff turning it to reveal its near-mummified abdomen. A black snake, its ribs stick from the leathery skin.

I assume the snake has been run over by a truck or car and this makes me think of Debi. Why in the world would a snake do that to your memory? you may be saying. Well, there are a couple of reasons. First, Debi is horrified by snakes. *Any* snake. So when she cut brush and raked leaves at Tanager last summer to make the trails there she wore silver bells around her ankles. She hoped the jingle-jingle would make the snakes in the woods leave her alone. I couldn't help but laugh at her sometimes, because she would also call out "Shooooo, Shoooooooo" as she worked her musical way through the bushes. I admire her, however, for confronting her fear, for isn't that true courage? Then, later that same summer, as we drove toward Chattanooga to have dinner she accidentally ran over a black snake and killed it. That snake curled up just like this one, as if it could strike the murdering car tire from the afterlife. Debi was so heartbroken that she started to cry. In today's world where there is rampant violence and many people are proud of having numbed themselves to feeling anything but anger and rage, I fell all the more deeply in love with Debi for having such sensitivity toward the snake. From that day forward she's been a vegetarian.

I'm lifting the dried black snake from the road with the tip of my staff when a pickup truck with two men roars toward me. I spot the shotgun on the rack behind their heads before I see their faces. I start to lower the snake to the ground and step farther toward the side of the road when the passenger in the truck sticks his arm out the window and gives me the finger. It jerks upward with the speed of a flushed quail and I behold an unshaven face, its mouth shouting:

"*F— you!*"

The truck zooms on past as adrenaline takes control of me and I swing the end of the staff skyward like a spear.

"*Go to hell!*" I yell at the top of my lungs.

The words are hardly out when common sense shakes me.

Why didn't I just keep my mouth shut and let the slimeballs keep speeding down the road toward whatever dark hole they were headed for? Now, if they circle back, I may have them and that damned shotgun to deal with.

There are no houses in sight in which to seek shelter and I don't feel right about running for cover in the woods. However, those thick kudzu vines down there by the blackberry bushes would make an ideal spot to hide. All I have to do is hurry to the bottom of this little hill and crawl in there as snug as the stuffed rabbit in my pack among my socks and jeans.

I'm not sure what to do so I take a few hurried steps forward, then stop to look over my shoulder. Thinking about Debi's warning that something horrible would happen to me on this trek doesn't help just now. I take more quick steps forward and turn back again to see if they're returning. I don't see them, but think I hear the truck motor changing gears. It's all happening so fast that I can't decide if the sound is in my imagination or not. Then there is no doubt. A backfire blasts the Georgia countryside and seconds later the beat-up and muddy truck looms around the wooded curve toward me.

I'm torn between dashing down into the woods or making a stand. Why didn't I just keep my big mouth shut? Is my pride worth getting myself shot or beaten up over? If you're a Southern male, brought up on the Civil War and the fact that your homeland was invaded by the Yanks, you know that's a hard question to answer. Southern boys are taught by their fathers from birth that they must always walk with honor and self-respect and never let anyone push them around. On the other hand, our Southern mothers have taught us that it's very impolite to show anger. Put those teachings in a boy, shake them up, and what you get is Southern charm, grace, and an inner tension that makes a Southern man a walking time bomb.

I've been arrested twice for fighting, and while that was a long time ago and nothing came of either incident, I'm still painfully aware that I can explode when pushed too far. As the muddy, dented truck rattles toward me, I'm becoming afraid —not so much of being hurt, although that's part of it. I'm afraid I'm going to hurt or kill these guys and be sent to prison

—a prospect even more frightening because I'd die if I couldn't roam whenever I chose. I want so much to be a man of peace, and I believe in turning the other cheek. I want to be as strong as a saint. But as that truck draws closer, I feel that same explosive mixture bubbling inside of me.

I look down once more into the woods and a part of me says hurry there *now* before it's too late, but another part of me refuses to budge. And then it is too late, the truck roars up beside me and the two men, both in their forties, are breathing in my face. Now that I get a close view of them, I don't like their looks any more than I care for what's happening. I drop the pack to the ground and hold the thick staff ready.

"You want something?" I say, hearing my words as if they were coming from someone else.

"What coon did you steal that hat from, hoss?" says the passenger, his speech slurred.

The driver lifts a pint of whiskey to his lips and grins like a dog licking himself. I smell the liquor on their breaths as I glance at the gun in the rack. My heart is pounding so hard against my chest that I hope they can't hear it. I feel like my insides will rip open any second, and when the passenger starts to open his door I can't hold back any longer. I kick the door shut.

"Come out of there," I shout, "and I'm going to beat your damned brains out with this stick. You got that?"

The driver cranes to show me his ugly face.

"That goes for you, too, asshole," I shout.

They stare in disbelief for a second or two and then the driver turns to his buddy.

"Get him," he says, as if commanding a dog.

The passenger looks at me with the eyes of a killer. He takes the bottle from the driver and raises it to his lips. Wound tight as a steel spring, I won't let my eyes so much as blink as I continue to gaze into his face. The windows are rolled down and if one of them reaches for the gun I'll ram the end of my staff into his head and—

"Let's go," the passenger finally says, lowering the pint of whiskey between his thighs. "He's just white trash walking the road."

They take off down the highway and I slip back into my pack, my whole body trembling. But if they come back with that shotgun aimed out the window, what am I going to do—shoot back with my walking stick?

Chapter Fourteen

As I walk on toward the Burge Plantation I can't get the whiskey drinkers out of my mind. Every time I hear a truck motor behind me I turn to make sure it isn't them coming back more drunk than before and with the shotgun sticking out the window.

To both rest and try to calm myself, I leave the side of the road and enter the woods. Ever since I was a child I have turned to nature to help heal me from disappointments, fears, scrapes with others or with myself. Rocks, roots, creeks, vines, birds, animals, plants, and trees of all kinds are medicine to Southerners. If you fail to grasp this, or if I fail to communicate it, we lack a most important link between us on this march to the sea. I would even go so far as to say that the bond a Southerner has with nature is second in importance only to the connection he feels for his family and friends. I certainly don't idealize farming, but since the industrial revolution hit the South and Southerners turned away from a more direct tie to the land, our souls have suffered in some ways. We are not as close to the home within our hearts as we once were because of this, and a kind of alienation grows within us without our being fully aware of what's causing it.

Stretched out on the ground beneath oaks and hickories, I begin to feel more at peace. But then I hear a snap in the thicket some forty yards in front of me. The whiskey drinkers with that gun?

I sit up, being careful not to make a sound, and try to see who or what moves before me. Then a small crash jars the woods, followed by another. Yes, someone is running this way at great speed. I now leap to my feet and— I'm relieved to find that the runner is a big deer. When he sees me, he freezes for a couple of seconds and we seem to become one, sharing a secret. We're both part of the forest and all its wonder, as timeless as the stars and the moon. Then, when he leaps over a mound of honeysuckle vines, I imagine that I'm him. My hair blows in the wind as I race forward. Moments later, however, the deer has vanished and I'm a man again, the sound of the animal's racing hooves fading into the brush.

Concerned that I may not reach the Burge Plantation by dark, I slip back into my pack to move on. I'm almost out of the woods when I hear the loud, high, shrill call of an Indian hen, its head as red as a rooster's crown. It sounds and looks identical to Clyde back at Tanager and it's as though Debi, who named him that, flies through the forest now to tell me that she's with me. But if that's so, she decides in a hurry to turn her back on me, for the giant woodpecker vanishes among the thick leaves, its exotic call already nothing but a memory.

The sun is setting when I arrive at the Burge Plantation and I'm exhausted, not only from the day's long, hot hike but from the stress of dealing with the drunks. Knock their brains out with my staff? Man, was I pissed. And how lucky I feel that no one was hurt, save for those inner wounds most of us try to hide. But, of course, the scars always show up sooner or later in our personalities, don't they?

Two massive wooden columns hold up the roof over the front door of the plantation's main house and I sit on the steps there to savor the evening breeze as I overlook the great lawn and await my hosts. A one-room slave's house sits some fifty yards away in the woods and is covered with vines. Its windows are broken and the porch is rotting away, crumbling to the earth to join the Old South.

Twilight begins to fall on the plantation when Sandy Moorehouse and his wife, Betsy, arrive from Atlanta. They're in their fifties and radiate a kind of warmth and security that a couple sometimes develops after years of mutual trust and love. Their facial expressions make me feel welcome. I come from the steps and shake their hands, thanking them for putting me up for the night.

"I'm sorry we have to leave so early in the morning," says Sandy.

"I apologize for not giving you more notice as to when I'd be walking this part of the route," I say, trying to show that my manners match his. In general, Southerners try to say they're sorry as often as possible. For example, right now I'm sorry that I don't know how this tradition got started.

"It'll be dark before we know it," Sandy says. "Want to see the place?"

"Sure," I say, hopping into his Jeep with him and Betsy.

"How many acres you got here?" I ask as we start down a dirt road behind the main house and pass a big lake, the water splashing and rippling when a fish jumps.

"Nine hundred," Sandy says as frogs croak and crickets chirp.

"Did you spend much time here as a child?" I say.

"Oh, yes," he says. "We live in Atlanta, but I always have one foot on this soil."

"We have to buy him rather long pants," Betsy says with a wink, "what with his legs stretching from here to the city."

"What's one of your strongest memories?" I ask Sandy.

"When I was a boy," he says, "we had an old black man who worked here I was fond of. He had a mule and wagon and I loved to ride with him when he hauled trash to the back side of the plantation to dump it in a ditch. On the surface, that may not seem like anything to cherish, but when I did that with him I felt a kind of freedom I've never known since then. There was just him and me and this land and the Georgia wind. He gave off a certain smell and so did that mule. Sometimes even today I find myself sniffing the air out here trying to find it again. That part of myself, I guess."

I feel a very personal connection to his memory, because my grandpa Buckles, Mother's daddy, was the last man in our county to travel to Fort Payne from his Sand Mountain home by horse-drawn buggy. I sometimes rode sitting next to him

and he'd pull a quilt over our laps to fight off the cool air.
When the buggy wheels hit a rough place in the dirt road,
which was often, our legs would bump against each other. But
I didn't mind. Rather, I liked it because it made me feel close
to him. What Sandy said about smell also runs deep in me.
I've never told anybody this before, but after Daddy died I'd
sometimes go to the mudroom at home, where we hang our
garden work clothes, and sniff one of his shirts. His unique
scent lingered and for brief moments he was alive again.

"You sound as close to this place as I am to where I was
raised," I say.

"I'd be lost without this land," Sandy says. "I've been
working on a curse to be chiseled on my tombstone as a warning to anyone who tries to sell this farm after I'm dead. I don't
have it all figured out yet, but the feeling is there and I think
the curse would work if I died today."

Sandy stops the Jeep and we get out to walk under a big
oak. Eight or ten rocks the size of human heads are placed in a
row some three or four feet apart.

"This is where slaves have been buried," Sandy says. "It's a
shame we don't know any of their names. Sometimes I stand
here and look across the fields and wonder which person at my
feet cleared the trees or moved the rocks from the pastures. Of
course I'll never know, but it doesn't hurt to think about such
things."

I like to think that I've learned a little since I was a college
student in the sixties and judged all businesspeople as heart-
less money grabbers. Sandy reminds me that even a stock bro-
ker, dealing daily in big bucks, can have a poetic side. For that
matter, romantic that I am, I believe most everybody has a
poet inside them, Reb or Yank; they just sometimes forget
where they've put him.

Lightning bugs begin to flicker yellow over the Burge Plantation as we climb back into the Jeep and move on past two
cabins that Sandy rents on weekends to city slickers who like
to blow the smog from their lives and hear doves cooing in the
fresh dawn. However, those songbirds don't welcome all who

come, for a 200-member hunt club on the vast estate also
helps pay the plantation's bills.

Darkness falls, and we go to a nearby restaurant for dinner.
I'm so tired that it's hard to keep my head up. But when we
return to the plantation Sandy gives me a copy of the diary
written by Dolly Burge, his great-grandmother, and I find I
have a little more energy than I thought. I go to bed and turn
its pages to see what Dolly experienced when Sherman and
his soldiers barged across the land:

. . . But like demons they [Union soldiers] rush in. My yards
are full. To my smokehouse, my dairy, pantry, kitchen, and
cellar, like famished wolves they come, breaking locks and
whatever is in their way. The thousand pounds of meat in my
smokehouse is gone in a twinkling, my flour, my meat, my
lard, butter, eggs, pickles of various kinds—both in vinegar
and brine—wine, jars, and jugs are all gone. . . . I ran out
and appealed to the guard.

"I cannot help you, madam; it is orders."

As I stood there, from my lot I saw driven, first, Old Dutch,
my dear old buggy horse, who has carried my beloved husband so many miles . . . and who at last drew him to his
grave. . . . There go my mules, my sheep, and worse than
all, my boys [slaves]!

One, Newton, jumped into bed in his cabin, and declared
himself sick. Another crawled under the floor,—a lame boy he
was—but they pulled him out, placed him on a horse, and
drove him off.

Sherman himself and a greater portion of his army passed
my house all day . . . they tore down my garden palings,
made a road through my backyard and lot field, driving their
stock and riding through, tearing down my fences and deso-
lating my home. . . .

Tonight . . . I could not close my eyes, but kept walking
to and fro, watching the fires in the distance and dreading the
approaching day, which, I feared, as they had not all passed,
would be but a continuation of horrors.

Placing the diary on the table by my bed, I dig into my pack and take out my journal to write about today's experiences. Since I'm writing this diary, in part, to share my trek with Debi, I sometimes begin the day's prose with a note to her.

My dearest darling Debi, for brief moments today I flew with you among the trees, your wings flapping as you called out, with Clyde, with the same passion you so often show when we make love. But for all my wonder at birds and their songs, I'd trade the worldful right now to hold you for five minutes beneath the Georgia stars at the Burge Plantation.

Chapter Fifteen

It's Saturday, Memorial Day weekend, when I awake at the Burge Plantation to what must be a flock of crows squawking just beyond my window. But when I look outside I see only two crows in the distance, black balls balanced atop the tips of pine trees. Two june bugs then buzz over the dew-covered lawn and the child in me wishes I had some sewing thread that I might tie around their legs so I could make them circle over my head like tiny green yo-yos forever suspended and spinning over my plantation.

Sandy and Betsy head for the Blue Ridge Mountains after coffee, and I start once again down the trail of fire that led to the sea. I soon discover a cotton field. Like many people my age who grew up in the Deep South, my parents were mostly raised in the cotton patch. They planted the seed, hoed and picked the cotton by hand. When I was twelve my father made me pick cotton one day because he wanted me to see what picking cotton was like so I would be thankful I didn't have to do it to make a living, as he did growing up. In only an hour my fingertips were bloody from pulling the sharp, pointed cotton bolls. We had a contest to see who could pick the most. When we placed our bags on scales at the end of the day I couldn't believe that his weighed so much more than mine. Then I discovered what put the gleam in his Alabama eyes—he'd placed rocks in his bag.

There's an ad on TV about cotton being "the fabric of our lives," and while it may be just a slogan to some, it always makes me recall that Daddy's brother's little boy died in a mule-drawn wagon of cotton. While his mother and daddy picked, he dug a cave in the load of cotton and it collapsed and smothered him in the same field. My older cousin confided to me that he got naked with a girl while she lay between the rows on moist, sandy ground. That she was one of our cousins only added to the cotton-patch mystique. For me the doors to sex as well as death were here. I have always been able to smell both in the soil, whether I wanted to or not.

I begin the day's hike between these cotton rows, and in less than one minute the red Georgia dirt offers me a quartz arrowhead, complete with a sharp point. It was probably made by a Creek Indian, a member of the tribe that once lived throughout this part of the state before it was forced to move to Oklahoma along its own Trail of Tears. I bet several Yanks walked over this stone point as they stomped through this very field.

I have hardly dropped the arrowhead into my jeans pocket when my shoe strikes a piece of rusty metal. I bend over and pick up a horseshoe that's almost as thin as paper from time and weather. Then, only a few feet away, nickel-size pieces of blue china brighten the red earth. I appear to have stumbled into a little gold mine of Civil War artifacts. Sherman's men often dragged more from the Southern homes than they could comfortably carry and later dropped their load. For all I know some Union soldier drank himself a cup of wine he poured from a Burge Plantation jug and then smashed the blue china on the ground just to see what kind of sound it would make.

Reaching the end of the cotton field, I leap a ditch to pick up the road toward Eatonton. I'm more than a bit jarred from the jump, apparently, because as I stand in head-high thistle, I hear music. It's a faint tune, and I've heard the melody before, but I can't put my finger on its title any more than I can determine where the music is coming from. Some of the purple thistle has matured and its silken threads float about the Georgia fields as if each one carries a musical note. That's not it, of course, but when I begin walking again the tune follows me. How can this be? I look about for someone playing a joke. Hey, I don't mind. I can always use a good laugh. Rarely have

I kicked a good grin out of my way. But there's no one there in the weeds or in the ditch. I take another step and the delicate music stays with me.

Then it dawns on me. I remove the pack and unzip it. The stuffed rabbit I befriended grins as if to say *I got you, Reb!* as a tiny music box inside him plays the last few notes of "Here Comes Peter Cottontail."

When the tune stops I squeeze the rabbit's stuffed body and feel the music box, about the size of a big strawberry, inside his chest. I press it with the hope of hearing the song again, but nothing happens. When I shake him, he still refuses to entertain me. Damned if he doesn't seem to grin again, as if he truly does have a mind and heart of his own and he'll not be pushed around by my whims. Well, sir, if those Yanks could march to the sea with a pet eagle they named Old Abe, I see no reason I can't name this little fellow Road Rabbit. Easing him back down into his home in my clothes, I zip up the pack and on we hop.

Late that afternoon I'm still six or seven miles from Eatonton, my water is gone, and my clothes are once again soaked with sweat. The rolling countryside is dotted with one- to two-foot-high mounds of red dirt as big around as telephone poles. I've rammed the tip of my staff into three or four of these mounds and uncovered fire ants by the thousands, racing through tiny tunnels. But I'm so tired and thirsty that I don't stop. My feet are covered with blisters and I can feel the heat rash on my legs. With every step I take, my jeans rub my inner thighs raw. My face, caked with sunblock, burns like pure hell despite the shade of my hat. My arms and shoulders are sore from carrying the walking stick and part of me wants to just plain flop down in the woods and be a lazy bum.

When a truck pulls up behind me, I think of the two whiskey drinkers and my heart begins to pound. A man with long red hair sticks his head out the window.

"Man," he says, "what in the world are you doing walking on a day like this? Hop in and I'll give you a lift."

I explain what I'm doing and that I hope to walk the whole way to Savannah.

"But do you have any water?" I beg him.

"No," he says. A floppy-eared beagle pup stands in his lap with his nose in the hot air, as if sniffing Road Rabbit snug in my pack. "But there's a store around that bend yonder. I'm on the way there now to get some more beer. That first six-pack had a hole in it. Can't you ride just that far?"

"Say that store's just around the curve?"

"A skip and a hop."

"I'll see you there," I say, and he drives away with the pup seeming to help him steer.

Red, as he called himself, was right about the store being just around the bend, but it's the longest curve I can recall ever walking. I swear, every step I take somehow makes it stretch farther down the road. Finally a dirt driveway littered with rusty bottle caps comes into view, and then two ancient gas pumps guarded by a wasp. The ice machine to the right of the store's door, however, is new and I drop my pack to lean against it.

It's the kind of grocery store that was once used as a gathering place for the locals to gossip, drink Cokes, eat Moon Pies, parched peanuts, pecans, and hoop cheese. Chairs were often wooden Coke cases set on one end, and in the winter folks gathered around a wood-burning stove like a bunch of Indians holding council. You can still find a little of this going on today, but it's only a shadow of what it once was and conversations must compete with the store's TV and the weird sounds of video games. I'm already curious as to what I'll find inside this grocery store.

Entering the store, I get stared at by the woman behind the counter. She puffs a cigarette and does something I haven't seen in a very long time. When the smoke rolls from her mouth she sucks it up into her nose only to blow it out of her mouth again. Guess she's one of these modern folks who's learned to recycle.

"Red said you're a Yankee," she says as I pay her for a cold bottle of orange juice.

"I didn't say that, Gloria," Red says, holding a six-pack in his right hand while the left one supports the beagle pup, squirming to get free. "I said he was following Sherman to the sea."

"Where you from then?" Gloria says, her eyes closing in on the Walker Investigation.

"Alabama," I say. "A little town called Fort Payne. You may have heard of it because the band Alabama lives there."

"Everybody from your hometown walk to get where they're going?" Gloria says, more smoke twirling up her Georgia nostrils.

"Just us who don't know any better," I say, finally getting some light in her eyes. "Mind if I sit down for a while?"

"Ain't nothin' to me," she says. "Take that other chair, it's more comfortable."

"How about me?" Red says.

"You can sit in the one that's broken," Gloria says. "Your hard ass can take it."

"Gloria has a crush on me," Red says with a wink.

"Hah!" Gloria almost chokes on her smoke. "And don't let that mangy dog down in here like you did earlier today."

"No danger in that," Red says. "I don't want him getting dirty again. Why don't you ever scrub these floors?"

"Why don't you cut that long hair of yours?" she says. "Hippies went out of style long ago."

"I'm a man with my own mind," Red says. "You live in the time period you want, and I'll live in mine."

"I wish I could," she says. "I'd go back before the Civil War."

"Have yourself a few slaves?" Red says. "Yes, Miss Gloria. No, Miss Gloria."

"Don't want any niggers working for me," she says. "I know enough about being a slave from running this store and waiting on the likes of you. I'd just like to go back to when life was simpler. Things are just too crazy in the world today."

"She's got a nasty mouth sometimes," Red says, "but she doesn't really mean anything by it."

"What?" she says, her eyes searching. "You mean me saying *niggers?*"

"That's insulting to blacks and whites today," Red says. "Where have you been the past thirty years?"

"Minding my own damned business," she says.

"Don't let her fool you," Red says. "She's got a big bark and a little bite."

I wish I could go inside her head right now and see what she's really thinking. Is she a racist or is something else keeping certain words tied to her tongue?

"I saw you walking up the road," she tells me, "before Red got here, Alabama. Thought maybe you's the son of the Goat Man. Don't guess you know who that is?"

"I saw him several times when I was growing up," I say. He used to come through my hometown with his wagon pulled by goats. On his faded hat and shirt he had pinned little things he found alongside the road. I remember a book of matches picturing a donkey and elephant fighting with boxing gloves fastened to the center of his hat. My school announced when he arrived and camped on the creek near the classrooms. My younger sister, Nita, and I would run there with other boys and girls as soon as the day's last bell rang. We gathered around the old bearded man and his teenaged son, who told stories about traveling all over the Deep South. I wished that I could've gone with them and it startles me just a bit now that I realize he may have been a major influence on me to wander as much as I have.

"I remember the Goat Man too," Red says. "Wow, I hadn't thought of him in years."

"You haven't had any thought in years," Gloria says, her eyes keeping score against Red.

It's great to be sitting down in an air-conditioned room, but my feet are killing me.

"Could I use that empty bucket I saw outside to put some ice and water in to soak my feet?" I ask.

"That's your business," Gloria says.

"Would you rather I do it out there?"

"Suit yourself." Her voice softens. "I've seen feet before. There's a bag of ice already open in the box. You can have it, if you want it."

"*You* giving something for free?" Red says. "Didn't think I'd live to see the day."

I get the plastic bucket—its label says DIXIE DOG FOOD— and fill it with ice and water. Back inside the store, I remove my shoes and roll my jeans up to my knees before sticking my burning feet down into the icy water.

"Ain't that cold?" Red says.

"Sure is," I say, pulling my feet out before a minute has passed, to rub them.

"Won't take the swelling out," Gloria says, "if you don't leave 'em in there longer than that."

"I don't blame him," Red says. "Ice is hard to take on bare skin."

"Some wimp you are," Gloria snaps.

"Guess you could do better?" Red says.

"I'm tougher than you," she says.

Red drops the beagle pup to the floor and slides the bucket of ice water over to Gloria at the cash register.

"Take a dive off the high board," he says. "Stick your feet in and I'll time you. Then I'll do it. Double or nothing on a six-pack every week till September gets here."

Chapter Sixteen

If I hadn't grasped how much Red and Gloria like each other
—well, in a way they do—they'd be getting on my nerves by
now. But I'm also hooked to see who can outdo the other.
Then, too, this reminds me that the soldiers of the Civil War
would bet on almost anything—cards, dice, foot races—to
keep themselves amused. They would even have lice races on
tin plates. One soldier was famous for having a prize louse that
always won. But his secret was discovered; he heated his plate
before each event to give his entry a hot-footed edge.

"Okay," Gloria says. "I'll show your little country ass what
tough is."

"Why don't you both put your feet in the bucket at the
same time?" I say, trying to get into the spirit of things.
"That'll be more of a challenge."

"Fine by me," Red says, already pulling off his shoes and
socks.

"Look how ugly his feet are," Gloria says. "I don't want
mine down in the same bucket with his."

"They won't hurt you," I say.

She frowns, but when she removes her socks I give her my
chair. She and Red square off like prizefighters around the
Dixie Dog Food bucket. In this corner, weighing two pounds
apiece, Gloria's feet, undefeated state champions from Eatonton Grocery! And in that corner, the challenger, Ugly-footed
Hippie Red! Yes, sir, it's as if I've stepped into a Brer Rabbit
story with Red and Gloria. And for all I can prove, the spirit of
Joel Chandler Harris—born and raised here in Eatonton and

creator of the Uncle Remus tales—is here in the store laughing at all three of us right now.

They lower their feet into the icy water and it does my heart good, frankly, to watch them begin to make faces that would scare the pants off old General Sherman himself. After two minutes, however, the champ can take no more. Gloria jerks her feet from the bucket, water dripping all over the floor. Red does the same right behind her, his smirk hard to hide.

"Stupid contest anyway," Gloria says, lighting a cigarette as soon as possible, smoke up her nose and out her pouting mouth.

"I sure do enjoy free beer," Red says, putting his socks and shoes back on.

"My God," Gloria cries, eyeing Red's dog chewing something as he runs from behind the row of canned goods near the rack of peanuts and Moon Pies. "I told you not to let that mutt down in here. Now he's gone and ate that rat poison I put out a couple of hours ago."

"*What?*" Red says, panic on his face.

"You'll have to get his stomach pumped at the hospital," Gloria says. "The vet's closed for Memorial Day."

"Shit," Red says, snatching the pup up from the floor. "He's a purebred. I paid a hundred dollars for him."

Gloria finally looks at me and winks.

"Take it easy, Cool," she says. "He just got a piece of candy some kid dropped."

"I thought . . ." Red lets the pup lick his nose.

"More than one way to skin the likes of you, Red Wilson," Gloria says, blowing smoke again.

With the cold beer under his arm, Red and the dog get back in the pickup and take off. I force my feet back into the icy water.

"Guess you got the last laugh on Red," I say.

"I like to mess with him sometimes," she says.

A huge black woman in a white dress and big hat with a red rose on it opens the door to enter with a black child about two years old in her arms. She wears a pretty pink dress and her hair has fifteen or twenty braids, each one adorned with a yellow plastic bow.

"How'd do, Gloria," the woman says.

"What are you all dressed up for, Ruby?" Gloria says.

"Going over to Mama's for supper," Ruby says. "Here, hold Sarah while I get a few things to take to Mama."

"I don't want to hold her," Gloria says.

"Now, you just shut up," Ruby says, "and hold her so she won't get her clean dress dirty."

The huge black woman sticks the child into Gloria's arms and speeds on down the aisles to grab a loaf of bread and a can of sardines.

"She's a pretty baby," I say to Gloria as I stick my finger near the child's little hand and she grips it.

"Pretty as a picture," says Gloria, her tone becoming tender and warm. "Are you pretty as a picture?"

The child lets go of my finger and puts her arms around Gloria's neck. Then Gloria kisses her cheek.

"Yes," whispers Gloria, "you're pretty as a picture."

"Don't slobber all over my baby girl," Ruby says, setting the loaf of bread, can of sardines, three potatoes, and a cabbage on the counter. "I want her fresh-looking for Mama to see."

"I ain't slobbering on her," says Gloria. "Here, take her back."

"Can I put this stuff on my bill?" says Ruby.

"I reckon," Gloria sighs, though a sign behind her on the wall says NO CREDIT/NO EXCEPTIONS.

When Ruby and her child leave I put my shoes and socks back on and prepare to hit the road again.

"You're an unusual lady," I tell Gloria. "You bad-mouth blacks in front of Red, but you treated that woman and little girl like they were your family."

"I grew up with Ruby," says Gloria. "In a way we are family."

"But what's with using the word *nigger* with Red?"

"You really want to know what I think?" she says.

"Yes," I say, believing that the little people all over America never get to be heard enough by the rest of the world and that she may offer some insight on today's Dixie.

"Red is an okay person," she says. "But he's a liberal and sometimes full of shit."

"I don't follow what you're getting at," I say.

"He thinks changing the word *nigger* to *black* or *African American* will help make America a better place," she says. "But that's all surface stuff. It's how we treat each other that matters. I never heard my daddy call a colored anything but a nigger his whole life. I never saw him mistreat a living soul either, but I've seen some liberals use all the correct words and cheat colored folks out of money. I ain't everybody's darling and don't want to be, but I'll tell you this much—I'm no hypocrite. You tell me what matters the most, what we say or what we do?"

"For my money," I say, "they should be one and the same."

"*Should be* and *is* are close cousins," she says. "But they don't always live in the same house."

"Now I got a question for you," I say.

"Shoot."

"What if you're just being stubborn," I say, "and refusing to let parts of the Old South die? What if you're simply afraid of the new?"

"I haven't considered that," she says. "You've given me something to think about."

"You've given me food for thought as well," I say. "Thanks for letting me get out of the sun."

"You brought some shade to me too," she says. "It gets pretty boring ringing up milk, bread, beer, and cigarettes seven days a week. You be careful out there, hear?"

I nod, then take the bucket outside and pour the icy water from it. Slipping back into my pack, I push on once again, the tip of my chestnut staff tapping to the sea.

Chapter Seventeen

Two miles down the road from the great icy Battle of the Feet, I'm disappointed to spot a sign saying that Eatonton is yet five miles away. While the rest at the grocery store did me a world of good, it fell short of giving me a new body. My feet are so sore again that I can barely walk. With the sun near setting and twilight on the way, it makes sense to sleep in my tent tonight and enter Brer Rabbit's town in the morning when I'm fresh and rested.

But finding a good place to set up a pup tent isn't always as easy as driving a car to a motel. I want to be away from houses tonight so I can have privacy and build a fire to cook dinner. Also, it's important that my tent not be seen from the road. After all, it is Memorial Day weekend and lots of folks are boozing it up. All of them might not be as kindhearted as Red after several cold beers and the last thing I seek tonight is a thrown rock or bottle introducing itself to the side or back of my head.

Lady Luck is with me, however. When the road crosses Little River, I spot a place to camp. To get there I must make my way twenty feet down a steep bank and thank goodness my staff comes to the rescue when my footing fails. My shoes make tracks in the sand as I follow the stream's bend to a beach with a perfect spot to pitch my tent. With that done, I begin to gather the driftwood, scattered all about as if waiting, like so many people, for someone to see its potential. Soon I have a fire going.

Hunger is closing in on me and I'm happy that I got two

sweet potatoes from Gloria at the store. She wouldn't let me pay for them, which happens so often in country stores once those working there learn what I'm doing. Just as old buck dancer Henry back in Covington cut a line in my staff to become part of the journey, people give food to participate in a walk that becomes a tiny notch in their own lives. I not only like sweet potatoes and raised them on Sand Mountain one summer to sell at the market along with sugarcane and watermelons, but I read more than once that the Yanks treasured them on their march. One Union soldier swore that the foraged Georgia sweet potatoes were the largest he'd ever laid eyes on.

I could sit on one end, he said, while the other roasted in the fire.

The potatoes Gloria donated aren't that big, but I wrap them in aluminum foil and place them in the fire with what might be the same joy that soldier felt as he licked his lips. While they bake I sit on the ground and stick my bare feet into the moist sand near the river's swirling edge. Hey, look at that! My right foot is mounded over with sand and looking just like the little frog houses my sister and I would build when we were children. Now if I can just . . . yes, my foot slides from the sand without the house falling in. It looks like an igloo and I haven't thought of this in so many years that I'm almost startled. It fills me with the same wonder and freedom I felt as a kid. Then I look around to make sure no one is watching a grown man play with his feet in the sand. But know what? I really don't care right now what people think. The past year was so painful with the death of my father that I'll take every carefree moment I can find.

Then, as so often happens when a man thinks he's found a place of total peace, I become alarmed because of laughter coming from the near distance. Has someone been spying on me and can't hold it back any longer? When the sound erupts again I can tell it's a woman's laugh. Then I hear a man's voice, followed by them both laughing and splashing just up around that bend, thick with trees and vines.

I sneak through the woods to see what they're doing. This

need to scout is more than just curiosity; I want to know what's there so I can feel safe here tonight. Twilight is falling and the thought of strangers in the dark—even those who laugh—doesn't sit right with me.

Their voices grow louder with each step I take and when a twig snaps I freeze from fear that they may hear me coming. But seconds later I'm prowling again and finally get to a spot where I can see them out in the river up to their waists. She is naked and her wet body has been blessed with great curves and firm, full breasts. Her boyfriend—they appear to be around eighteen or nineteen years old—disappears under the water to emerge with his head between her thighs, lifting her high into the air on his shoulders. She seems to fall toward the river in slow motion and her long wet hair dangles as her slender legs stretch toward the darkening sky to kick at just the second she splashes. When she comes up again, he tries to dunk her but she swings her arms around his neck and he begins to laugh. When she kisses him on the lips I start to head back to my tent because I feel guilty about invading such a delicate privacy. But sometimes I'm too drawn to people to dismiss them so easily. I linger a moment more to watch her lips slide from his mouth and down his neck to his chest, where she licks his nipple. He holds his arms around her with such tenderness as he kisses her head that it hurts as much as it excites me.

Finally, I ease back through the trees to my fire and tent, their laughter once again drifting through the falling night like a secret they think only they share. Some five minutes later I hear a car or truck door slam near where they were playing and then a motor starts. It fades into the woods along with their innocent and sensual laughter. I'd like to know if he's taking her home or simply down a dirt road deeper into the trees so they can continue to celebrate their youth in a more discreet fashion among the lightning bugs that now begin to sprinkle the night with flashing yellows.

I'm not certain if it's from night falling or from the closeness I saw in the river's lovers, but I feel a trace of loneliness. This isn't a bad thing, for sometimes I find such a state, if not overpowering, leads me closer to those I cherish. I envision my mother now, back home in the mountains, and see her aging hands, wrinkled and spotted from years of exposure to the sun. I think of all the clothes they washed for me, the meals they've cooked. In my mind I try to stroke those hands just now and ask her to forgive me for the times I've been impatient with her or raised my voice. Lifting the staff, I hold it overhead with both hands toward the faint stars. With my heart, I try now to send love through the heavens and back over Lookout Mountain to my mother, so she may be safe and not worry about me. There may be those who would question my means of prayer, but let each man, I have long believed, reach up to the Great Spirit in his own way.

As for Debi, I see her, too, though she is clear on the other side of the Rockies. Thinking of her lips, I kiss the staff, and then, holding it like a baseball bat, sling it that the kiss might sail over the moon and fall into her lap, a warm, tingling sensation on her thigh that, I hope, will make her feel my presence . . . make her heart warmer. And if these little rituals do nothing more than allow me to feel closer to those I love, then they have done their deeds and made me believe that I'm more than just a Rebel alone in the Georgia night.

The darkness is thick now and I add more driftwood to the fire to brighten the flames. Sitting on the ground, I pull Road Rabbit from the pack and place him on a nearby rock. The world would truly be a different place if all people were as gentle as he looks.

"Any music for me tonight, Road Rabbit?"

I reach over and squeeze him, but he is silent. I fear that maybe I pressed on him too hard earlier today and broke his music box.

The fire, blazing higher now from its new wood, begins to play its own popping and crackling tune. And in only forty-five minutes it gives me two baked sweet potatoes. When they cool, I don't need a fork. I simply hold one in my hand to eat, skin and all, each piece as sweet as honey. Save for the occasional mosquito biting me, dinner couldn't be better. I'm not even haunted by my childhood memory of seeing Sherman with horns in the flames when my father fried fish by a lake. To a distant observer, however, I might look like a man by a fire communing with nature as he tries to knock some sense into himself, a smack in the face every now and then.

With my stomach full, I grow sleepy among the sounds of croaking frogs and chirping crickets. Because clouds drift overhead, I suspect rain and pull my pack and Road Rabbit into the tent. Inside the sleeping bag my tired body surrenders and my eyes get heavy until Road Rabbit falls from the top of the pack and rolls to my head. I start to place him back where he was when the music once again rises from his small chest as if to show me that he is still very much in control of his own destiny. The pack, only a foot from me, is much too far away for my talented friend to sit all by his lonesome. I put him just a few inches from my face as his song and that of the river join hands to lead me to sleep.

Chapter Eighteen

Morning fog rises from the river and the distant bridge looks ghostly, a link to another world. In fact, I have started to feel that I'm living in two worlds at once—that of the present and that of the Civil War. Last night I dreamed that I was a soldier in the Confederacy but wore the uniform of a Yank. In reality it was common for both North and South to wear the other's colors because clothes were hard to get. Rather than wear rags a man would take a uniform from his dead enemy. But in my dream I sensed that I was wearing the Union colors for another reason. Then, as it happens in dreams, I floated out of the dark woods into a Union camp where fires burned outside tents as far as the eye could see. The moment my feet touched the ground I found myself walking straight toward Sherman, who was perched on a cracker box, his usual seat, while he smoked a cigar, its tip glowing red.

"What do you want?" he said.

"A message for you, Uncle Billy [as his men often called him]. One from my father. Your men shot his bird dog today."

"But this is war," said Sherman. "I promised that I would make Georgia howl."

"Yes, sir, that's why I brought you this message."

Then I pulled a pistol and placed it to the general's head. When I squeezed the trigger, however, the gun exploded to make the sound of a dog yelping.

I awoke in a heavy sweat and for several seconds I couldn't distinguish the past from the present. I believed that I had killed Sherman and the Yanks had thrown me into a dark dun-

geon. Was I now to be shot or hung by the neck till dead?
When I sat up and wiped the sweat from my forehead, however, I heard the very real sound of a dog howling in the distance. I pushed my fingers against my nylon tent to make sure
I really was in my little traveler's home and not the jail I first
imagined. Then the gentle sound of Little River itself assured
me that I was okay. I pulled open the tent and let the breeze
cool my sweaty face. While relieved to be back in the world I
knew, there was some part of me that didn't want to let go of
the dream. That same part of me wanted to be back in the
Civil War; it wanted to remove Sherman from the face of the
earth. Then, at last, as I came fully awake, the horror of war
and the darkness in men's hearts shook me. I crawled from the
tent and splashed river water onto my face. In the distant
moonlight the dog continued to howl.

Sherman's soldiers usually broke camp around four or five
each morning, but a one-man army can do as he likes so I
don't crawl from my tent till seven. Digging in last night's fire
with a stick, I uncover a few red-hot coals and place driftwood
atop them. When the flames appear I set a two-cup coffeepot
there, caffeine not too many minutes away.

I didn't eat all of the second sweet potato at dinner and had
tossed it a few feet from the tent. This morning it's been
replaced with possum tracks leading into the weeds. I'm following those claw marks when a splash in the swirling river
grabs my ear. I spin that way, almost expecting to behold yesterday's lovers, but only the tail of a fish lingers in the air and
then that, too, becomes the water's secret.

Once my coffee is gone I stuff my tent and Road Rabbit
into the pack and climb the foggy bank by the bridge to get to
the road. I've hiked only a mile or so when a Jeep pulls over
only a few feet away. A man sticks his head out, and I won't
pretend that I don't watch closely to make sure a gun doesn't
come next.

"Are you the one looking for Sherman?" he says, making
me uneasy because it seems that he somehow knows about
last night's dream.

"I'm following his route," I say, trying to see deeper into the man's eyes.

"A friend of mine heard about you back in Covington and phoned me," he says. "My family and I would be pleased to put you up for the night and feed you at our old farmhouse. It's nothing fancy, but the sheets are clean and I've got a story or two about the general that might interest you."

I like his voice and face, but I'm careful not to commit myself till I learn more about him and the situation. If there's one thing that bugs me it's to be with people I'm not comfortable with. By the time I discover that he has three children and is a counselor at the local high school where his wife teaches math, however, my gut and common sense tell me I'd be wise to accept his generous invitation. We agree to meet in Eatonton outside the Uncle Remus Museum after school this afternoon.

As I march into Eatonton, Joel Chandler Harris comes to mind again. Born just twelve years before the Civil War, he was red-haired and freckled—why, imagine that in a Southerner! Joel was brought up by his mother and grandmother on a dirt-poor farm. Shy, with a slight stutter, one of his greatest pastimes, besides playing in the woods near birds and animals, was to hang out at the general store, which doubled as a post office. Here he could get an earful from those who came and went and read the newspapers that were left behind. His life was changed forever when he read an ad in *The Countryman:*

> *Wanted:* An active, intelligent white boy, 14 or 15 years of age, is wanted at this office to learn the printing business.

Joel answered the ad and the publisher of *The Countryman,* Joseph Addison Turner, hired him to set type and let him live on the Turner Plantation nine miles north of Eatonton. After working hours, Joel roamed about the slaves' cabins and sat by their fires, listening to their folklore. Years later, when he became a writer in Atlanta for the *Atlanta Constitution,* he began a series of stories based on those cabin yarns that made him, Uncle Remus, and Brer Rabbit world famous. Joel swore that it was an accident that his writing became such landmarks of Americana, but the public still hounded him at his home, alternately called Snap Bean Farm or the Wren's Nest, because that bird once built a little home in Joel's mailbox. While Joel stayed modest to his death in 1908, he did once accept an invitation to the White House because the children of President Theodore Roosevelt were so in love with his tales.

My sister, Nita, and I were taken with the Uncle Remus animals to the point that we'd pretend we were them. Just which one of us got to be Brer Rabbit, however, was sometimes a hair-yanking discussion. Personally, I thought she made a great tar baby, though she would never stay stuck to a tree as long as I would have preferred.

Walking down Main Street in Eatonton, I'm thinking what good friends my sister and I have been all these years, when something stops me in my tracks. There, in the center of the courthouse lawn, standing on his hind legs, is Brer Rabbit. He's almost three feet tall and grinning as if he's about to pull a trick. The weathered sculpture is so lifelike that for a moment or two I think I feel Road Rabbit punching my pack in hopes of getting out to play. But then again, it may just be my coffeepot poking me in my back.

I lower the pack to the ground, take out my camera, and take a snapshot of Brer Rabbit, smoking a pipe. As I march on down the street toward the Uncle Remus Museum I get the strangest feeling that Brer Rabbit is tiptoeing only a foot or two behind me. But when I turn to check, I find only my shadow, the staff looking like a giant snake standing on the tip of its tail. Hmm, I must've seen too many cartoons or daydreamed too much when I was a kid. My family didn't get a TV set till I was in the third grade, so Nita and I had to make up our own stories to entertain ourselves. When we finally got the Talk Box we'd put it on the front porch sometimes at night and sit on the lawn pretending we were at the drive-in theater. Mother made us popcorn, and we'd burn a rag to make smoke to keep the mosquitoes away.

The Uncle Remus Museum is in an old log cabin and I enter it to behold pictures and carvings of all the birds and animals, as well as Uncle Remus himself, inside glass display cases.

"I read about you in the newspaper," the woman overseeing the museum says. "Welcome to 'Uncle Remus land.'"

"Glad to be here," I say.

"We're right proud to have two famous writers from Eatonton," she continues.

"Who's from here besides Joel Chandler Harris?"

"Oh, don't you know? *Alice Walker.*"

"Alice Walker?" I say, rather impressed, since she won the Pulitzer Prize in fiction in 1983 for her novel *The Color Purple.* "Does she still live here?"

"No," the woman says, "but her mother lives just a few blocks away."

"Can you tell me how to get there?"

"Why, yes, I suppose so."

She gives me directions to the Walker house. I leave my heavy pack in the museum, but head that way with my staff. When I walked the Trail of Tears I was attacked by a Doberman pinscher and had no stick with me to defend myself. I don't care to have a repeat performance.

I soon arrive at a brick housing project and knock on the Walker door. A large black woman about my age appears behind the screen.

"Yes?" She squints as if my hat and staff are suspect.

"I'm sorry to bother you," I say, telling her my name and what I'm doing. Alice Walker is one of America's most noted authors and I thought it would be fascinating to talk with her mother.

She continues to squint as if trying to size me up.

"You may have heard of my first book," I say. "I'm part Cherokee and walked the Trail of Tears to write about it."

"Yes." She nods. "Come on in. We're part Cherokee as well. My name's Ruth, Alice's sister."

Feeling I've had a very lucky break that we're both of Cherokee descent, I enter the small but cozy apartment. Does this Native American connection surprise you? Thousands of slaves intermarried or interbred with Indians in the Deep

South. I'm a member of a state-recognized Cherokee tribe in Alabama and we have black members in it. Hundreds of runaway slaves fled to the Florida swamps to join the Seminole there, and over five thousand slaves went with my Cherokee ancestors when they were forced to Oklahoma. Along the way black witch doctors sang healing songs in African tongues to the sick while Indian medicine men chanted in Cherokee and rattled dried gourds.

"I'm afraid Mama won't be able to talk with you," Ruth says. "She's sick in bed and I just arrived from Atlanta to take care of her. But please sit and cool off a little and you and I can say hello. Could I offer you some iced tea or a cold Coke?"

"Nothing to drink," I say, and when I hear Ruth and Alice's mother cough in the nearby bedroom I'm not so sure I was wise to have come here. "I'm sorry your mother isn't feeling well," I continue. "I always worry when my mother's sick. Is that a picture of your mother up there?"

On the wall over the couch hangs a photo of a woman seated on a bench with a white picket fence behind her and yellow and red roses blooming all around her. She's laughing as surely as if she were sitting in the Garden of Eden.

"That's Mama," Ruth says, her voice concerned.

"She looks more like you than Alice," I say, and her face brightens.

"Alice lives in California now," Ruth says. "But I cared for her when she was little. I cooked and washed clothes. Sometimes she still calls to confide in me, the older sister. Guess you're wanting to hear a story about her?"

Something in her tone makes it dawn upon me that perhaps Ruth is often in the shadow of her famous sister. Do people have trouble seeing her for who she is rather than who they think Alice is?

"I'd really rather hear a story about you," I say. "I bet there's something special that happened when you were growing up here in Eatonton."

She seems moved that someone cares about her own history, the attention giving it new or deeper meaning. Judging by her eyes, she drifts back into the past, opening its squeaky doors.

"I do recall one story," she begins. "I was in the eighth grade and had this crush on a boy in the ninth. Oooh, how he made my heart jump every time I saw his face. Thought I would die when he invited me to his prom. Then the school objected to him wanting to bring somebody my age. We got that worked out, but I felt like I didn't have anything nice enough to wear. I'd go down to this store window every day and stand looking at this pretty dress. When I stood in the right spot on the sidewalk and held my head just so, I could see my reflection in the glass and put myself inside that dress. But when I walked away it stayed there. The price tag said eighteen dollars, and back then that was a lot of money. We were poor and it took all we had to make ends meet. Mama worked as a maid for a doctor and I couldn't believe that she scraped together enough to buy that wish dress for me. When she brought it home in a box I placed it on the foot of my bed and wouldn't even try it on till the night of the prom because I was afraid I'd hurt it. Oh, but what a time me and that boy had at the dance. He'd gotten to take a bus into Atlanta to rent a tux and we were on top of the world."

Her face is aglow with the memory and now she seems to once again float over the dance floor, her date spinning the moon on the tip of his finger.

"Are you still friends with that boy?" I ask, thinking how kind her mother had been to buy that dress.

"After years of being apart we got close again after we each experienced a divorce," she says. "But he's gone now."

"Gone?" I ask as her eyes lose the gleam and the moon falls from her date's finger, a lightbulb shattering on a concrete floor.

"Murdered," she says. "Ten years ago today."

"What happened?" I say, startled that what began as such a sweet memory ends in horror.

"No," she says, as if some spirit has been released that now owns her. "I can take you to the dance, but not to the killing."

Her mother coughs again from the nearby bedroom and Ruth looks that way.

"I better go so you can check on your mother," I say. "I hope she feels better soon. Sorry about you losing your friend. I had a lover shot in the back some years ago and she can never walk again. It still haunts me."

"Oh," she says, as if having second thoughts about telling me what happened to her prom date. But then her mother coughs again and I open the door to leave.

"Be careful out there," she says. "Hold on to your staff like a prayer itself."

"I will," I say, tipping my hat to her as I move on, my hand around the stick a bit tighter than before I entered the Walker home.

Chapter Nineteen

"I forgot to tell you something this morning when I invited you to spend the night," Joe says outside the Uncle Remus Museum that afternoon.

"What's that?" I ask as I load my pack and staff into his Jeep and we start down the street, passing the Brer Rabbit statue on the courthouse lawn. "I have to sleep with your grandma?"

"Nothing that drastic," Joe says. "But we're having study night for seniors in American history and Spanish in our home. As many as forty or fifty kids may show up. Their finals are tomorrow and some of them need last-minute help. Think you can handle that many teenagers at once?"

"Don't worry, Mr. Eeeeeeeellis," eight-year-old Little Joe says, slowly drawing my name out until I feel that he sees something in me that others can't. "I know places we can hide if those big kids get in the way. Sometimes they're too loud and Duchess and me—she's my dog—get under the magnolia limbs. I have to lead her 'cause she's blind."

"She's not blind," Joe says.

"She is, Daddy," Little Joe says. "She just doesn't want you to know it. She smells her way around to look like she can see."

"She just has a little trouble seeing." Joe shakes his head.

"She's blind," Little Joe whispers to me as if his father can't bear to hear the raw truth again.

We arrive at a beautiful old two-story farmhouse surrounded by towering, massive pecan trees. Their branches tremble be-

cause a strong wind is blowing. Black clouds boil and the front
porch swing sways back and forth, creaking as it does so.

"I better hurry on to the barn and milk," Joe says, "before
the rain starts. Little Joe, will you introduce our guest to your
mother and two sisters?"

"Yeah," Little Joe says.

"What did I hear?" comes Joe's warm but firm voice.

"I mean *yes, sir.*"

"Thank you," Joe says as he hurries toward the barn. Lightning flashes yellow over the giant pecan trees.

"Come on in, Mr. Eeeeeeeeeeellis. But be careful of the
loose board on the back porch. You'd think Daddy would find
a nail. I don't like hammers, do you?"

"They're good for building things."

"See up there in that pecan tree? That's where Daddy's
promised to put me a treehouse. I'm going to have a rope
ladder and pull it up at night so my sisters can't climb it. I'll
have a television up there too."

"I have a cabin that began as a treehouse," I say. "My father and I built part of it together."

"Wow, Mr. Eeeeeeeeeeellis, you're the first man I ever met
who lives in a treehouse. You do that and walk a lot, don't
you?"

In the huge kitchen he introduces me to his mother, Melody, and his two sisters.

"Where should I put my pack?" I ask.

"Just drop it in the hallway for now," says Melody. "No,
I'm sorry, I'm not thinking straight. I had an argument with a
student last period today and I'm still frazzled. Little Joe,
show him to the guest room."

"Follow me, Mr. Eeeeeeeeeeellis. Your bed is just below
the bee room. That's where the bees used to swarm every
summer when they came from the chimney. Sometimes moths
fly around the light in your room, but they don't sting."

Little Joe leads me to a room with a high ceiling and a
fireplace. The wooden bed, made during the Civil War, is covered with an antique quilt and the mattress is stuffed with
goose feathers. I wish it could talk, for I'd like to know who

slept there and what they whispered during winter nights long ago.

"Are you cold, honey?" says the man as he runs a tiny goose feather from the mattress down her smooth back.

"Not as long as you do that," says the woman. "It makes me warm all over and when I close my eyes I see a flock of geese gliding over a full moon in October."

I ease my pack to the floor by the window overlooking the front porch and place my hat on the mantel to make myself feel more at home. When I lean the staff against the mantel as well, however, Little Joe takes it.

"This is a big stick," Little Joe says. "Can you hit rocks with it?"

"I haven't tried," I say.

"When you get grown you forget fun stuff, huh?"

"Sometimes," I say, recalling what a blast children can be. "What gives you the most fun?"

"I like to climb trees," says Little Joe. "When I get big I want to become a professional tree climber or a baseball player. I haven't decided yet. Want to see me climb a tree? Come on," he says, placing the staff against the mantel, "I'll show you."

Little Joe and I go to the front porch where we can see there are many trees to pick from, but the wind is wild now and rain begins to pour. Joe shakes his head as water runs from the roof. But quick as the lightning around us his face brightens and he climbs up to stand in the center of a rocking chair. Back and forth and back and forth he rocks like a death-defying acrobat high above a breathless crowd with no net to catch him.

"Can you do this, Mr. Eeeeeeeeeeellis?"

"I doubt it," I say, "and if I could it wouldn't be as good as you do it."

"I couldn't walk as far as you. I'd get tired."

He climbs down from the rocking chair and leans his head from the porch to open his mouth and catch raindrops. I don't mind that he's showing off. I like that he feels comfortable enough around me to play so openly. It makes me warm all

over inside knowing that Little Joe has such a secure place to
live. I believe in looking the harshest reality square in the eye,
but sometimes I get sick of all the news on TV and in the
papers about children being beaten, locked in closets or base-
ments, and sexually abused. I think sometimes Americans are
so bombarded by such headlines that we forget how innocent
and wondrous life is for most children. These Norman Rock-
well pictures of Little Joe playing on the porch, in the rocking
chair, and with the raindrops become truly complete when his
dog, Duchess, runs from the rain and into his arms.

"I'm sorry she's blind," I say as she licks my hand.

"Well," Little Joe whispers, "I guess she can see a tiny bit.
But don't tell Daddy. Look, Mr. Eeeeeeeeeeellis, it's stopped
raining. I can climb a tree for you now."

I hear my mother's voice inside me.

"That's not a good idea right now," I say, rubbing Duchess
behind her ears. "The limbs are wet. You could slip and fall."

"Not me," Little Joe calls as he runs down the porch steps
toward the magnolia tree clustered with giant blossoms.

I start to call out again, but before I get another word out he
has started up the tree with such speed and agility that a monkey might drop his peanuts to watch in awe. On and on and up
Little Joe climbs toward the very top, the shaking branches
dripping water all the way as Duchess jumps beneath him and
barks.

"Look!" Little Joe yells from the treetop.

He holds a limb with his left hand while he reaches for one
of the tree's big white flowers with the other. His fingers almost touch it when he slips and I'm sure he'll fall some thirty
feet to the hard ground. But he catches himself and yanks the
flower from the branch, all in a day's work for a professional
tree climber.

"It's for you, Mr. Eeeeeeeeeeellis," he says, hurrying back
to the porch and placing the magnolia blossom into my hand.

"It's beautiful, Little Joe."

Indeed, I'm so moved by the gesture that it almost over-
powers me. It takes several moments before I realize that my
father is here with us among the petals. A man who had great

difficulty saying in words what he felt, he often would walk into the field behind our home and gather wildflowers to set in a vase on the kitchen table. Never would he point to them or brag about his getting them. His Cherokee instinct was to behold the beauty of nature from a silence in the soul.

"Smell it, Mr. Eeeeeeeeeeellis."

I raise the magnolia to my nose and sniff a fragrance that will stay with me till the day I die and beyond, as I drift through eternity with Little Joe, my father, and General Sherman. This moment, these petals, hold the magic of the journey. Not a magic trick like pulling a rabbit from a hat, or sawing a body in half . . . but a magic that lets us see how simple things—Joe giving me a flower—are profound. More than that, as this magic sinks in deeper, I realize that I have now had a tenderness touch my heart that I have not allowed since Daddy died. Yes, a greater healing has begun.

Chapter Twenty

I take the magnolia blossom to my room and place it in a glass of water on the mantel by my faded hat, its snake rattler and crow feather only inches from the snow-white petals. When I go into the kitchen I find Joe has returned from the barn with a pail of milk. He places it in the refrigerator and puts a pot of water on the stove to cook pasta for tonight's teenagers.

"I hope Little Joe didn't get on your nerves," Joe says, eyeing him in the adjoining den where he watches cartoons on television.

"He's probably a good kid when he's asleep," I say loudly so Little Joe will hear me. He simply looks at me and grins like we share a secret as tall as a tree.

"We tried for five years to have children before our first daughter was born," Joe says. "I was so sure the third birth would be a girl, too, that I had started to make out the hospital check saying *for third daughter* when Little Joe was born."

Pieces of onion and garlic Joe had placed in a saucepan minutes ago have started to fill the air with a rich aroma and I'm getting hungrier by the second. I had no lunch today.

"It's good to see that some men can cook," I say. General Sherman himself was something of a chef. When he attended West Point he'd sometimes treat his friends to an oyster dish he'd cook in his room.

"I learned to cook because I love to eat so much," Joe says. "If I didn't jog every day I'd be fat. When I was a kid I was overweight, and clumsy as well. In baseball I always got stuck in the outfield and the whole time I was sweating in the hot sun I'd hope that the batter wouldn't hit one my way. I had trouble catching a basketball, let alone a ball as small as an apple. Guess that's one of the reasons I like being a counselor at school. I understand that kids struggle sometimes. I didn't think I'd ever end up on these three hundred acres. Daddy asked me one time when I was a boy what I'd do with this farm if I owned it. I told him I'd blow it straight to hell."

This amuses me because I see I'm not the only one who went through Dixie Denial when he was growing up.

"But I couldn't do that with this farm now," Joe says. "It's been in the family since long before the Civil War. This house began as a two-room building for the people who operated the gristmill. Up there on the hill, just above the barn, is where the big house stood. My aunt Lalee, who raised me as much as my mother, would get me out of the house anytime she wanted by telling me that up there on the hill was where all the gold had been buried to hide it from Sherman and his soldiers."

"You looked for it?"

"I dug more holes in that piece of ground than Georgia has peaches," he says, pouring quartered tomatoes into the sauce pan. "Thought every new try I'd finally strike it rich. My shovel finally got dull."

"There is gold up there, Daddy!" Little Joe shouts. "You just didn't dig in the right place."

"Melody has a way of getting him out of the house sometimes too," Joe whispers once his son has turned back to a *Road Runner* cartoon. *Beep! Beep!*

Melody and her two daughters have been to town to shop for graduation presents and they soon return with a carload of teenagers. Within another thirty minutes the home is packed with high school students. There's so much excitement in their talk and laughter that I'm amazed the old farmhouse itself doesn't begin to rock and roll. That old cliché that it's a small world hits home again when I spot the boy and girl I saw in the river last evening. She sits at a table with an American history book. He's in a chair next to her and their fingers weave together on her bare knee under the tabletop. I don't know how this couple will score on the American history test tomorrow, but they sure are passing Mustard 101 with flying colors.

I'll tell you something more about this couple. The girl is about nineteen and has bright, clear blue eyes with jet-black curly hair falling to her shoulders. Her lips are thick and I recall in great detail how inviting she looked wet and naked last evening in the river. Even her voice is sensual as she repeats those boring dates in American history that kids so often have to know for tests. I can just imagine what she's really thinking as she continues to sit close to her lover, his fingers now stroking her thigh under the study table.

While I must commend Joe on his fine hospitality in asking me to spend the night, I can't brag on his manners when it's time to serve the pasta. I thought I was an elder to these kids, but Joe serves them first, and I stand nearby with a plate in my hand, a humble Rebel pilgrim with clinched teeth masquerading as a smile. But what really bothers me more than waiting is the fear that the pasta won't stretch far enough to get to my starved mouth.

Okay, okay, I overreacted and am calming down now that I finally have some food on my plate. I also apologize for the growling, but if that girl over there wearing the University of Georgia T-shirt leaves that piece of French bread untouched on her plate it's a dead duck.

When a chair becomes empty at the big round table where six students, including the river lovers, sit, I join them and tell them a bit about my march and how I've roamed the earth since I was seventeen. If I've learned anything about youth it's that they feel a kind of bond with anyone who shows a passion for living. With all their hormones taking them on a daily roller-coaster ride, I doubt they have little choice. In any event, it gives me a charge to be around their high energy.

"How do you feel about growing up in the South?" I say. "Do you want to follow in your parents' footsteps or take a new road?"

"I'm dying to get out of Georgia," one boy says. "I'm joining the Air Force to see the world. Daddy wants me to stay here and take over his dairy, but I've already seen enough cows' tits to do me a lifetime. I might come back home and open a business of my own in a few years to be close to Mother and Daddy. We get along real good, but you can have those cows."

"I'm just the opposite," a girl with red hair says. "I want to get married this summer and have babies. The world scares me. Just look at the news. People kill each other for nothing. I couldn't leave my grandma anyway. She's getting real old and I want to spend all the time I can with her before she passes on. I want her to hold my babies. I hope the first one's a girl so I can name her after Grandma. She's already made her a pretty little baby quilt with ducks and geese on it. I mean, I believe in women's liberation and all that, but I always feel free. I wish you could meet my boyfriend. He's away at Georgia Tech, studying to become a dentist."

"We want to buy a car and drive to Colorado," says the boy who holds his river-lover's hand under the table. "We'll work there this summer and start college in the fall."

"Yeah," his girlfriend says. "We've been here our whole lives. The people are okay, but they gossip a lot and if you think anything different than they do they look at you funny. Things are just changing too fast for them to get a grip on it. My grandpa's the sweetest man alive, but he still doesn't believe we've put a man on the moon."

"How do ya'll feel about blacks?" I say.

"Depends on the person," the river girl says. "Just like whites. Some I like and some I don't. I sure don't believe in racism, if that's what you're driving at."

"The ones on TV who are so angry bother me," her boyfriend says. "Like when they had those riots in Los Angeles and there was so much looting. That's not right. Stealing is stealing, and that's wrong. Maybe if I was black and lived in a big city I'd see it a different way, but . . ."

"It's wrong to steal," the boy who wants to join the Air Force says. "But if my folks had been slaves and whipped all their lives and I lived in a ghetto, I think I'd be mad at the world too. I'm glad I'm not black. It would be rough in this country."

"Yeah," says the girl bent on having babies, "but you got to use your mind to get ahead in today's world. You can't feel sorry for yourself and take it out on others and think they should pat you on the back. Both blacks and whites should be beyond the past. The only way we can change things for the better is to focus on now and the future. Whining just won't cut it."

I'm fascinated by what these kids have to say and am encouraged by their basic optimism, for they are the New South of tomorrow. Their values will help determine what Dixie becomes. But right now I'm more concerned with Little Joe. He has tears in his eyes as he opens the refrigerator and pulls out a piece of watermelon.

"What's wrong?" I ask him.

"I don't want to talk about it," he says, and takes off across the back porch, making the loose board creak on purpose, his foot stomping at just the right time.

I give him a few seconds to get outside and then follow Duchess to find him sitting on the ground under the magnolia limbs. Nibbling on the ripe red watermelon, he doesn't look too happy to see me or his dog.

"I put the flower you gave me in a glass of water and set it on the mantel in the room where I'm staying," I say. "That was the finest gift anyone has given me in a long time."

"You don't have to be nice to me," he says, wiping a tear from his eye.

"I'm not," I say. "You got the last piece of watermelon, and I wanted some."

"There was more in the fridge," he says.

He studies me for what seems like a long time before he breaks the slice of melon in two. He gives me the smaller piece.

"That boy called me *Little*," he says. "My name is Joe or Joseph or Little Joe, but not just *Little*."

"When I was your age," I say, "I was smaller than you."

"You were?" A trace of hope lights his face. "I wish I had arms as big as yours. I'd show that boy."

"What would you do?"

"Punch him," he says, another tear coming from his eye.

"That's all? I think you should nail him by the ears to the side of your house so that his feet dangle. Then we should take off his shoes and socks and build a fire under him and leave him there till he swears to call you Big Joe for the rest of his life."

."Ah, Mr. Eeeeeeeeeeellis, you don't really mean that, do you?"

"But before we let him down we should line up all the kids from inside the house and let each one pound him with a rotten egg."

"Aaaaah, Mr. Eeeeeeeeeellis . . ."

"Well," I say, "maybe just this one time we could let him slide."

"Maybe," he says, wiping his eyes dry as he studies the side of the house and grins as if envisioning some sweet revenge. Then he scratches Duchess on the head and says: "How high can you spit a watermelon seed, Mr. Eeeeeeeeeeellis?"

Little Joe takes a bit of melon and raises his eyes toward the sky. A black seed shoots from his mouth toward the newly risen moon. I then find a seed and do the same, and there we are in the Southern twilight trying to leave our tiny marks in the heavens. Those who only get their learning from books will swear that all the seeds we spit fell back to earth. But I will never be convinced that we didn't put a couple of new stars in the Georgia night. At least, I'm sure Little Joe did, and that Duchess sees them shine, her bark a bugle calling out *long live Dixie lights.*

Chapter Twenty-one

Itching to get to Milledgeville, capital of Georgia when the Civil War erupted, I part company with the Deloach family the next day as they scramble to deal with the last day of school. As I walk down the road I can still see Joe in the kitchen at dawn churning butter, the stick in his hand going up and down in the five-gallon crock.

Road Rabbit doesn't seem to mind sharing the pack with a magnolia blossom as we march on toward the sea, and when I'm fully out of Eatonton and back in the rolling countryside I hit a couple of rocks with my staff in honor of Little Joe. A farmer in a pickup with a pig in back stares as if I've been out in the sun too long, but I just wave and knock another home run over a barbed wire fence. The much impressed pig—this batter takes his fans wherever he finds them—sticks his big nose over the truck's tailgate and his giant ears flop in the wind. I appreciate the recognition, but the porker also reminds me of one of Sherman's most noted foragers, a tall and slender Cherokee named Joe. One afternoon as Joe and a party of bummers roamed the Georgia countryside he sniffed inspiration in the air, jerking his horse to an abrupt stop.

"Men," he said, "we got pork chops on the fire."

"You're dreaming," said one of his comrades. "We haven't seen a hog for days."

"There's one near here," said the Tennessee Cherokee. "I smell him."

"You're just smelling some old Reb in the wind. Now, let's move on before we get cut off from the rest of the men."

"I'm tired of eating chickens and turkeys," said the Indian. "I tell you I smell a pig and I'm having myself ham for dinner."

"Maybe you'd like Lincoln to bake you some biscuits and serve them with butter and strawberry jam?"

The bummers laughed, but the Cherokee slid from his horse to the ground and sniffed the air again. He then followed his nose across a field till he heard a hog grunt.

"There's dinner." He pointed to the ground.

All were amazed as he uncovered a fat pig that had been buried in a hole and covered with boards and earth. The men then butchered the hog and Cherokee Joe rode toward the Union camp with hams and pork chops dangling from his horse.

Most of the Cherokee who fought in the Civil War, however, sided with the Confederacy. In fact, the last general to surrender was Cherokee General Stand Watie. At the Battle of Pea Ridge in Arkansas he and his three thousand men downed the gun-toting Yanks with their bows and arrows. They could shoot two or three deadly points before the Union soldiers could reload their muskets. It sends a chill down my back to recall this story, because I hiked across that battlefield when I walked the Trail of Tears and I could've sworn that I heard men crying out in the autumn wind, as arrows and bullets tore their flesh and bones.

It has never been easy for me to talk about my Cherokee heritage, because it involves my spiritual side; I feel and experience things that cannot be easily explained. But to pretend such things do not occur would be to deny a vital part of my Southern heritage. I'm saying all this now because as I enter the city limits of Milledgeville, my Cherokee roots are wrapped around my march to the sea far more than I could dare dream in a hundred years. Just how these roots will lead me to a startling and historic discovery is perhaps best revealed a small piece at a time. Otherwise, it might boggle the mind. Besides, for all our blabbermouth tendencies, us Southerners sometimes like to escort folks down the path a step or two before we spill our grits.

I get a room at the Jameson Inn, shower and change into sweat-free clothes. Then I have only to walk across the road to find a mall with a bookstore. I not only like to see what new books are on the shelves, but I remember my good fortune at the bookstore back in Covington when Don got me invited to spend the night on the Burge Plantation. Don't we often circle back to the same honey tree?

After thumbing through a couple of books on the Civil War, I move over to the Native American section. I'm pleased to find a copy of my first book, *Walking the Trail,* which is about my walk along the Cherokee Trail of Tears. But what really intrigues me is the customer next to me.

"Have you read this book?" she says, pointing at my book.

"Let me see," I say, taking it from the shelves and opening the book. "Hmm, this is an unusual book. It has a mirror in it."

The woman is in her early thirties and wears jogging shorts. A blue bandanna is wrapped around her head and her skin is aglow with a tan. Her eyes are as dark as a night made for looking up at the stars.

"A mirror?" she says. "I've read it and don't recall any mirror."

"See for yourself," I say, handing her the book opened to my picture complete with the hat, crow feather, and snake rattler.

"It's you," she says. "Isn't it?"

"I guess I've changed a little since that picture was made," I say. "But, yeah, for the most part it's me. I couldn't help but play a little. I'm pleased to meet you," I add, holding out my hand to shake hers.

"That's okay," she says after telling me her name is Sally. "I love to play, and I feel like I know you so well. I made that whole walk with you from Oklahoma to Alabama."

You may already think I'm the most sentimental sap in the world, but I am now moved almost to the point of tears over meeting this woman and having her respond with such warmth and excitement. Yes, for all my independent and Rebel ways, I have such a need to feel close to others. Now here before me stands Sally, looking right into my heart as well as my lusts because I was so open with my thoughts and feelings when I wrote *Walking the Trail*.

"What became of Crow Dog, and how are your parents?" she asks. "You talked about them with such tenderness."

Crow Dog, the black Lab, loomed out of a Georgia pine thicket when I neared the end of my nine-hundred-mile hike. He insisted on walking home with me and we became the best of friends. In a few days, however, I began to worry that his owner might be looking for him, so I put an announcement on the radio and a man came forward claiming that Crow Dog was his, that someone had stolen him. It broke my heart to place the beautiful black Lab in the backseat of the man's car. Three days later, when I returned the backpack I carried on the Trail of Tears to its owner, Susan, who was also Cherokee, she asked how I was feeling about the loss of Crow Dog. I had told her the story on the phone and now admitted that I missed him terribly, that I hoped he was well and liked his alleged master. I hoped I had not made a horrible mistake in giving him up.

"He has missed you too," she said.

"How do you know?" I asked.

She then led me into her living room. There sat Crow Dog. He had appeared the day before as if he knew just where to come, though it was miles from the home of the man who claimed he owned him. Crow Dog then stood and placed his mighty paws upon my stomach, ready to hit the trail again where things happen beyond instant comprehension.

"Crow Dog is living with Susan," I tell Sally as customers come and go in the bookstore. "He seems happy and I sometimes visit him. I cut a few black hairs from his neck before I left for this trek and placed them in my medicine pouch. You asked about my parents. Mother is doing pretty well, but misses Daddy a great deal. He died last summer while planting peas in the garden."

"I'm sorry," she says, her tone saying even more. "I wish I had the courage to take off by myself like you, even if it was just in a car."

Her eyes are so warm, vulnerable, and hungry that I want to give her something to help her. I feel I have so little to offer, however. Then I recall that my medicine pouch is in my pocket. I take it out and open it to reveal little pieces of walnut shell my father cracked on his special rock at the barn, tobacco from his pouch, hairs from Crow Dog, and three peas from the bag of seeds Daddy was planting when he died. The last item is the tiny feather of a dove. Cherokee lore says that the bird is sent from the Spirit World to coo for those who feel alone; the song is said to tell them that they are loved. Save for the hair from Crow Dog, this is the same kind of medicine pouch that my mother, my sister Nita, and I kissed moments before I placed it in the peaceful hands of Daddy on the morning we buried him.

I take a pea from my pouch and place it in the center of Sally's palm.

"You said you wanted courage to hit the road," I say. "I hope this will help you find it."

She seems overwhelmed as her fingers wrap around the pea. Medicine, like beauty itself, is in the eye of the beholder, and sometimes simply giving someone a little attention is a tonic. The world is filled with people needing just a slight rub on the back to believe in themselves.

"This means more to me than you can understand," she says, "because I'm part Cherokee too. You can really see the Indian in my sister. Here, I'll show you a picture of her."

She opens her purse, places the pea inside a tissue there, and removes a photograph. She hands it to me and I behold both Sally and her sister in bikinis on the beach with great waves foaming behind them. True, her sister could pass for a full-blooded Indian. But what really holds my attention is how seductive Sally looks in that brief swimsuit, spotted like a leopard. She has one of the best-looking bodies I've ever had the good luck to see.

"Yes," I finally say. "She looks very Cherokee."

She drops the photo back into her purse.

"How long will you be in town?" she asks, looking at me as if I'm the embodiment of the proverbial open book.

I've received hundreds of letters from women who've read *Walking the Trail* and have responded to its erotic and spiritual qualities. Some of those women have sent photos of themselves and have asked to meet me, saying that they share a like passion for living. How beautiful they are to me, not only because they've been blessed with inviting shapes of flesh but because they write so openly from their hearts. Debi has shown amazing strength in not getting too jealous about these invitations. She understands that I share some things only with her. Still, I can't deny that I'm tempted at times—just as I am now with Sally.

"I'm not sure how long I'll be in town," I say. "Maybe a few days."

"Well," she says, writing her phone number on a piece of paper torn from the bag she's carrying. "If you have any free time, give me a call. I know a great spot in the woods where we could spread a blanket and have a picnic. Wow," she adds, eyeing her watch. "I'd better hurry or I'll be late for work at the pharmacy. Thanks for the seed."

She gives me a quick kiss on the cheek and races away. I fold the piece of paper with her phone number and slide it into my front pocket.

I find it true more often than not that once we give something to another it comes back to us doubled in size and quality, though things of the heart aren't always easily measured. I'm saying this now because after Sally vanishes out the mall door a woman comes from around the bookshelves.

"Forgive me for listening," she says. "But I overheard your conversation and I'd like to cook you dinner tonight to make your journey across Georgia a bit more enjoyable."

We talk for a while and I accept the kind invitation from this lady, Ruth Carter, who is a professor of international studies at the local university. Her house sits on a lake beneath towering pines and the crabmeat baked in a white wine sauce she serves is excellent. The real treat, though, is her personality.

"I like to jump atop my desk to get my students' attention," she tells me at the dinner table.

"Oh," I say, "like Robin Williams's character did in the movie *Dead Poets Society*."

"Yes," she says, "but I was doing it ten years before that movie came out."

"I have something for you," Ruth says after dinner as she places a box no bigger than one for pocket matches on the table.

"What is it?"

"Open it," she says as candlelight flickers over the box.

I lift the tiny lid and behold a golden angel, spreading its wings like Clyde does when he calls out to Debi and me at Tanager. While the angel is bigger than a lightning bug, it isn't as large as a june bug.

"You might have need of her before you get to the sea," Ruth says.

"Yes," I say, feeling that the angel came to me by way of the pea from my medicine pouch. "But where shall I place her?"

"Maybe in the shade of your crow feather?"

I take my trail hat from a nearby chair and pin the celestial creature behind the feather. If it's only a finely crafted piece of gold and has nothing to do with the divine, I don't think any less of it. Receiving it has already lifted my soul a little, as surely as Clyde will fly tomorrow through the trees and sing out for all who care to listen.

Chapter Twenty-two

On the outskirts of Milledgeville, Sherman jumped from his horse, Sam, and ran into a plum thicket for shelter from the icy November wind. His orderly raced alongside him, carrying the general's saddlebags filled with campaign maps, underwear, cigars, and a bottle of whiskey.

Sherman downed a shot of the booze, then struck a match and lit one of the cigars. He took a puff and noticed smoke swirling from the chimney of a slaves' cabin across a cotton field. A crow squawked atop a towering pine as he started walking toward the one-room house, cigar ashes vanishing in the cold wind.

Inside the cabin, the general warmed his hands by the fire. The slaves who lived there were careful not to look the white man in the eye for fear they might offend him. Their ragged clothes and cowed faces touched Sherman.

"Whose plantation is this?" he asked.

"Dis be Massah Cobb's plantation, suh," said one of the slaves.

"Howell Cobb?" said Sherman, his voice rising.

"Yes, suh, dat right."

Howell Cobb owned six plantations, had been the governor of Georgia, and was considered to be one of the big-dog generals in the Confederacy.

"Strip the plantation bare!" Sherman shouted to his soldiers. "Give the wheat, corn, and molasses to the Negroes! Then burn the place to the ground—every last bit of it!"

As the Yanks closed in on Milledgeville, Governor Joseph

Brown hurried to the local prison and released 126 convicts who swore to fight for the Great Cause. While they raced to catch the last Confederate train to leave Milledgeville, the Georgia secretary of state, N. C. Barnett, dared to stay behind in hopes of saving the state's great seal and some important documents. From inside the capitol he watched the Union soldiers invade his town and then he sneaked the seal and papers down to a river bluff. He hid there till dusk and sneaked back home where he and his wife placed the seal under a pillar of their house. The wrapped documents were buried in a pigpen with four hogs.

Georgia's capital fell into the Yankees' laps; they literally paraded into town as their band played "Yankee Doodle." Then the soldiers cheered the 107th New Yorkers, who ran their flag up the flagpole atop the capitol's dome.

Freed slaves crowded into town to behold their new heroes. Great day in the morning! Everything's going to be just fine and dandy now. Still, some of the Milledgeville blacks were terrified because their masters had told them that the Union soldiers had horns sticking from their heads and had roasted the kicking and screaming Atlanta slaves to a crisp golden brown when they burned the city.

The Yanks almost forgot the bloody battles of the past three years as their festive spirits continued to soar. After chopping up the pews from St. Stephen's Episcopal Church for firewood, the soldiers filled the pipe organ with molasses. Their fingers dipped into the sweet goo for a little holy dessert, and their boots left sticky tracks on the floor.

At the statehouse the troops held a mock meeting of Georgia's legislature and appointed Sherman to whip the state back into the Union. The brandy-inspired parody ended with toasts and a group of soldiers storming into the room; they shouted that the Yankees were coming. The party ended with the men tossing hundreds of books, including Audubon's *Birds of America,* out the windows to the muddy earth where one soldier forced his horse to trample them. Major James Connolly of Illinois wrote this about the literary bash:

It is a downright shame. . . . I am sure General Sherman will, some day, regret that he permitted this. . . .

Anna Maria, whose father was head of the nearby state asylum, noted:

We were despondent, our heads bowed and our hearts crushed. . . .

Neither Major Hitchcock nor General Sherman, who arrived with the 14th Corps, attended the mockery in the statehouse, though years later in his memoirs Sherman would write that it was a good joke. If the general did much laughing that night, his ribs may have taken a beating, for he slept on the hard floor of the governor's mansion which had been stripped bare, except for the heaviest furniture, by Governor Brown and his family right before they jumped aboard the getaway train to Savannah. Sherman and his men feasted that evening, nonetheless, over a table made from boards stretched across camp chairs.

I'm pondering these things as I stand under the leafy limbs of an oak only ten yards from the governor's mansion. It's 97 degrees and sweat is dripping down my face. Removing my hat to let the slight breeze blow around my head, I spot my tiny new traveling companion, Hat Angel, cool as a cucumber in the shade of my crow's feather. I wonder where Sally placed the pea I gave her from my medicine pouch. When the breeze dies, I place my worn hat back on my head and walk on till I come upon a green chameleon resting on a black wrought-iron fence in front of an antebellum mansion, its massive columns twenty feet tall. The reptile starts to turn brown right before my very eyes, and its throat swells like a small balloon. When it leaps to the grass, I think I see someone spying on me from the porch window. Who would do this? Why? I decide that I was fooled by sunlight on glass playing with a white silky curtain. But am I right?

Around the corner from the mansion, on the campus of the

university where Ruth, the angel giver, teaches, I find a pay phone and dial the office number of Bud Merritt, an administrator at the state asylum and a local artifact hunter. Ruth gave me his name, thinking that he might shed some light on Sherman's march through this part of Georgia. When he answers, I tell him about my cause and ask if he'd honor me by meeting for lunch. The very long pause that follows makes me suspect that he has no interest, and I'm disappointed but—

"Okay," he finally says. "Where do you want to meet?"

The inn where I'm staying has a restaurant and I suggest that Bud and I get a bite there today. I arrive before he does, and I'm still curious as to why he hesitated to meet me.

Bud stands six feet tall, is about my age, and looks like a cross between Clint Eastwood and James Taylor. He sits down across from me at the table and his dark eyes are as suspicious of me as I was of his long pause on the phone.

"You're a historian?" he says, his tone on edge.

"Not exactly," I say. "History fascinates me greatly but I think of myself more as a writer and nickel adventurer. It's what's inside Southerners right now that grabs me the most."

"Oh," he says, his tone warming as his shoulders relax a little.

"I love to look for artifacts," I continue, trying to find a vital link between us. "I found my first spearhead when I was in the second grade. It was as long as my hand and its edge was sticking from a dirt bank I often climbed to get into a sagebrush field to play with my sister. It filled me with a kind of wonder I can never get enough of, like I was part of whoever made it and we were brothers, but just in other times and other worlds. Does that sound strange to you?"

"No, not at all," he says, in a tone that's completely friendly now. "I first started collecting artifacts by finding arrowheads myself. When I'd see one on the ground, and I still do this today, I study it for a while before I pick it up, as if it's alive and I don't want to scare it away. I appreciate what you are saying about feeling a brotherhood with a stone and the soil. It's sometimes hard to beat walking across a plowed field with a stick in my hand to see what I can turn up."

That's a true Southerner for you. He's compelled to scratch in dirt, whether for farming, gardening, or relic hunting, or he'll practically dry up and blow away. In fact, a man or woman who grows up in the South and wants no part of dirt is in the grip of Dixie Denial. These individuals may even refuse to have potted plants in their homes or apartments for fear of crop failure.

"Sorry if I was cool to you on the phone," says Bud. "I didn't fully grasp where you were coming from. I thought maybe you were a pure historian and some of them, not all, bug me because they seem to have no sensitivity; it's all objective academic stuff. Then, too, I've met some who consider relic hunters like myself little more than tumblebugs because they think we destroy historical sites. Some may, but I think most of us help preserve history with the artifacts we find. Now that we're getting to know each other I must ask you to speak up a little because there's so much noise in here with the dishes rattling around us, and I damaged my hearing sometime back in the sixties when I played in a rock and roll band."

"I listened to some loud rock back in the sixties myself," I say, feeling more comfortable with Bud by the minute.

"Today I play bluegrass with my wife," he says. "She's got a great voice."

"My girlfriend sings as well," I say. "She writes songs and plays the piano. I'd give two of my fingers to sing like she does."

"We have more in common than I imagined we would," says Bud. "After lunch, how'd you like for me to take you to the site of the Battle of Griswoldville?"

"I'd like that very much."

"I've found hundreds of artifacts there," he says. "One of my favorites is a Confederate Tennessee belt buckle. I came across it after a little swamp was drained. I had been hunting that whole area for several years before I dug far enough into family records to learn that both my great-grandfathers were wounded there. Both were also shot in the right arm. One died three months later from gangrene. I've studied official Civil

War records and have determined within one hundred yards where they stood fighting when they were wounded."

His story sends goose bumps up my arms, because I've studied the Battle of Griswoldville and it's one of the eeriest and most moving stories of the entire Civil War.

Chapter Twenty-three

Finishing lunch, Bud and I hop into his pickup and hightail it south. The Georgia sun is so brutal that he turns the air conditioner up full blast; it blows on my naked arms and I drift back to the cold November wind of 1864. As Sherman sipped whiskey from his bottle in the plum thicket overlooking Howell Cobb's plantation, the outer fringes of his right wing swept through Griswoldville. They turned homes, depots, and factories—makers of pistols, sabers, soap, and candles—into ashes. The wagons that accompanied them had been fighting mud, their marred wheels scattering them along a line of forty miles. Because the wagons were vulnerable to attack from the Rebels, fifteen hundred Yanks were sent to guard them. Most carried new and lethal Spencer repeating rifles, something few Confederates had ever laid eyes on.

Those rifles remind me of a story I encountered when I researched the March to the Sea. When darkness fell, two Union soldiers sharing picket duty were the young Theodore Upson and the elderly Uncle Aaron Wolford, both of the 100th Indiana. Wolford eyed the cold moon; he was as silent and distant as its craters.

"You're usually happy-go-lucky, Uncle Aaron. Are you not feeling well tonight?"

"My time's come," said Uncle Aaron. "I was thinking about my wife and eight kids back home, how I liked for us to sit around the table and eat together."

"Now, what kind of foolish talk is this?" said Upson. "The war is as good as over. I bet we don't even see another battle.

You'll be back home at that table fighting over the last piece of apple pie before you know it."

"I'm too old to lie to myself," said Uncle Aaron. "I can feel it in my bones and it's not the same cold that comes from winter. I want you to send my things to my wife and kids and write her all you can about me. Will you do that for an old man?"

"I will," said Upson. "But I think you're just tired tonight and there's nothing to worry about."

The following day the men were putting up a barrier of logs and fence rails and building fires to cook lunch when muskets exploded in the near distance. Uncle Aaron and Upson jumped to their feet to behold a line of Johnnies marching toward them through a cotton patch, their steps bound for glory.

The Rebels, numbering 3,700, came from Macon and were too young or too old to fight in the regular units. They knew next to nothing about killing and their seven brigades were under the drunken leadership of General P. J. Phillips. Believing that Sherman was headed for Augusta, they hiked that way in hopes of defending the city when they stumbled into the bluecoats.

The proud Rebs formed several lines and their bugler played as if to open the gates of heaven itself. The drummer boys then shook the air with the same gallant music their heroes had heard when they gave Rebel yells on the slopes at Gettysburg. On and on they marched toward the Yanks with their muskets held ready, the Confederate flag flying high in the November wind. When the first line fired, they almost vanished in the smoke as they reloaded and the next line moved forward. Most of the bullets whizzed high above the heads of their enemies, but some found their marks and Yanks moaned, slumping over the barrier of pine logs and split rails.

Finally, however, the blues opened fire with their Spencer repeating rifles and Rebs began to be cut to pieces before they realized what they were up against. Having come too far from their base to race back, the Johnnies scrambled for shelter in a ravine only fifty yards in front of the Union soldiers. But in that desperate race they became target practice for the repeating rifles. Bodies fell atop each other, jerking about in the blood-soaked mud, and men cried out as if from the fiery pits of hell, their backbones blown apart, eyes gone, arms and legs severed.

Theodore Upson's dear friend Uncle Aaron was indeed killed. Later, he wrote about the Rebs on the battlefield:

> It was a terrible sight. Someone was groaning. We moved a few bodies and there was a boy with a broken arm and leg— just a boy 14 years old; and beside him, cold in death, lay his father, two brothers and an uncle.

Upson wanted to build Uncle Aaron a coffin, but there wasn't time because the troops had to hurry on. He refused, however, to simply drop him in a cold, wet hole in the earth. Using an ax, he split a hollow sycamore log, then placed his friend into the makeshift urn and folded his arms over his chest. On a rail, Upson carved AARON WOLFORD, 100TH INDIANA. Honoring his promise, he sent Uncle Aaron's ragged Testament, pocket watch, and a few dollars to his wife and eight kids. The letter that went along to tell about the battle and burial was stained by Upson's tears, which smeared the ink when he tried to wipe them away.

"He had a rare soul," Upson told his Union comrades. "I hope his wife and kids know it."

General Phillips, now sober with a pounding headache, cracked ego, and clawing conscience, led what was left of the ragged Johnnies back to Macon by the light of the moon. There they limped aboard a train and steamed toward Savannah to help General Hardee defend the city in the event that Sherman made it that far.

While Bud and I speed down the Georgia highway, I find myself studying him from the corner of my eye. I wish I could see deeply enough into his soul to grasp all that he thinks and feels about being a Southerner and a descendant of Confederate soldiers who were victims of the March to the Sea.

"What are your thoughts on Sherman?" I ask, once again amazing myself with my discreet and subtle investigative style.

"Well, I don't like revisionist history," Bud begins. "I think to really love history you have to look at it in the context of the times. In his time Sherman was something people had never seen before. If you look at him through the eyes of today, he seems pretty mild. He moved through enemy territory and didn't slaughter men, women, and children. His burning had some sort of rhyme and reason, so some people think, what's the big deal? But Colonel Rains offered Lee a land mine he had developed and Lee turned it down. He said, 'I will not make war on noncombatants.' I mean, Lee wouldn't even consider it.

"If you look at what Sherman did from that perspective, he's a big pill to swallow. After we've been through Cambodia, Bosnia, and the Holocaust, Sherman might not seem like that much. But when you go back to 1864, to a small hamlet like Milledgeville, and 30,000 soldiers with 5,000 teamsters and wagons storm in and leave families scratching in the dirt in the heart of winter hoping just to find a little cornmeal or something to feed themselves and their children, then you don't exactly have the prettiest picture in the world. I just don't think you can look at history with today's values and reinterpret it to suit your own outlook. You have to think about Sherman the way people in his own lifetime did.

"I'm not a person flash-frozen in 1865 who walks around mumbling out the side of his mouth *if only the South had won The War*, as my grandmother always called it. No, I even have some admiration for Sherman's strategy. This was the breadbasket of the South. But he didn't have to destroy all the food, because the railroads were being wrecked and there was no way to get supplies to Confederates after he left. With all the people moving into Georgia now, I suspect in time all this will just be a footnote in history anyway."

The Georgia countryside is but a blur outside the speeding pickup. The Old South seems to greet the New South when I spot a Confederate flag blowing atop a pole in front of a TV satellite dish.

"We've talked enough now," I tell Bud, "for me to see that you're something of a thinker. How do you feel about all this controversy over the Confederate flag?"

"I can't help but wonder," says Bud, "if we don't need to draw a line *somewhere*. If the flag is shot down, will the Civil War monuments in every Southern town square be next? Those stone figures weren't placed there to celebrate the Old South or slavery, but to honor the soldiers who fought in the war. I can't see tearing them down and dragging them to a monument graveyard like a bunch of wrecked cars because some say they're offended by them. I see nothing wrong with recognizing the three hundred fifty thousand men who died. That's seven times the number of men who were killed in Vietnam. You look at the population of the South during that time and I bet there wasn't a family that went untouched by one or more deaths. All this has become so politically incorrect that people are afraid to even talk about it. It's not my fault or the fault of any of the Sons of Confederate Veterans that the Ku Klux Klan gets out there and waves the battle flag. I agree with Lewis Grizzard that if they took those hats off, their heads would be shaped just like their hats. I have no affinity with these kinds of people whatsoever. There are blacks I can sit down and discuss such things with and they understand. Just as African American heritage is important to some, my Southern heritage is crucial to me."

Hear, hear.

Chapter Twenty-four

"We're almost to Griswoldville now," Bud says as he slows the truck on a road bordered by towering pines, kudzu vines, blackberry bushes, and modest farmhouses.

"It must've haunted you when you discovered that both your great-grandpas were wounded here," I say, feeling kinship to Bud, since both my great-grandpa and great-uncle were wounded in Georgia fighting Union soldiers.

"Oh, yeah," he sighs. "It made me rethink every bullet I had ever found where they fought. And the amount of spent bullets was incredible for a four- or five-hour battle. I could go out there on a Saturday and find over a hundred bullets."

Bud stops the truck by the railroad, and we get out. I follow him some fifty yards to the rock foundation of an old building.

"This is where the gun factory stood," says Bud. "It manufactured Griswold pistols that were copies of the .36-caliber U.S. Navy Colt. Over three thousand were made and that pistol is so collectible today that a good one will bring as much as ten thousand dollars. Over here on the tracks is where the Rebs were walking toward Augusta when they happened upon the Union soldiers."

Bud and I both began to sweat as we march down the railroad tracks. The wooden ties have been soaked in oil to preserve them, and its smell is almost as strong as that of a dead possum just up ahead. Two enormous black buzzards peck its carcass. On either side of the tracks stand pines and blackberry bushes already heavy with dark fruit. Four or five bees buzz in and out of a yellow-blooming honeysuckle vine, and the buzzards lift their mighty wings to flap into the woods as we get closer to the possum.

"As early as the 1940s people were digging up tons of earth here," Bud says. "Then they'd drag giant magnets through it to attract artifacts."

"Capturing the ghosts of Griswoldville," I say.

"Yes," Bud says, taking a seat under the shade of a pine. "I have one of those ghosts for you, if you'd like it."

I nod, but I'm not sure just what he's up to. I take a seat on the ground a few feet from him and he reaches into his pocket. He removes something, concealed in his fist. Then he places a bullet in my palm.

"I found it right over there," says Bud. "It's a Yankee bullet. One that was dropped, not fired, during the battle."

"That's *one* human being who wasn't killed," I say.

"When the battle started," Bud says, "there was so much smoke at first that the Rebels thought the men in front of them were Yankees. They began to fire on their own men. Here where we're sitting is within fifty yards either way, left or right, of where my great-grandpas were shot. You may ask how I know this, but if you look closely you'll see a slight rise before us, which was a landmark on the official records and a massive cotton field at that time. Anyway, judging by the rise, and where I have found dropped bullets of both North and South as well as spent ones, I can pinpoint to within a hundred yards of where my great-grandpas were shot."

For what seems a very long moment Bud and I study each other as though we have touched something we both feel, but is best said in what we're already doing together this afternoon.

When the big buzzards fly back to the tracks and start pecking their possum, I ease the bullet down into my pocket. I'm wiping the sweat from my head when Bud takes my hat. He ponders Hat Angel and the snake rattler.

"Your hat makes me think of an old man I used to see when I was a boy," says Bud. "His hat held little things he had found on the side of the road. He traveled all over America in a wagon pulled by goats."

"You mean Goat Man?"

"You've seen him?"

"Several times when I was growing up. You're the second person who's mentioned him since I left Atlanta. He was a kind of folk hero to me. I wish I could have talked with him man-to-man before he died."

"He's not dead. Not unless he passed on recently. Last I heard, just a few months ago, he was still alive and kicking down in a Macon nursing home. He has a young girlfriend there. She's in her eighties."

In *A Streetcar Named Desire,* Tennessee Williams's Blanche says that she has "always depended on the kindness of strangers." I can't deny that I, too, must often thank strangers for guiding me down the right path. Bud has not only given me an artifact and a direct link through his ancestors with the March to the Sea, but he's planted a red flag on the map at my next destination. I'll walk to that Macon nursing home, meet my childhood folk hero, and see just what he and other elders there recall about the war. Why, he might even be inspired to come out of retirement and straddle a billy alongside me.

It is a hot, exhausting two-day walk from Milledgeville to Macon. But after I get a motel room and shower I feel refreshed and excited to see the Goat Man. I visit the public library to research him. His real name is Charlie "Ches" McCartney, and he's followed the twists and turns of more roads and had more lovers than I dared dream of.

Born in 1901 near What Cheer, Iowa, the Goat Man was often picked on by other kids because he didn't act like they did. At the age of fourteen he ran away to New York City where he married a twenty-four-year-old Spanish knife thrower. They scratched out a living in bars and pubs where the Goat Man worked as her target. The closer she stuck the long silver knives to his head, the better their tips were. He filed the blades daily to make certain they'd stick in the wood so she wouldn't have to repeat a throw to appease the boozed-up audience.

"Those were the *easy* days," the Goat Man tells me after I

arrive at the Eastview Nursing Home, a modern brick building a few miles east of downtown Macon, where he's been since 1988. "After I divorced the knife thrower I went back to Iowa and wrestled at county fairs to make money. One day I took on a black bear."

"A bear?"

"I wanted to back out. But two men pulled me by my hair onto the platform. I spit bear hair from my mouth for two days. I beat him only because I was so scared and God Almighty took mercy on me."

The Goat Man rubs his left elbow, which is deformed with a knot as big as a lemon. We're sitting in the lobby of the nursing home and I'm totally entranced by this gentleman who is now ninety-two years old. This living legend has a strong and yet gentle presence, and he connects me to my Southern roots in a way no one else can.

I first met the Goat Man when I was nine years old. My older sister, Sandra, came home and told me that the Goat Man and his son were camped just down the road by a creek. I had never seen the Goat Man before, but I had heard that he looked like a mountain man with a long beard and he slept with his goats on winter nights to keep him warm. He could speak Goat and understood everything his animals said. If he wanted, he could turn himself into a goat and hide from people. He lived mostly on goat milk, but he could also turn plain old field rocks into delicious soup simply by dropping them into a pot of boiling water and stirring them with the same staff he used to drive his herd. He knew many other secrets, too, but wouldn't tell anybody unless they gave him food and he liked them a lot.

I sneaked through the woods toward the creek and heard the goats calling out long before I saw them. There I spotted the Goat Man with his long beard and overalls. He was bending to place a car tire on a fire, and then he stood, bigger than life itself, surrounded by thick black smoke. I looked for his son, but saw no one except him and some fifteen goats. Had he turned the son into a goat? Atop two small wagons were signs reading: JESUS WEPT and GOD IS NOT DEAD. His clothes were covered with buttons, whistles, tinfoil, cigar wrappers, Coke and RC bottle caps, pencils, and even a spark plug dangled from a string tied around his neck. Getting a close look at him, I wasn't so sure that I wanted to sample any of his homemade rock soup. But my curiosity was heating up to fever pitch.

"What are you doing out there, boy?" he called, and I would've run back home right then but I was too frightened.

"I brought you something, Goat Man."

"Come out where I can see you better."

My heart was pounding as I stepped from the woods and held up a brown paper sack.

"Don't be afraid," he said. "Children are the joy of God, and I mean no harm to anyone. What do you have there?"

"Something to eat," I said, eyeing him, the goats, and the wagons as if they might vanish before my very eyes. The metal wheels on the wagons had no rubber, and pots, pans, signs, cans, buckets, gourds, birdhouses, mirrors, hubcaps, wire, and more were tied to the wagons' sides and tops as if the Goat Man ran a traveling junk store. I was still uneasy, but when he stepped closer I could see into his eyes. They were warm and kind and I offered him the bag. When he bent over to take it, the spark plug, tied to the string around his neck, dangled forward and rocked back and forth like a pendulum to an old clock. Around eight of his fingers strings were tied. I figured he had so many secrets that they were there to remind him.

"My mother made it," I said, after his fingers gripped the paper sack.

He reached inside the bag and pulled out a big piece of peanut brittle. My uncle had raised the peanuts and my grandfather had raised the cane for the molasses that went into the candy. The Goat Man took a bite and nodded. I was sure I had won his favor and he would now tell me one of his secrets. But Nita appeared from the woods.

"Mother said for you to get home right now," she called out, "or she's going to whip your behind with a hickory switch."

It was rare that my mother ever lifted a finger against us, but I had sneaked off from the house and I didn't want her to worry. Then, too, Daddy would be home any minute from work and one of his main rules was that his children be there when he arrived so that we could all sit down together at the dinner table. He didn't tie string around our fingers to remind us, but a lick or two from his leather belt had an effect on my memory.

"Will you be here tomorrow?" I asked the Goat Man.

"Only the morning light knows that," the Goat Man told me. "I might not be alive tomorrow."

I told him I hoped he stayed and that I'd come back, but early the next morning as I brushed my teeth to prepare for school I heard the musical rattle of the wagons and the eerie cries of the goats as they passed in front of our house. I ran to the front porch and waved as the Goat Man and his son—he hadn't been turned into a goat after all—disappeared down the road with the animals and a secret I feared that was lost forever.

Chapter Twenty-five

"I know a story about Sherman," shouts an old woman hobbling forward as she braces herself with a metal walker. "It's more interesting than anything that old goat will tell you."

"She can't help it," the Goat Man says. "It's human environment. That's all it is, human environment. She wants attention."

"*Well,*" the old woman snaps again, "do you want to hear my story or not?"

Gossip about my journey has spread through the nursing home as fast as a wildfire and I'm both touched and a bit put off by this bundle of nerves who shakes her witchy finger as she speaks.

"What's your name?" I ask.

"Helen," she says, her tone softening.

"I do want to hear your story," I say, "but it would be better if we waited till I've finished talking to Mr. McCartney."

"You don't have to lie to me," she yells. "If you don't want to hear my story, just say so. I've been lied to before and survived. If you think goats know more than people, then just go right ahead and keep fooling yourself. It's no gravy from my bowl. I can still hootchy-kootchy like I did sixty years ago."

Helen, in her eighties, begins to shake her whole body while she holds on to the aluminum-frame walker, and eight or ten others in wheelchairs or with canes begin to gather, a couple of them clapping their hands. One elderly gentleman has black skin, red hair, and a growth on his forehead about the size of a grape; it's purplish-blue. The bizarreness, how-

ever, is overshadowed by a radiant innocence in his face. And
on his lips is one of the most curious little grins I've ever seen.
It may be only wishful thinking on my part, but he seems to
find everything amusing as if he had learned long ago from a
mirror that humor was his salvation. Judging, too, by how calm
the Goat Man is staying during this outbreak of celebrity envy,
he's experienced it more than once and has learned to sit it
out with grace.

"How do I look?" Helen shouts, her shoulders rocking back
and forth faster by the heartbeat as her narrow hips try to keep
the beat.

"You need to be in Las Vegas," says an old man in a wheelchair. "You're hot."

"I think it's disgusting," says an old woman leaning against
her cane. "A lady shouldn't carry on that way."

"Human environment," says the Goat Man as he shakes his
head. "Human environment, that's all it is. She means no
harm."

"I never made it to Vegas," shouts Helen, "but I was a main
attraction in a carnival for over three years. Madam Hoochi-
coochi they called me, and my picture was as big as an elephant on the side of a truck. Let's see you shake like this,
Goat Man. You can't do it, can you?"

More and more of the old folks are arriving by the second
and I'm trying to decide what to do when Joyce, who operates
the nursing home hair salon, dashes from her little room down
the hall to take Helen by the arm.

"Oh," Joyce says, "if I could dance like you I'd never cut
hair another day to make a living. If I could do even half as
well, I'd be pleased with myself. Won't you finally please show
me some of your steps?"

"You really care?" Helen says.

"I do," Joyce says. "I care about anything you want to talk
about."

"That man back there don't." She points at me. "I got a
Civil War story but he won't listen."

"I met him earlier," says Joyce. "I think he's just so interested that he wants to have you all to himself later."

They disappear into her salon and she closes the door. The others begin to go about their business and I turn to find the Goat Man holding a copy of *USA Today* rolled up within six inches of his eyes; his lips move as he reads.

"Mr. McCartney?"

He lowers the newspaper and I once again behold his wondrous, kind eyes. Only two teeth are left in his aging head.

"I'm sorry we were interrupted," I say. "You were telling me how you hurt your arm?"

"I was working for the WPA," he says. "A tree fell on me. It's just nature's way. When I was found several hours later, I was out cold with my arm twisted and broken. They took me to the morgue and started to stick me to drain my blood, when I woke up. God had sent an angel to rub my eyes."

Unable to do much work now that his left arm was ruined, and refusing to go on welfare, the Goat Man decided to explore America. Inspired by Robinson Crusoe, he persuaded his new wife to make him, her, and their son, Albert Gene, goat-skin clothes in which to greet those they met along the roads they traveled. Averaging twelve miles per day with his goat caravan, he supported himself by selling postcards of himself and his family with the goats. Everywhere he camped people flocked around him to scratch their heads and perhaps wish they were as free as this prophet, poet, and self-made gypsy king.

"Most people were good to me," says the Goat Man, "and some brought me food and money. But more than once I was beat up and hit over the head at night. Sometimes people threw bottles at me from their cars or trucks. They turned my wagons over at night."

In 1941 the Goat Man and his son moved to Jeffersonville some thirty miles east of Macon on Highway 80. In addition to the money he made from the postcards, he received donations from those who heard him preach. His church was usually the shade of a tree and he encouraged men to love each other and try to overcome their greed. Hundreds of spiritual signs nailed to oaks and pines throughout the Deep South were his handiwork, and they proclaimed GOD IS KINDNESS and JESUS IS YOUR

FRIEND. When he and his goats wandered into the isolated mountains of north Georgia, some living there claimed that the Goat Man was Jesus Himself.

"I never said I was," says the Goat Man. "But when they decided I wasn't, they tarred and feathered me. I was a hell of a mess. Down in south Georgia in World War Two people thought I was a Nazi spy and the sheriff searched my wagons. He didn't find a shortwave radio because there wasn't one. People can't help being weak and suspicious. It's just human environment."

He finally built a little church of his own with a dirt floor in Jeffersonville and called it the Free Thinking Mission. It doubled as his home, but burned to the ground in 1978. He and his son then bought a school bus and lived in it near the church site. That was ten years after the Goat Man stopped traveling with his caravan. Back in 1968, on Signal Mountain near Chattanooga, Tennessee, he was mugged and the wound on his head required twenty-seven stitches. The same thug slashed the throats of eight goats. Days later, headed to home sweet home, the Goat Man awoke in Conyers, Georgia, to find two more of his goats had vanished. Rumor said one was barbecued. The second had been tied to the railroad tracks and departed Georgia with the early morning train.

"I just never had the heart to keep going with my goats after that," the Goat Man tells me. "But I didn't stop traveling. I just started walking and hitchhiking."

Indeed, he didn't stop. When he reached his eighties, he thumbed all the way from Macon to Los Angeles. Already the ex-husband to at least five wives—the Lord works in mysterious ways—the Goat Man had a crush on the starlet Morgan Fairchild. Bound and determined to marry her and bring her back to live in Dixie, the Goat Man found himself in an L.A. hospital after being beaten and robbed of his U.S. savings bonds. He flew home to Albert Gene, who was still living in the parked yellow school bus.

In forty years the Goat Man and his billies wandered across forty-nine states and Canada.

"I would've gone to Hawaii," says the Goat Man, "but my

goats couldn't swim. Anyway, if we'd made it they would've just eaten the grass skirts off the hula dancers."

His eyes get big when he speaks of those grass skirts being eaten away and I love the fire that still heats this old man. At the age of ninety-two, he has more passion for living than some folks in their twenties. And as I sit here beside him, rubbing his aching and deformed left arm where the tree fell on him, I feel as though I have completed a kind of circle and come home in some rare and special way. Almost forty years ago I gave him some candy in hopes of getting one of his secrets, but he disappeared down the road. Life's true secrets are, of course, found in the sum of our experiences, and for thirty years now I've been on the road learning those secrets through the joy, sadness, thrill, intrigue, and reflection of those I have met. I'll never know how much this now-delicate old man influenced me to follow the life I've been leading, but I suspect it's a great deal. How blessed I feel to behold his living legend, one of my roots still feeding from his spring.

Chapter Twenty-six

The Goat Man promises to introduce me to his girlfriend after lunch, and as he walks down the hallway toward the cafeteria I behold his aged body and the small, careful steps he takes. He's still able to move about without a cane or walker. Strings are fixed around two fingers. Whether they are to remind him of some treasure yet buried in his heart or simply there as gypsy rings to fly him to another state in the blink of an eye, I don't know. For all my pushy questions there are some best left unasked. He's almost to the cafeteria door now and I stand frozen, studying him, wondering how many more times he will make that little hike to the hot and freshly baked bread I smell drifting from the kitchen. Perhaps true wisdom to the traveler—and all of us are on this journey called life—is to have the humility and peace to eat each meal as if it were the last before we begin that greater trek down the path beyond the grave.

In the TV room, more than a dozen of the nursing home residents gaze at *The Andy Griffith Show*. Andy is explaining to his son, Opie, why he must release the baby birds he's been nurturing.

"I taped a robin's wing one time," an old woman in a wheelchair says. "Some kid had shot it with a slingshot."

"I made many a slingshot in my day," the elderly gentleman seated across from her says. "One winter we were so poor I fed us squirrels and rabbits I killed with it."

"I'll eat a tender squirrel with some dumplings and mashed

potatoes," the old woman says. "But I never tasted a rabbit that wasn't as tough as shoe leather."

"Got to get 'em when they're young to be sweet and juicy," the old man says.

"I reckon the only ones my husband, God rest his soul, ever shot were nursing-home rabbits," the old woman says.

"I don't know what became of my last slingshot," the old man says. "I think one of the grandsons took it. I had it hanging on a nail over the fireplace. You know how kids start off asking you for stuff, but then they're just like snowballs rolling down a hill. They start picking up whatever's in front of them like it was theirs all along."

"We didn't do that to my grandparents," she says. "They lived with us till the day they died and if us kids wanted to as much as touch any of their things we asked permission like we'd been brought up to show a little respect."

"*Respect*," the man says. "Now, *there's* the difference between our generation and these new ones coming along. I don't think they even respect themselves."

"I got a good lick across the fanny with a hickory switch if I misbehaved," the woman says. "Now children take you to court and sue you."

"I'm glad I lived when I did," the man says.

"Ain't that the truth," the woman says.

When they turn back to the TV to behold Opie letting the birds fly free from the cage, I walk on down the hallway to the beauty salon and knock on the door. Joyce opens it.

"If you're looking for Helen," says Joyce, "she's gone back to her room."

"That was sweet of you to care for her a while ago. You seem to really be in touch with these old folks."

"I've been here doing hair for twenty years," she says. "They're my family and always doing something to keep me on my toes. I like to touch their hair and see if I can make them feel better. It's more for me than for them. See that mirror there? Well, when I first had it installed, the home had a new arrival, Mrs. Baker. She was in her upper eighties and hadn't said a word. I didn't know if she'd had a stroke or what.

But I talked her into letting me wash her hair and curl it one afternoon. When I turned her around to see herself in my new mirror, she said, *'My God, I'm pretty.'* Well, I was so happy that I just sat right down and had myself a good cry. Another lady kept begging me to promise that I'd do her hair when she died. I loved her, but I couldn't say I would. I've got this horrible phobia of dead people. I've had it since I was a little girl and there's just nothing I can do to get over it. Anyway, one day I was rolling her hair and her head fell forward. I mean, just like that. I took one look at her face and it scared the living daylights out of me. I ran out of here like a chicken with its head cut off. I was halfway to the front door when I finally got the nerve to run back in here and dump her purse on the table to look for her heart medicine. I was shaking so much I didn't think I'd ever get her nitroglycerin tablet into her mouth. I was so relieved when I did and she opened her eyes. Now, just listen to me, carrying on like I was preaching at a revival. Want me to show you to Helen's room?"

"If you have time."

As we leave the little salon I glance at the calendar on the wall, picturing a rolling meadow filled with sunflowers. Over it is written: TODAY IS THE FIRST DAY OF THE REST OF YOUR LIFE. The room fills me with sweet sorrow. I'll bet that many of the women who come here to have their hair cut and washed and get a permanent are rarely touched outside this room. How lucky that they have Joyce and her needy fingers for that crucial human contact. Can any of us at any age truly deny that there have not been moments in our lives that we felt as though the simple, tender touch of another would make our day?

I follow Joyce down the hallway and peek through the many open doors. Road Rabbit would be very much at home here, because almost all the little rooms have stuffed animals— bears, dogs, cats—on the beds, in chairs, or on chests of drawers. When we get to a room with a stuffed raccoon, I become spellbound by an ancient lady wearing a big red hat as she rocks back and forth in an oak chair.

"Daddy?" she calls out. "Daddy, is that you?"

"It's Joyce," my guide says, "and a friend. How are you today?"

"Daddy's very late," the ancient lady says. "He should have been here long ago. He's taking me home today."

"Let me know if you want your hair washed," Joyce says. "I'll give your head a good rubbing."

"Daddy?" she calls again. "Daddy, I'm down here in this room."

"Her parents have been dead for many years," Joyce whispers as we continue on down the hallway.

"Doesn't she ever call out for her mother?"

"No, because her mother couldn't drive."

We stop before a closed door and Joyce knocks. A voice tells us to come in and Joyce motions for me to go alone, that she'll see me later. I open the door and find Helen brushing her hair before a cracked mirror. Stuck in the corner is a postcard from Texas with a bull as big as a house on it. Atop it sits a cowboy waving his hat.

"Sorry I didn't get to talk to you earlier," I say.

"Not many people like to talk to me," she says, her brush easing through her hair.

"Do you have children?"

"A boy in Texas," she says. "He came last month and stayed a couple of days. He has his own life to keep him busy. Did Joyce tell you that somebody stole the gold watch he gave me?"

"No."

"They'd steal time itself from you if they could."

The demanding tone I heard in her voice earlier when I talked with the Goat Man has vanished. It's been replaced with a softness, as though she has let go of something that was eating on her. Perhaps she's simply a bit embarrassed by how she acted.

"You used to travel with a carnival and be a hootchy-kootchy dancer?"

Her brush stops and she begins to pick gray hairs from the bristles. She drops them into a plastic basket near the edge of her bed.

"I just made that up," she says. "It doesn't seem fair that a goat man should get so much recognition. I'm sorry that I said what I did. I'm just lonely sometimes."

"It's okay. I get lonely sometimes too. I think we all do."

"But when you get old, it's different. You have so many memories and no one to share them with. Not really, not the way you do when it's someone who loves you. The story about Sherman is real. Do you still want to hear it?"

"That would very much please me."

"My grandmother was very frightened when the Yankees came, because my mother had just been born. She was smaller than most babies and more delicate. Granddaddy was away fighting with Lee and Grandma didn't know what to do to protect Mama. When she saw the soldiers coming across the cornfield, she put dirt on the flames in the fireplace and hid Mama up in the flue. When Mama got big enough to talk she asked Grandma why she did that, and she said Sherman was taking so many things with him she figured he'd take her, too, if he ever saw how pretty she was. I had a rag doll Mama made me when I was little and my favorite game was to play that the Yankees were coming and I'd have to hurry that doll up into the same flue before the soldiers got her. She stayed covered black with soot and my cousin called her a slave doll, but I always said she was as free as me."

"What became of that doll?" I ask, finding it eerie that her cousin saw it as a slave.

"I had a little friend," she says. "We called her Crawfish 'cause she was always in the creek turning over rocks, looking for crawfish. She was a colored girl and lived in the old slave house by the pond with her grandma. She'd put those crawfish in a mason jar with water. Her grandma would then kill them by pulling their heads off. She dried them in the sun on a broken piece of glass that they said came from the old Snyder mansion that had burned to the ground. Her grandma ground up those dried crawfish with a rock and mixed the powder with roots and leaves she got in the woods. Then she wrapped it in little pieces of newspapers and sold it or traded it to colored people for curing sores or taking off warts. Once she traded some of it for ice cream so Crawfish and me could have some. It was the first ice cream we ever ate and it hurt our teeth but it was so good.

"We'd let it melt in our spoons and suck it out. We had a contest to see who could make the most noise doing that. Her grandma was real old but she could hear good and she stuck her head out of that old cabin to see what the fuss was. Me and Crawfish thought she'd scold us, but know what she did? She got a spoon and did the same thing. She was a noisy somebody, but the three of us got to laughing so hard that tears came to our eyes. The next month Crawfish's grandma got sick, real sick. We made her soup, like she told us, out of the crawfish and roots she mixed up. My mama liked that old woman and sat by her bed, feeding her the soup. But she died one night while Mama slept in a chair by her bed. Grandpa made her a coffin out of boards. We couldn't afford her a tomb-stone. Crawfish stayed with us for a couple of weeks after that. But then an uncle came to get her and take her to Chicago. I begged Mama to let her stay with us, but Daddy said it wasn't right because she was a colored girl. I couldn't see the differ-ence. I loved her like my own sister. The night before she left on the train I washed that rag doll to give to Crawfish and some of the cotton stuffing came out. Mama sewed her back together and when I asked why she was crying she said she stuck herself with the needle, but I never believed her."

"Did you ever hear from the girl again?"

"Once. She couldn't write, but her uncle addressed a letter to us and Crawfish had drawn me a picture with a blue crayon. It showed her, her grandma, that doll, and me sucking ice cream from spoons."

She turns to me as if waiting for judgment to be passed on her story, on her life and its contribution to my journey.

"I walked forty miles out of my way from Milledgeville to see the Goat Man," I say. "But if he hadn't been here it would've still been worth the time and energy to meet you and hear that memory. It's the only one like it I've found. That makes you unique."

"You're not just trying to make me feel good?"

"No, and when your generation is gone all those firsthand accounts will vanish with you. You're worth more than gold."

Her face takes on a beauty that can come only from inside when a person feels that he has meaning and that another cherishes it.

"I'll tell you something I never told anybody," she whispers. "Sometimes when we have ice cream for dessert in the cafeteria here, I bring it back to my home to be alone with me and my spoon and . . ."

She stops as though what she thinks is too personal to share. I respect that and it's easy to see that she joins Crawfish, that old woman, and the rag doll in her private world. As for myself now, I'll never eat ice cream again like I did before this afternoon. Will the New South, or all of America for that matter, ever be so free that people of all colors can sit together and slurp melted ice cream, tears of joy running down our cheeks?

"Joyce is going to wash my hair," she says. "Would you help me to her salon?"

Helen puts aside her brush and gets behind her aluminum-frame walker. I move beside her down the hallway and at one point she stops to rest and takes my hand. Her hand is warm and soft, and I guess somewhere along the way on this march I slid over the edge, because for a very long moment I cannot distinguish my mother from this old woman. I can't help but think of my mother back home in the hills of Alabama with a hoe in her hands working in the garden. They and all other elderly women are one soul, and I am but a single breath in their passage on earth.

When we get to the salon, I help Helen into the beauty chair. Joyce lights up, once again ready to turn someone's hair into a crowning glory.

When I exit the little room I discover the Goat Man pushing a wheelchair down the hallway. He introduces me to the woman in that chair, his girlfriend, Virginia Turner, a retired nurse.

"I have to twist his ear every now and then to keep him in line," says Virginia.

"I always did like a woman with a good grip," says the Goat Man.

They look at each other with all the fire and magic that young lovers have when they first leap from the cliff. Standing behind her, the Goat Man strokes her hair and she grins like the cat who's about to eat the canary.

"Did he tell you we were crowned the King and Queen of the nursing home?"

"No," I say, "but I can sure see that you are."

Before I leave I stop by the salon to tell Joyce and Helen good-bye. Helen's head is under the dryer but she waves. I pull Joyce aside and ask her if she thinks the Goat Man is truly as happy as he seems.

"Oh, yes," she says. "He never complains. Not since he fell in love with Virginia. You see how they are together. The only time I've ever seen him sad was once after his son, Albert Gene, came to visit him. We couldn't find Mr. McCartney anywhere in the nursing home and we finally discovered he was walking down the side of the road trying to find his way back to the school bus. I guess all those years of traveling with his son got his fever up. But when we brought him back, he was at peace again."

When I slip into my pack and lift my staff to hit the road I spot the Goat Man pushing his girlfriend toward the TV room. I just can't resist getting his autograph.

"Would you sign my hat?" I ask.

"Be happy to, son," says the Goat Man.

He pulls a pen from his shirt pocket and with great flair writes his name along the brim between Hat Angel and the snake rattler, the tip of the crow feather pointing at the prized signature.

"Mr. McCartney," I say, "when I was a little boy living in Cleveland, Tennessee, you camped near my house and I gave you a bag of peanut brittle. Do you remember that?"

He rubs his well-trimmed white beard and seems to probe his many years for the answer. He finally shakes his head and laughs.

"There were so many children who gave me things," he says.

"That's okay," I tell him. "*I* remember."

He hands me my autographed hat and I walk outside into the scorching Georgia sunlight. I'm a few steps down the road when I turn back to see if he's watching, itching to come along. All I find is my own reflection in the big nursing home window. But that doesn't dampen my spirits in the least, for mine eyes have seen the glory of the coming of the Goat.

Chapter Twenty-seven

I hike to downtown Macon and enter the Canary Cottage, a café where the Goat Man enjoyed breakfast for seventeen years. Dot, the owner, never charged him for his daily biscuit and cup of coffee and he claimed a special chair near the door by the window. My third time here, I sit in his historic spot.

"How did your visit go?" asks Dot, whose cash register is only six feet away. Above it on the wall hangs a drawing of the Goat Man.

"Good," I say. "Seeing him was a kind of dream come true. It made me feel whole again."

"You two may be cut from the same cloth," she says. "God does funny things with His scissors."

A waitress brings me a biscuit and a cup of coffee. When she leaves, Dot comes to me and lowers her voice.

"I'm happy to hear he's doing well," she says. "You see, I'm the one who contacted the state to put him in that nursing home. Only did it because he was having trouble taking care of himself, and it was breaking my heart to see a man of such strong spirit go downhill."

"You probably did the right thing," I say, wrestling with my words. "The people who work there are kind."

A customer takes out money to pay his bill and Dot returns to the cash register. I put some peach preserves inside the biscuit and take a bite. It's not as good as the biscuits my mother makes, but I like sitting here in the Goat Man chair for one more thrilling ride.

"Since we talked yesterday," says Dot, returning to my table, "I got to thinking more about your walk along the Trail of Tears. It's really a shame the way we treated the Indians and threw them out of the South."

A woman in her seventies at a nearby table turns to face me. She's well dressed and has big, dark eyes; smoke from a cigarette in her hand streams into my face, and I begin to cough.

"You're the man who walked the Cherokee Trail of Tears?" she says.

"That's right. Now I'm walking the route of Sherman's March to the Sea."

"Where do you go from here?" she says, finally lowering the cigarette so its smoke doesn't swirl into my eyes.

"Back to Milledgeville."

She opens her purse and pulls out a business card.

"Look me up when you get there," she says. "I live in the house built by the man hired to force the Cherokee from Georgia to Oklahoma. He died in the same home. You might want me to show you around."

I take the card from Rowena, but I'm put off by the invitation. While my own journey along the Trail of Tears was remarkable, I still sometimes envision the horror of the Indian removal and all those who died along the way. I have the personal belief that human spirits can linger or come and go from where their bodies died, and the thought of entering the home of a man who helped destroy my Cherokee ancestors makes me uncomfortable. When Rowena leaves minutes later, I lift the card from beside my cup of coffee and study the address. I don't recall seeing that street. While I'm most curious that my path should cross that of a woman so related to such an important part of my life, my instincts continue to tell me to stay clear of her home. I fold the business card and toss it into the trash can behind the cash register when I try to pay Dot for breakfast.

"No charge," she says. "It's on the Goat Man."

I gather my gear and start for Milledgeville. It's another long, hot day for marching and my feet won't let me forget it either. But I feel so blessed that my trek into Macon went well that it empowers me to push on. I have a great tendency to reflect on my most recent encounters as I hike along the road-sides, and today is certainly no exception. I keep seeing the Goat Man pushing his sweetheart down the hallway in her wheelchair and the tenderness he showed when he ran his string-tied fingers through her hair. This makes me long for Debi and I decide that I'll call her when I have the luck to find a store with a pay phone.

All along my journey I have been entering post offices to make photocopies of my diary and mail the pages to Debi so that she might feel part of my walk and possibly gain some insight into the South, me, and my love for her. I also sent her a map of the route of my march to the sea in hopes that she would write me care of general delivery. But so far not a single post office has had a letter for me. As much as I have longed to hear her voice, I haven't phoned her because I felt she needed a little time to get over my taking the trek without her. I've been telling myself that sharing my journal with her will win her over, and that everything will be okay. But I don't totally believe myself, and some of that fear is loose in me now.

I finally spot a grocery store and it has a pay phone on the side of the building. I lower my pack to the ground and dial Debi's number. She's staying in a trailer on her parents' property by a lake near Tacoma, Washington. Her parents are building a house there to live in when they retire from teaching in China. When Debi answers the phone, her very voice excites and entices me. I can taste her lips and more.

"I thought you might like a direct field report from the Rebel front," I say.

"Yes." Her tone is warm and I'm encouraged.

I tell her about my visit with the Goat Man and how seeing him and his elderly girlfriend together inspired me to phone, a lasting future between us becoming all the more important to me.

"Oh, darling," she says. "I'm not so sure about that."

"Haven't you been getting the mail I've sent?" I say, finding it difficult to accept that I may have failed at my trade as a writer to reach her heart and mind and relax her fists once

again into the gentle and unafraid fingers I have come to know
so well.

"Yes," she says, and her lack of saying more makes me feel
that there is much she needs to say but dreads it.

"How's your job at Taco Bell going?" I ask, stumbling for
conversation.

"I can't wait to get out of there and start the new job cooking at Huck Farm," she says.

"Really appreciate that college degree when you wrap those
wild burritos, do you?"

"*Sí, señor,*" she says.

"Debi?" I say, reaching for my courage.

"Yes?"

"What's going on?"

"Dad phoned a couple of days ago," she says, and I know
whatever it is I don't want to hear is coming. "His school in
China has an opening in the library and I can take it this fall if
I want it. I could teach English part-time as well and make a
great deal of money. There's a piano at the school and I could
work on my songs. I could start learning to speak Chinese. I'd
have to commit for a year and I have to let the school know
my decision by the end of this week."

"What about us?" I say.

"I don't think you fully realize how much your doing this
walk has confronted me with who I am as well as who we are,"
she says, her tone kind but firm.

"Don't make a hasty decision," I say, imagining reaching
for her hand.

"If I don't leave now I'll be late for work," she says. "I can't
afford to lose this job."

"I can wire you some money," I say.

"No, that's not it," she says. "I've depended on you too
much already and . . ."

"Don't make a decision till you get my letter," I say. "I'll
write you today and send it by overnight mail. Okay?"

"Okay," she tells me.

The little grocery store with the pay phone fades as I walk
down the country road, the voice of Debi as near as my

thoughts of her. I try to put myself in her shoes and imagine how I'd feel if she were on a journey and I was receiving news every few days of how exciting and magical it was becoming. (I forgot to send her the pages about the whiskey drinkers— yeah, sure.) Perhaps my plan to share my trek with her through my journal has backfired on me. If I were feeling stuck at Taco Bell and got such news, I might feel cheated by my lover as well. Of course, my ideal self says, *No, love always embraces another's joy and freedom.* But then again, how often do we really live the ideal?

When I pitch my tent at sunset deep in woods far away from the road, I remove my shoes and socks and rub my blistered feet. Recalling how Debi had bathed them with such care when we first met in Denver, I take pen to paper and write her that letter.

My Dearest Darling Debi,

I've decided that you were right about coming with me, but since you've already promised to take that new job in a couple of weeks to cook at the kids' camp—what'd you call it, Huck Farm?— we'll just wait till that's over and I'm back from stalking Sherman before we hit the road together. To make up for my absence and rekindle our romance I'll fly to Seattle and we'll trek all the way across America to New York in a wagon pulled by goats. If anyone has the makings of a good Goat Woman, honey, it's you. I can just see you now up at sunrise milking those critters to make yogurt. Maybe we can invent a flavor of ice cream called "Baaaa!" which Ben and Jerry will beg to market from coast to coast. I'm almost sure we'll roll into snow-covered Minnesota to appear on Prairie Home Companion *with Garrison Keillor; you know how fond he is of homespun lore. I think, too, we must be gracious when Ross Perot asks to join our grass-roots caravan to greet the American people firsthand without frills or lace. Should we have a little saddle made for the lead billy so he can sit atop it and guide us? I'm pretty certain that by the time we roll into Washington, D.C., Bill and Hillary Clinton will want us to stay a few days with them to get a firsthand account of the hands-on wisdom we've gathered along the way. Then in New York I can see us as guests on* The Today Show, *Katie and Bryant fighting over who gets to hold the most kids at once.*

Okay, so I might be pulling your leg just a little here. What I'd really like is to have both your legs stretched across mine so I could ease my fingertips over your skin and bend over from time to time to lick your ankles, knees, and all in between—not forgetting or overlooking for a single moment the great territory that lies north of there. Indeed, my darling, I'd like to have all of you stretched out naked on a bed with just enough candlelight to see your pretty eyes. I would start there in their delicate corners with the tip of my tongue and trace your nose down to your lips. More times than you can dare dream I have, as I walked beneath the Georgia sun, pretended that the sweat running down my face into my mouth was you squeezing an ice cube. From your lips I would let my tongue slide down your chin to your neck, a spot I often study when you're not looking because it houses your vocal cords, and your voice has taken me places others might find forbidden, your moans telling more erotic tales than some want to admit exist in their private fantasies. It is your very boldness to be so real and open both in flesh and spirit that keeps hammering me back to you. Even now as I write and the lightning bugs begin to flicker in the trees around me, my mouth waters because I can see you here beside me as my tongue eases from your throat to your breasts. Did I ever make it clear how your nipples have rescued me from the world's sea? At times when I've felt pulled into its madness— perhaps by my own selfishness, ego, vanity, or greed—those rare circles of sweetness have been not only lighthouses to guide me from the storm, but anchors to all that is holy and truly matters because there with my head on your chest I could hear your heart beating . . . and feel your breath come and go to calm my undertow. Leaving your nipples, my tongue would slide down your stomach to your navel and lick there the mystery of woman's ability to create man before daring to go lower into the cave of eternal joy where more than once you have invited me in to behold not only the strength you inspire, but my deepest humility and peace. Debi, my darling, without you I would wash back out to sea and be but the foam atop the crest of a wave. Please see my hand forever reaching for you, longing to feel your grip of understanding, pa-

tience, and care. These things I say not only in honor of Tanager and the Courting Tree there, but for all our dreams yet to come true that our love might call out like a song that has at last found its home.

Never before feeling that I have so much at stake, I place the letter in my pack and build a small fire as darkness settles around me. An owl begins to hoot in the great distance and somewhere down in the hollow a whippoorwill calls out. Lightning bugs flicker yellow in every direction I turn, and the croak of a tree frog soon joins the night's choir.

My endurance has greatly increased since I left Atlanta, but today's walk has tired me and I crawl into the tent to get some rest. I snuggle up next to the pack, the newly written letter inside it offering me a kind of comfort because it takes me closer to Debi.

I awake, however, in the grips of a dream that feels so real, I can't at first swear it's not. I was back home in the garden, and Daddy sat smoking his pipe in the chair beneath the pear tree while Sherman—an obsessive oil painter in real life—painted the picture of a seagull, a fishhook caught in its beak. Then Crow Dog walked across the garden through the corn with my staff in his mouth. Rowena—the woman I met in the café today—followed him with her hand around the tip of his tail.

I'm so moved by the vision that I can't sleep, because anytime I dream of my father and feel this close to him I believe that he may be trying to tell me something from the Spirit World where he walks among our Cherokee ancestors. I leave the tent to place another stick on the glowing red coals. Sherman was an insomniac and often stirred about campfires in the night in his pajamas. It's eerie that he seems present now. His face isn't in the flames as I saw it when I was a child, but his presence is in the shadows cast by the fire.

The flames die down into the glowing coals, and I crawl back into the tent. When I awake refreshed the next morning, hearing a dove cooing in the near distance, I feel the aftermath of the dream. That Rowena was in it makes me wonder if I was hasty in dismissing the invitation to see her home.

When I arrive in Milledgeville I take my letter to the post office and send it Overnight Express to Debi. I then walk to the address that was on Rowena's card and am a bit startled to discover that it's right across the street from the old governor's house, where Sherman and Hitchcock stayed. When I open the wrought-iron gate to approach the mansion with its massive white columns, I also spot what appears to be the same chameleon I saw here before as I drifted by unaware that I was becoming part of yet another one of life's curious circles.

Chapter Twenty-eight

I press the buzzer and soon hear footsteps. The massive door squeaks as it opens and Rowena appears.

"Oh, so you did decide to say hello. Here, come in at once and get out of that horrible sun."

"I'm afraid I'm rather sweaty," I say, entering the cool hallway where a grandfather clock ticktocks. Across from it on the wall is an ornate gold-framed mirror so huge that a giant could straighten his tie in it before strutting down the sidewalk into town.

"Well, yes, of course you are, but that's only natural. Set your pack down and we'll find something cold to drink," she says, making certain that her cigarette smoke doesn't stream into my face. "Do you like tea?"

I nod, my eyes finding hers.

"Lemon?" Her accent isn't Southern.

"Sounds good," I say.

"Have a seat and I'll be right back."

I leave my pack and staff in the hallway and take a chair in the room to my left. Except in magazines and antique stores in New Orleans I've never seen so many elegant pieces of pre–Civil War furniture. The dining area joins this room and the sunlit table is so long and wide that it seems to beg for a feast. On it sits an Oriental bowl twice as big as my hat, painted with branches holding birds so lifelike that I hear their songs drifting about the mansion. No, wait a second, maybe it's not them singing at all, but the music box playing on the buffet to the right of the table. Whatever the source, tinkling music fills the house, even if it's only the ice cubes rattling against two glasses of tea as Rowena returns.

"This place is a knockout," I say, after I see that she's barefoot and offering me one of the glasses with a twinkle in her eyes.

"It's home. I'm glad you like it. Does your tea suit you? I can put more sugar in it, if you'd like."

"It's just right."

I got up when she entered the room, but now we both sit and raise the glasses to our lips at the same time. Rowena is about the age of my mother, and just like my mother and many other women of that vintage, she radiates a beauty that comes only with the years. It is centered in the eyes but flows into the entire face, every wrinkle vital to the stories told there. Those who do not yet realize that the skin ages to reveal what is in the experienced heart are cheating themselves when they look at another or at their own likenesses in mirrors. How can I feel so good about being in this historic house now, when only yesterday the very thought put a bitter taste in my mouth? I'm not sure, but I'd bet last night's dream has something to do with it. It's also possible that the Great Goat has played a trick on me, reminding me that when it comes to trusting first impressions I'm as blind as anybody else sometimes. Whatever, I'm most happy that I came here. It feels all the more right when, after talking awhile longer and finishing the tea, Rowena invites me to spend the night.

"You can have the room just above this one," she says.

"I'd like that," I say. "I'll be able to see the house across the street. It looks haunted. How long has it been abandoned?"

"I can't speak to its being haunted or not. But it hasn't been deserted. It's where Flannery O'Connor lived. Her mother is still there. She's in her nineties now and pretty much stays hidden from the world. I think it's her niece who looks after her and they refuse to answer the front door at all. Would you like more tea now, or shall I show you to your room so you can . . . do whatever you care to do?"

I'm almost sure she started to say *so you can shower*, but had the grace and kindness not to be pushy about my sweaty appearance. I hand her my glass, a lemon wedge in its bottom among three ice cubes.

"I'd sure love to clean up," I say.

"When I was a child," she says, "we were poor, but Mother, after working in a cafeteria all day, would always bathe and put on the only nice dress she had for dinner. My older sister and she took turns wearing it when they went out in the evenings."

I can already see in her eyes and hear in her voice, as well as infer from her conversation, that she longs to truly communicate who she is, was, and is becoming. This is just perfect for me and when we start up the stairs for her to show me my room, I'm not embarrassed by stopping to stare at the life-size bust of a man with a big mustache who sits atop an antique bookcase with glass doors.

"That was my great-uncle Will. He wrote for *The New York Tribune* during the late 1800s and got his leg blown off during the Civil War when he followed Union soldiers into battle to do research for a book he was writing. He and Thomas Edison were dear friends and used to travel a great deal together. I just recently came across a handwritten letter he had gotten from Edison about his new invention, the phonograph. I inherited one of the first ones from Uncle Will and earlier this year sold it and the letter to some man who travels around the world showing Edison exhibits. I'm not even sure how he found out I had it. I didn't especially want to sell it, but I needed the money to help settle my late mother's estate. Uncle Will was really rather a sad man who lost far more than a leg. His wife and three daughters were killed by scarlet fever and from that point on he had a grudge against God. Actually, he became an atheist. I'm afraid the kind of light his friend Edison invented didn't shine on the darkness he lived in."

"You'll have to watch me," I say, starting up the stairs behind her. "I'm full of questions when people fascinate me."

"Oh, I don't mind. It's good to meet someone alive enough to notice the things around him."

"Your uncle Will worked for *The New York Tribune*. Are you from New York?"

"Washington, D.C. But I spent all my childhood summers here in Georgia at the Glen Mary Plantation several miles north of Milledgeville. When I sold it, I bought this house. I told you its builder, John Sanford, was appointed by Governor Gilmer to herd the Cherokee from Georgia to Oklahoma. Sanford built this place in 1825. It didn't start out with the twelve columns you see today, but only four. He used to joke that he'd have to sell another slave every time his wife wanted two more."

When we reach the top of the stairs I find myself confronted by a large framed picture of a Yankee general. The old buzzard looks so grand and stately that I'm tempted to salute him. I'm also puzzled that he looks so familiar. Where have I seen his picture before? I'm about to pop that question to Rowena when we arrive at my room.

"You'll see the clean towels," she says. "But if you need anything else, don't hesitate to call out. I'll just be downstairs in the kitchen."

I close the door to my room and set the pack on a chair with my staff leaning against the arm. Following this journey's tradition, I place my hat over its tip, the tiny golden angel peeking out from behind the crow feather. I then unzip my pack and pull Road Rabbit from his hideaway. I set him on the mantel between two antique urns, and he begins to play his tune as if to say how much he likes his new view of the world. On the wall, only inches over his long, floppy ears hangs a silk painting of an elderly gentleman with a white beard. Seated, he holds a loving arm around a boy of about five or six years old who stands beside him. The long red candles in the brass holder on either side of them aren't aflame, but the painting's intimacy is so lifelike that it seems to fill the room with a light of its own.

The more I study the delicacy of the silk figures the more I realize just how grimy I have become walking in the scorching sun. What a luxury to step into the shower. It feels so good to get clean that I stand here long after it's necessary. I open my mouth and face the spout to fill my mouth with water and let it overflow on the times my canteen came up empty and I was miles from a store or farmhouse to replenish it. And I swear that skin has a soul of its own, thriving on hands of water when a woman's fingers can't quite stretch from Washington to Georgia. And a big fluffy towel, mind you, isn't simply a piece of cloth for drying the body but a dance partner as smooth as breath and as limber as a snake eager to show all the right moves.

Getting dressed, I look out the window at the O'Connors' house, separated from the old governor's mansion by a vine-covered fence and surrounded by elms. It's a three-story house with a brick chimney towering above a red tin roof. The windows are dark as if light is forbidden inside the house, and I'm surprised that children, itching for a break in the summer boredom, haven't thrown rocks through the panes. Then, as fast as a witch, a swallow shoots twittering from the chimney.

I'm a bit of a snoop myself as I head for the kitchen and stop at the head of the stairs to ponder the Yankee general. I'm sure I've seen him or someone who looks very much like him before. His gaze seems to follow me down the stairs where Rowena feeds a big yellow cat, rubbing against her ankle.

"Who's the general?" I point upstairs.

"One of my relatives, Ethan Allen Hitchcock."

"Hitchcock?"

She nods, a question in her eyes.

"I'm carrying a diary written by a Henry Hitchcock who traveled with Sherman on the March to the Sea. Are they related?"

"Henry? Hmm, I don't know. Could I take a look at the journal?"

This rare coincidence seems too good to be true. But I run upstairs, get the journal, and give it to Rowena.

"Mind if I look around outside while you thumb through it?" I ask.

"Oh, no, make yourself at home."

As I walk out the back door Rowena pulls a pair of glasses

from her purse and hurries to the kitchen table. I've come out here to walk among the pecan trees and blooming gardenia bushes because it's my country way of pacing the floor while Rowena gets to the bottom of this Hitchcock mystery.

"Hey," she calls out the back door before I've taken many steps. "Get yourself back in here. We've made a dandy discovery."

"They're kin?" I dash back into the house.

"We're all three related," Rowena says. "The General Hitchcock upstairs was my distant uncle and a friend of Sherman's. He's the one who got Henry Hitchcock, his nephew, a position with Sherman on the March to the Sea."

Goose bumps run up my arms, and Rowena and I stand staring at each other as though she and I are related in some fantastic way. We have stepped, or been led by Fate, it seems, into a realm that presents itself very few times, if at all, in the course of a man's life. It makes me feel somewhat like I did when I was a child and I believed that anything and everything was possible.

"After the Civil War," Rowena says, "the General Hitchcock upstairs is the one who bought the Glen Mary Plantation where I spent my childhood summers. I inherited his things and there's a small trunk in the back room with a bunch of his stuff. I've never gone through it. Shall we look?"

Chapter Twenty-nine

"This is fun," Rowena says with excitement and anticipation when I lift a small leather-bound trunk from a closet and carry it to the kitchen table.

The ancient luggage is covered with mildew and its brass locks are tarnished and apparently broken, for three or four layers of tape have been wrapped around the trunk's center as if it were a mummy.

Rowena tries to pull the wrinkled tape free, but it's as bound to the leather as our imaginations are to the trunk's contents. I'm amazed that she has let it sit in some dark closet all these years collecting dust. I give her a hand with the tape, but it pays no more attention to my tug than hers and that only makes me want to see what is inside all the more.

I'm no stranger to old trunks, for when I lived in New Orleans for eight years—only two blocks from the house where Confederate President Jefferson Davis died—I hit the junk stores and donation centers every morning. I once paid seven bucks for a trunk that turned out to be filled with 8 x 10 photographs taken in the 1930s by one of Europe's finest photographers. The exhibit contained rare pictures of Pablo Picasso, Albert Camus, and a dozen other famous artists. The collection had come from Paris to tour America and just how it got lost for so many years is beyond me; sometimes man seems to work his hardest at loss. A struggling writer at the time, I was almost broke and became ecstatic when the photos proved to be worth a small fortune in New York and Los Angeles galleries. So here now, leaning over Rowena's kitchen table, I'm once again on fire to see just what's in *this* trunk.

"I've got a pocket knife," I say. "Want me to cut the tape?"

"I don't see why not," Rowena says.

I pull my red-handled knife—it belonged to Daddy—from my pocket and open the blade. It slices through the tape and we lift the lid, a musty smell rising from bundles of letters tied with pink and yellow ribbons, a dozen or more leather-bound photographs the size of my hand, and—

"My word," she says, "look at all this Confederate money."

She pulls a stack of bills tied with string from the trunk and, Lord love a watermelon, I smell a closet Rebel somewhere in her esteemed Yankee family tree.

"Can I hold it?" I ask, and the words are hardly out of my mouth before we start to laugh, not only at me but at each other for being so sucked into the Civil War through this amazing time machine that looks like a dusty old trunk. While our bodies are still in chairs, our psyches are twisting and twirling at great speed through a tunnel that for all I know may at any moment dump us into the lap of Scarlett O'Hara in a hoopskirt. This sensation is fed all the more as Rowena and I look into each other's eyes, widening with the thrill of mutual discovery.

"I've never held Confederate money before," I say, putting the currency to my nose to sniff the romance of Once Upon a Time. "Wouldn't you love to know who-all held it and what it bought before it bit the dust?"

But Rowena doesn't seem to hear me, for she's now digging deeper into the trunk to pull out a straight razor and then an ancient package of needles and thread. Next comes a black silk umbrella and she pops it open, no bigger than my hat. Its handle is made of brass and molded into the shape of a dog's head.

"It must've belonged to General Hitchcock," she says, raising the umbrella over her head. "And was used to keep the sun from his face and eyes."

I place the Confederate money on the table—not out of sight—and reach for one of the many leather-bound photos.

Opening it, I behold a daguerreotype of General Hitchcock that was made back in the 1850s. Proud, in full uniform, he's much younger here than in the giant picture at the head of the stairs. The detail of his face is extraordinary and I wouldn't put it past him to wink any second now.

Rowena, perhaps after strolling down some peach- and plum-blossomed sidewalk before the Battle of Atlanta, lays the black silk umbrella on the table by the Rebel money. I hand her the general and reach for another photo. Despite the artifact lust still sweeping me off my feet, I somehow manage to squeeze in a moment to be touched by how generous and innocent Rowena is during this delicate rampage. Not once do her eyes harden or scold that I must be careful not to damage anything. I certainly wouldn't mean to harm, but I suspect many folks with such valuable pieces might cringe at seeing a stranger's fingers crawling through the family.

"I realize now why the general looked so familiar when I first saw him upstairs," I say. "He looks like Henry Hitchcock, who's pictured in the diary I'm carrying."

"You're right." She studies the photo of the general and I open another leather-bound case to find him, at an older age, staring back once again.

"I look at his eyes and I think how many times they looked into the eyes of Sherman," I say.

"And his lips," says Rowena. "I'd like to know all that they said to each other."

I open the next little leather-bound case to uncover a photo of Major Henry Hitchcock himself. Still somewhat stunned that our paths have crossed in such an intimate manner, I can never read his journal now without feeling some personal connection, that first crucial and vulnerable thread of human affection. My God, has the South totally gone to hell now, a Rebel like myself letting a damned Yank into his heart? I just hope my great-grandpa Croft has mellowed in the Great Beyond and understands that I'm not conspiring with the enemy, but only trying to show a little Southern hospitality in my soul for those who have not had the great fortune to be born in Dixie.

"Many of these letters were written during the Civil War," says Rowena. "Here's one from some navy man named Porter."

"Can I see?" I ask, becoming more astounded when she gives me the letter. Yes, it was written by Admiral David D. Porter. He was in charge of the Union boats that blasted the Rebel forts just south of New Orleans before the city fell to the Yanks. He was also head of the flagship that took President Lincoln to Richmond after the Confederate capital fell. Porter's men guarded Lincoln with rifles as he toured the city.

"Oh, and take a look at this one." Rowena lights up. "It was written by General Hitchcock to Henry Hitchcock."

"Yeah," I say, as if we're dueling with literary pistols, "but this one *here* was written by Henry Hitchock himself. And here's another one by him."

"Oh, oh, oh, oh." Rowena waves a letter overhead as though one has only to touch it to get the thrill of a lifetime.

"What? *What?*"

"We've hit the jackpot. It was written by Sherman himself."

Dear Madam, I have learned with deep sorrow of the death of my old friend General Hitchcock near Sparta, Georgia. No purer man or better intellect ever graced our old army, and I feel better for knowing that his last days were watched tenderly by those who knew and loved him in his best days. I beg you will convey to his widow my assurance of sympathy and sense of gratitude for her unweary and unselfish devotion. Nearly all his old comrades have gone and few remain who knew him well. But those few can bear their testimony to his great worth. Truly your friend, W. T. Sherman, General.

"It was written," Rowena continues, "to the sister of Mrs. Ethan Allen Hitchcock. Oh, no . . . ."

"Now what?"

"I got ahead of myself. This is a copy of the letter Sherman wrote. I bet my mother sold the original during the Great Depression, because Glen Mary was in financial trouble. I was still very young then, but seems as though she said something

about Sherman giving us a helping hand with a letter long
after he died."

"What a wonderful twist," I say, "General Sherman rescu-
ing a Southern plantation."

"General Hitchcock didn't get to enjoy the plantation for
very long," she says. "He bought it in 1869 and died only two
years later."

"Is he buried there?"

"He was, along with other family members, but he had
graduated from West Point and some years ago the school
asked that his remains be moved to its cemetery."

"That must've been some experience for you, a Northern
child spending summers in Georgia."

"Oh, yes, it was a funny horse to ride. Growing up in D.C. I
had never gone barefoot till I came to the South. Nor had I
played in a creek or climbed a tree. I used to search the barn
hayloft for chicken nests. One egg got me a penny piece of
candy. My aunt, who passed Glen Mary on to my mother, had
a way with chickens. When she went to kill one for Sunday
dinner she would hypnotize it first."

"You taking me for a ride now?"

"No, I tell it for the whole truth. I don't know how she did
it, but she did as well as any snake charmer. She'd grab that
chicken by its feet, turn it upside down, and look into its eyes
till that bird would get glassy-eyed. Then she'd place its head
on a wooden block, raise the ax, and whack its neck in two
before I could close my eyes or turn my head. Other times she
would just grab a chicken up and squeeze her hand around its
head as she twirled it to twist its head clean off. That bird
would hit the ground jumping all around with blood shooting
out its neck as if it still had a mind of its own and was determined to keep flopping till it found its head again."

"I saw that done many times myself when I was a child," I
say. "It always both scared and fascinated me. When the body
would finally stop jumping about, my mother or grandmother
would pluck the feathers and singe the body, holding it in one
hand and a burning newspaper in the other. I was told I had to
bury the head or the beak would peck out my eyes in the

middle of the night while I was sleeping. But I never saw anybody hypnotize a chicken. It must be a Yankee thing."

"I don't know about that. But when I was little I was careful about how I looked my aunt in the eye."

As Rowena and I study each other it's now all the more apparent that we don't have to be too cautious about how we look into one another's eyes. At some special point in our leap into the historic trunk we crossed more than the Mason-Dixon line.

"Pick a card," she says as she pulls a stack from the trunk and spreads it as if we're playing poker. "Any card at all."

I pull a card from her hand and find it holds a faded picture of General Hitchcock. She then turns her hand to show that all the eight or ten cards have the same picture. Yes, sir, another one of those Northern tricks.

"It's yours if you want it," she says.

It's considered very bad manners in Dixie to refuse a gift, but a Rebel taking a Yankee general with him as he marches across Georgia? Oh, mercy, the things a humble pilgrim will do in the name of Southern literature.

Chapter Thirty

Almost overwhelmed by the twirl through the time-machine trunk, I now see everything around Rowena with a heightened awareness. She's more of a Southerner than I first realized, too, for she confesses that she has named this grand old mansion Mara's Tara. She not only lets me swing about the limbs of her family tree, but is opening her heart wider by the hour and I cannot yet begin to guess what tales will rattle their bones if she grows to trust me enough to waltz skeletons from her closet.

"I'm sorry I have to leave for a while," says Rowena. "But I arranged to play bridge before I knew you were coming."

"Don't feel like that," I say. "I don't want to be in your way."

"Oh, but I'm enjoying your company. When I get back, perhaps we could have a drink and sit out on the porch. The sun will have set, and if we're lucky, maybe a breeze will join us."

The whole concept of time is different when a journey becomes an odyssey, and that transformation happened long ago on this trek. I'm not even certain exactly when, but I think it was around the time Little Joe and I placed new stars in the great Georgia sky as we spit watermelon seeds over the Milky Way. In any event, I'm no longer conscious of the age of Rowena or myself; I only know that it feels good to play with someone who realizes that we're all only passing through and that each moment counts. Okay, so it doesn't hurt either that I have a place to duck the sun and lay my head—Mara's Tara one cool shade.

When I head for my room and come face-to-face with General Hitchcock at the head of the stairs, he's not at all the stranger he was before Rowena and I dug into his heirlooms. The card with his picture I picked from Rowena's tricky hand is now a prized keepsake and I take it into my room to use as a bookmark in Henry Hitchcock's journal. Now feeling a connection with Henry, I'm compelled to see if I can find anything he wrote about his uncle Ethan Allen. I dig into the diary and get lucky right away through a letter Henry has written to his wife back in St. Louis only days after first joining Sherman's staff near Rome, Georgia:

> . . . my seat at the table has been occupied for more than half an hour by the telegrapher who attends the General [Sherman] taking down dispatches from his dictation. If you could read these you would have some idea both of the magnitude of the area over which his thoughts, plans, precautions, provisions range and of—what is to me—the wonderful range, celerity, and vigor of those thoughts. If ever a "live man" has commanded any of our armies, he is one. I do not wonder that Uncle E. [General Ethan Allen Hitchcock] called him "my glorious friend Sherman."

I hear the massive front door squeak as it opens and closes and I peek out the window to watch Rowena go through the wrought-iron gate, get into her car, and drive away to her bridge game. I have often walked by houses at night and seen human shadows there, making me wish that I were invisible so I might drift into those homes and learn what goes on behind closed doors. Now, with Rowena gone, I feel that Mara's Tara is an opened oyster, a pearl every which way I turn. I place the picture of General Hitchcock inside Henry's diary and go downstairs. Don't get me wrong, I won't ramble through drawers or enter rooms where I have not already been invited. But the spy within leads me down the stairs to see what I can find that hid behind Rowena, her personality more enticing than *things*. Back in the room where I first sat drinking iced tea, my eyes fall upon a flint spearhead some six inches long and two inches wide. It rests on a whatnot shelf and I pick it up, wondering what was the name of the Indian who made it hundreds of years ago. He was probably Creek or Cherokee; how many children did he have? What was his greatest dream, pleasure, heartache? How did he die? *How will I die?* Will someone one day spot my brass Confederate States belt buckle collecting dust on a shelf, lift it and wonder, *Where in the world did this come from?*

Returning the spearhead to its spot, I wander on into the hallway where I behold myself in the huge mirror on the wall. The ticktock of the nearby grandfather clock echoes as my reflection reminds me that I need to shave, but I must buy some razor blades first; my old ones are dull. Then it dawns on me that it might be more interesting to let General Hitchcock give me a hand. His straight razor is still laying on the kitchen table by the silk umbrella with the brass dog head handle.

I go upstairs to my bathroom, apply soap to my face, and stand staring into the mirror with the razor's edge to my skin. I've never used a straight razor before, and I'm not certain how hard to push to get only whiskers (this Rebel is still a bit sentimental about his own blood). But I ease the sharp edge against the skin and it leaves a smooth trail through the soap. Old General Hitchcock's not a bad barber at all. Debi, in a way, is here with me now as well, because from time to time she likes to shave me, her fingertips applying lather to my skin. But this intimacy goes deeper than that, for my older sister, Sandra, would sometimes shave my father and I can never recall seeing him more at peace. Perhaps it's nothing new that only through those we love the most can we surrender the hardest lines in the face. And I have yet to meet a man who doesn't at times feel a strong need to start over fresh, a clean, close shave sometimes cutting him free of his bum—though he has been known to reappear before his five-o'clock shadow.

I'm grateful when Rowena returns from her bridge game—

she won—because the old mansion, as unique as it is, just isn't the same without her.

"It's cooling off outside and the sun is setting," she says. "Let's pour ourselves a strong one and kick off our shoes. What do you drink?"

"A bourbon and water would hit the spot."

She fixes herself the same and we stroll onto the porch to kiss the day's blaze farewell, the chameleon a beautiful green as it darts across the lawn. I haven't allowed myself to have even a cold beer so far on this journey both because alcohol raises the body's temperature and because I've wanted my head as clear as possible at all times. But sipping the chilled booze with fine company now only serves to enhance the visit to Mara's Tara, my hedonistic side slapping me on the back— what a good guy you are. Have another.

"Oh, goodness," says Rowena as she squints at my neck, "you've cut yourself."

I touch my skin to find a tiny forgotten piece of tissue paper I stuck there to clot a nick. I'm a tad embarrassed.

"I have a small confession to make," I say. "I used General Hitchcock's straight razor to shave and was doing a smooth job of it till I got so confident that the blade decided to remind me what I was made of."

"I recall my father using one and was always so afraid that he would slit his throat. I could see his heartbeat there just about where you cut yourself."

"I lost my father just last year. We were very close."

"We have several things in common," she says, rattling the ice cubes in her glass. "I worshipped my father."

"You only get one."

"Yes, but in my case . . ."

"Is something wrong?" I ask.

The chameleon races up a nearby gardenia bush, shaking three or four old petals to the ground. Most of the flowers, however, are new and their sweet fragrance drifts across the porch, blending with the smell of bourbon.

"It's not easy to talk about," she admits, sipping her drink.

"So many things aren't," I say, hoping that she'll let me in.

She rattles her ice cubes and then studies me for a moment as if to see if I'm still listening.

"I told you that I used to come to Glen Mary when I was a little girl to spend the summers," she began.

I simply nod, for a sound might frighten her away.

"When I was seven years old I stayed a whole year there with my great-aunt and grandmother because my father was very ill in Washington, D.C. He had a seizure on the street and the doctors weren't sure what to do for him. I'd lay awake some nights on the plantation wishing he would hold me. The call of the whippoorwill in the darkness sometimes made me so lonely I felt like I would die. I couldn't tell anybody and kept it all buried inside. I wanted the moonlight to take it away. But after a year he got better and I went back home. I was so happy to be with him, but his seizures got bad again. He and Mother didn't get along and when I turned nine she packed a bag one day and said she and I were moving to Georgia to live at Glen Mary forever. I begged her to let me stay and my father came home just as she was pulling me out our front door. He took me from her and pulled a pistol, telling her to leave for Glen Mary without me. I hated to see them have trouble, but I was relieved to be with my father. Mother left for the train station and Father carried me upstairs. In less than an hour he had one of his seizures, a very bad one, and fell to the floor. I was horrified and ran next door to tell our neighbor. But Mother had already asked her to be on the lookout for a chance to steal me away to the train station and she did just that. My mother was boarding as we arrived, and it was a nightmare to be pulled from the city and headed to the South. I never saw my father again. He died on the street in D.C. the next year during another seizure. I was never able to forgive my mother or the neighbor after that and Glen Mary became less a palace than a prison till I turned fifteen. That's another story, but I've already given you an earful and I limit myself to one confession per sunset. Can you smell the gardenias?"

I nod, careful not to look too boldly into her eyes, most vulnerable now.

"My father was fond of gardenias," says Rowena. "Sometimes, when the breeze is just right, I can come onto the porch, close my eyes, and smell him only a few feet away."

Chapter Thirty-one

It's considered rude in the South to stay longer than two nights with someone unless he's next of kin, and even then you run the risk of wearing out your welcome. After all, as the Civil War proved too well, us Rebels are touchy about our personal space. So, with that in mind, I plan to depart from Rowena and the elegant Mara's Tara after two days have flown by, but . . .

"The radio said it'll reach a hundred and one today," Rowena says. "People are dying from heat strokes and the newspaper advises everyone to remain inside and take it easy. Stay at least another day or two till it cools off a little. Besides, I thought early in the morning before the sun got too high, we'd go for a drive so you could see Glen Mary, if you'd like. Oh, that reminds me. I have something I must show you right now."

She rises from the dining table and hurries from the room. Frankly, I'm delighted and relieved that she's invited me to stay longer. I've dreaded hiking beneath the severe sun and there's not another town of any size along my route till I get to Savannah itself.

"Can I bring you more coffee before I sit back down?" she calls out from the kitchen.

"No, thanks, I still have plenty."

"How about more catfish?"

This morning she panfried finger-size catfish in cornmeal to perfection. They were tender and sweet, served along with scrambled eggs and cheese grits. I love to eat, but what made

them taste truly great was the excitement she showed in serv-
ing them, as if that dish were the single feather in her cap.

"I probably have room for a couple more," I say.

She returns with a plate of catfish and what appears to be
two old letters framed behind glass.

"Have you had any personal experiences with the KKK?"
she asks, after placing the framed letters on the table and
pushing three pieces of catfish onto my plate.

I'm surprised both at her question and how quickly it hurls
me back into the past. I feel like I'm living it, as if the memory has been waiting all these years for just the right breath to
carry it to the surface.

"When I was four or five years old," I say, "I went to town
with my father and we had to stop the car on Main Street
because a parade was passing. There were dozens of men
wearing white hoods and robes and carrying torches. I thought
it was a kind of circus and Daddy let me stand on top of the
car so I got a closer look. I waved at them and they waved
back. Everybody who was watching seemed happy and I told
Daddy I wanted to follow them and see what kinds of tricks
they did at their circus. The year before, in a big tent, I had
seen a man shot from a cannon and a woman turn a flip atop a
horse. Daddy said it wasn't a circus, but he didn't or couldn't
explain what the men were doing and I thought he just didn't
want to take me because it cost too much. When we got home,
I was still so taken by the men with torches that I persuaded
Mother to give me a torn sheet. I cut holes in it for my eyes
and placed it over my head. I marched around the house saying I was part of a circus. But when I went outside to show my
sister Sandra, she became mad and told me to take the hood
off.

" 'But I'm playing circus,' I said. 'I saw men doing it in the
street today.'

" 'They weren't part of a circus,' she said, pulling the sheet
from me. 'They were men with the heads and hearts of animals and were hiding so you couldn't see what they looked
like.'

" 'How did they get that way?' I asked, totally confused.

" 'By hating people,' she said. 'And when you hate people you start to hate yourself and that turns you into an animal.'

" 'But they were nice. They waved and said hello.'

" 'They only pretended to be friendly. They do that so you'll follow them and start hating people before you realize what you're doing. But once you turn into an animal, you stay with them because you feel no one else understands you.'

"My sister had a way of scaring the hell out of me," I tell Rowena, "and that was the last time I played circus. It was years later before I had any grasp on what the Klan was really about. Even today when I see a picture of one wearing a hood I imagine he has the face of a hyena, because that's what I was afraid I might start looking like when I was a child because I had worn that sheet one afternoon."

"What a haunting memory," says Rowena.

"Yeah, but that's part of growing up in Alabama. Don't worry, I went on to make my share of good memories with sheets as well. Why did you ask about the Klan?"

"Something happened at Glen Mary with the Klan that I've always found a bit sad and funny at the same time. Back in 1875 my family donated three acres to the local blacks to build a church that could also act as a schoolhouse. Many people frowned upon blacks learning to read and write, and three months after the building was completed, the Klan wrote a letter to my family and nailed it to a tree at Glen Mary. Here, take a look at this."

Now our advice to you is to stop those night meetings and unless you do put a stop to it we will put an end to your existence . . . death will be your portion, it will. . . . We have been resting in our graves three years but have been aroused again by your misbehavior. . . . When we come there will be a tornado to be remembered. . . .

We are your friends that fell on the battlefield of Virginia.

We are the KKK from Augusta, Georgia.

"Real sweet talkers," I say.

"My family had the good sense not to take it too seriously either," says Rowena. "Look at the letter that was written back to the Klan and nailed on a pine at the well so all the neighbors could read it":

Monday, Sept. 6, 1875

To the "Mythical KKKs" of Augusta, Georgia . . .

I have had the honor and edifying privilege of reading with some little effort your communication. . . .
As I have long since rid myself of Ghost-fear will the spirits of those friends whose bones lie on the battlefield of Virginia condescend to make me a personal visit, and if it be not convenient for all of them to do so, perhaps they would deputize some respectable medium . . . in the carcass of a jackass.

"I don't know if the Klan ever read it," says Rowena, "but there was no more trouble after that."

"These letters trigger another memory for me," I say. "When I was attending the University of Alabama, I owned a chopped Harley-Davidson. I usually rode alone but became friends with a guy from my hometown who had a Triumph motorcycle. He was one of the kindest people I had ever met. I felt very close to him. After college I hit the road and thumbed all over the United States. Years later, when I was back home visiting my parents, he stopped by to say hello and introduce his wife and daughter. He was wearing a pistol at his side. Two days later he phoned and asked if I'd come to his home to discuss my possibly doing a favor for him. I went out to see him and had been there for only a few minutes when he complimented me on the brass belt buckle I was wearing.

" 'I have one I'd like to show you,' he said.

"He disappeared into a bedroom and returned a moment later with a leather belt rolled up in his hand. He gave it to me with the same gentle nature I had seen years before when we first met and he had handed me a screw driver to tighten a screw on my Harley. I unrolled the belt to discover a brass buckle with KKK printed in its center. It was so hard to believe, I stood staring at it as I tried to think what to say.

"'You joined the Klan?' I said.

"'Yes,' he said, 'all my life I've wanted to feel that I was part of a group of friends I could depend on. Now I feel that with these men and my wife feels it with the women. Now that we have a little girl I want protection with others if the blacks take to the streets to hurt us. I asked you out here today to see if you'd write a story about the Klan. I trust you and know you'd write it in a fair and honest way. All the stories that have been written for newspapers so far make us out to be one-sided.'

"A sadness went through me," I tell Rowena, "because I felt like I had lost a friend. And it wasn't hatred I saw in his eyes or heard in his voice as he talked, but love of his family and a fear of the world and its variety of people that makes a man feel very small, especially if he thinks he's too alone. I chose not to write the story, and for days I was haunted by this experience because it released a kind of fear in me as well. Not so much a fear of violence as of the intolerance that pushes men, even old friends, apart. It made me question where friendship begins and ends. Some would quickly ridicule my old buddy because he joined the Klan. Should I now be against him? If I'm not, should others be against me? Of course, most of us don't make rational decisions about such things. It's like love, sex, and religion; we act out of emotion, and the more of that we have, the more passion empowers us to be self-righteous."

Rowena listens like a real friend and I feel I can trust her not to judge me too harshly. That, along with the promise I made early in the walk to tell you "The Confession," now leads me forward.

"Something happened almost thirty years ago," I tell Rowena, "that I've never told anyone but one person. It altered my life and it's not easy to discuss. Could I confide in you?"

"Please," she says.

"It was back in the sixties," I begin, "and I was seventeen

years old. I had just started to run around with my cousin
Rodney, who was my age. He lived just up the creek from me
and I'd always had a warm spot in my heart for him. His
mother was Daddy's twin. Once she shot herself on purpose in
the chest back by their garden near the woods. She decided
she wanted to live and walked back to her house. She was
rushed to the hospital and lived, but a few years later died of
cancer. I felt sorry for Rodney, having no mother when he was
only ten years old. After she died he started getting wild. Well,
when we both turned seventeen Rodney went to work at a big
grocery store in my hometown and I worked next door after
school in a gym as a weight lifting instructor.

" 'Let's have some fun tonight,' Rodney told me during our
lunch break one Saturday.

" 'Sounds good to me,' I said. 'What's up?'

" 'Mojo.' He grinned.

" 'You mean the black guy you work with?' I said.

" 'Yeah,' said Rodney. 'He's a meat cutter and has been
sneaking cleaned chickens home from the store—says he's got
a barbecue sauce he makes that's so good it could put a smile
on an angel in hell.'

" 'He's cooking some chickens for us tonight?' I said, getting hungry.

" 'No,' said Rodney, 'we're cooking up something for him.'

" 'What do you mean?'

" 'Last week I started telling him that the grocery store is
owned by the Klan,' said Rodney. 'That's bullshit, but he's
not sure whether to believe me or not. So I want to scare the
hell out of him.'

" 'I thought you liked Mojo,' I said. 'He seems like a nice
guy.'

" 'I do like him,' said Rodney. 'He's put several big steaks
in the trunk of my car. But I want to pull a joke on him.'

" 'Joke?'

" 'We'll set a cross on fire in front of his house,' said Rodney. 'We'll nail a chicken to it so he'll think it's the Klan
giving him a warning to stop stealing from the store.'

" 'I don't know,' I said. 'That sounds pretty mean, and besides the Klansmen are nobody to mess with. Not here in Alabama anyway.'

" 'Don't be so damned serious,' said Rodney. 'The Klan will never know about it, and after Mojo has sweated for a couple of days I'll tell him the truth. He'll be relieved and think it's funny.'

" 'I don't know. . . .'

" 'Oh, come on, it'll be a hoot,' said Rodney. 'You don't have a wild hair on your ass if you don't help me on this.'

"That evening I sawed some boards at the barn and nailed them into a cross. I tied a burlap sack around it and Rodney brought a fluffy white chicken he killed at his barn with the same gun his mother had shot herself with. We wired the chicken to the cross and put it in the trunk of Rodney's car. When it got dark we went to the bootlegger and bought a pint of 'shine. By ten that night we were ready for our fun. We drove to Douglas, the black part of town, and looked for Mojo's house.

" 'Which one is it?' I said. 'You told me you'd given him a ride home and knew which one it was.'

" 'I did,' said Rodney. 'But it was daylight then and all these little houses look alike at night. Wait, that's it—that one right over there.'

" 'Are you sure?' I said.

" 'Yes—hell, yes, I'm sure.'

"He parked the car in the dark under a tree some fifty yards from the house and we got the cross, chicken and all, from the trunk. Then we splashed a little gasoline on it.

"There was a single light on inside Mojo's house and we sneaked to the front yard and drove the sharpened cross into the ground with a sledgehammer. Rodney lit it with a match and it made a small explosion, blazing four or five feet into the air as the porch light came on. Then, as the door opened, I was horrified because I saw the old, wrinkled face of Sparky, my childhood friend. He dropped to his knees when he saw the cross burning and let out the most haunting cry I've ever heard in my life.

" 'Sweet Jesus,' he called out. 'Please don't hurt me. I's just an old man.'

"I stood frozen for a moment, staring at Sparky on his knees on the porch with his hands woven together. He held them overhead as if God Himself might lift him from earth.

"I finally ran and jumped into the car with Rodney. I couldn't sleep that night, for I felt I had done such a bad thing. The next day my conscience made me tell Daddy what I'd done. I feared what he might do, but he simply looked at me.

" 'I guess you already know the right thing to do now,' he said.

"I nodded.

"I got in my car and drove toward the house where we'd burned the cross. When I got there, what was left of the cross was sticking from a garbage can by the street. The chicken was charred and its beak was open, its eyes closed.

"I stepped up on the porch and knocked. Sparky soon appeared, his expression timid. He didn't recognize me from years ago. I explained what I had done, how it had started out as a joke and I didn't mean to hurt anybody.

" 'Can you forgive me?' I said, holding out my hand with the hope that he might shake it.

" 'Yes, suh,' he said, taking my hand. 'I's forgive you. The rest be between you and yourself. And maybe that chicken.'

"I'll never forget how his old wrinkled hand felt in mine, but I wasn't sure if it was his or mine that was trembling. Maybe it was both of ours. I've never had any hatred or racism in my heart whatsoever for anyone, but it took years to forgive myself for that night. I try to see the good in everything. I tell myself that event is what helped me open my mind, because only days later I ran away to New York to stay with Sandra for two weeks before heading back home. That trip made me hungry to learn about other people and the world, and a part of me was changed forever."

I feel that my very soul is naked before both you and Rowena now. Have I told too much?

"We all have our ghosts," says Rowena, her wisdom most

welcome. "Without them we'd just be pictures in magazines. I do hope you'll stay for a couple of more days. Won't you?"

"I'd like that," I say. "Seeing Glen Mary will be a treat."

My decision seems to make Rowena happy, for she smiles and rakes the last catfish onto my plate. But I haven't been completely truthful with her. It isn't really Glen Mary that I want to see, but simply more of Rowena. I'm somewhat entranced by her, and when on such rare occasions that happens with someone, I have learned not to assume that another gift of equal magnitude will be awaiting around the next bend.

Chapter Thirty-two

Night falls on Mara's Tara and I exit the grand old mansion to walk the tranquil streets where the citizens of Milledgeville once carried lighted candles through the dark in support of Georgia seceding from the Union. No such flames burn tonight, but lightning bugs flicker yellow in all directions just as they did long before the Civil War.

As I walk down the street behind Rowena's home, I catch a firefly and hold it in my cupped hand, caged in the bars of my fingers. When I arrive at the Memory Hill Cemetery, two blocks away, I open my hand and the insect flies free over the tombstones, ghostly in the moonlight.

A wire fence surrounds this huge graveyard and the iron gate is locked. But it was open when I came here earlier today to meet Louis Andrews, who is eighty-three years old. Retired from the Internal Revenue Service, he has followed in his father's footsteps to become the cemetery historian. Each afternoon he comes to Memory Hill for two hours to offer his services, free of charge, to anyone trying to locate a departed relative. A thin, small man with a great musical voice, Louis wore red suspenders and carried a wooden cane. In his other hand he held a fan like the one he gave me; one side pictured a roaring waterfall while the other side advertised a funeral home. He was quick to point to the granite stone at the entrance, which bears his name to honor him as the Memory Hill historian.

"Only two problems with it," he said. "People I haven't

seen for a while think I've died and every dog in Milledgeville pisses on my name. But I like dogs so that's no big deal."

As we walked across the cemetery his cane led the way, my staff following. From time to time he'd stop to rest and we fanned ourselves, if only to hurry the sweat faster down our faces and necks.

"Those links of chain you see yonder sticking from each concrete block belonged to the slave beneath them," said Louis. "It was the same chain he was shackled in. Three links means he was born, lived, and died in slavery. Two says he was born and lived in slavery, but died as a free man. One link you can figure out for yourself. Now, underneath all those chains are hundreds of slaves buried in a mass grave. We don't know anything about them."

"Did you know many blacks when you were growing up?" I asked, seeking insight into the Old South.

"We had an ex-slave living in our home," he said. "My whole family almost died one winter with a killing kind of flu. She nursed us back to life. Back then blacks and whites got along. We respected each other. All the racial trouble started with the civil rights marches. It got people mad at each other and confused."

I thought he spoke from his heart, and I didn't care to confront him. But I wondered if some of what he said was true simply because blacks "stayed in their place," as some racists used to put it. Or was he right in saying that some folks, both white and black, have let anger and confusion blind their brotherly love?

"See that brick wall over there?" he continued. "That's a kind of mass grave too. Twenty-seven Jewish boys have been put to rest there. They were the sons of four Waitzfelder brothers and suffered from hemophilia. On Jewish holidays the family used that brick wall as a wailing wall. The town elders used to say you could hear them mourning a block away. And over here, that tall monument by the cedar is the Methodist guardian angel. She protects the Methodists from the Baptists. We have to be careful around this next grave because it's where Dixie's buried. She lived during the Civil

War down on the river just outside of town here and began to
have spells the doctors couldn't figure out. She could lift six
men on a table with one hand. When the governor saw her
strength, he sent her to show President Grant. Queen Victoria
herself got to behold this Georgia witch, but was careful not to
get too close."

Alarm then streaked across Louis's face and he pushed the
tip of his trusty cane against my leg.

"I don't mean to be rude, son," he said. "But you're block-
ing the sunlight from Dixie and a witch feeds on that.
Wouldn't want her to get mad and give you webbed feet or a
hump on your back so you couldn't carry that pack. You got a
piece to go yet before you get to the sea. Now, regarding your
mission, let me point out that all the graves face east because
it's long been believed that the Lord would come from that
direction on Judgment Day. All graves, that is, but *these* three."

"They face south," I said.

"Why, son," he said, a twinkle in his blue eyes, "there may
be hope for you yet. You appear to at least know the directions
of the earth. Indeed, they do face south because three Confederate soldiers insisted on it."

"At your age," I said, "you must've known folks who fought
in the Civil War."

"Many of them," he said. "When I was a boy they were
already old men, but on Confederate Day, as many as were
able would walk from the courthouse to Memory Hill to a
gazebo where a speaker would honor their valor, and then
they'd have lunch."

"Can you show me where the gazebo stood?"

His cane tapped the earth as he led me past the graves of
Flannery O'Connor and Susan Myrick—who taught the *Gone
With the Wind* cast the correct Southern dialect. I can almost see
her now, coaching the character of Prissy, the whining black
slave who cried out, *"Oh, Miss Scarlett, I don't know nothing 'bout
birthing babies."* When we arrived at a flat stone barely visible
above the earth, Louis stopped, leaned on his cane, and
fanned himself with the waterfall fan.

"This rock was part of the foundation of the gazebo," he

said. "I recall one day in particular I helped an old gentleman who had a bad leg hold himself up. As the speaker drew to a close, with his voice rising on each word he said, *'You were not defeated, no, no, you were only worn out from victory after victory!'* The old man let go of me and stood as straight as an arrow . . . for a few seconds. Then I helped him over to a chair in the shade and brought him a plate of food. He didn't have any teeth and I mashed his potatoes and green beans with a fork so he could gum them. 'I was once a little boy like you,' he told me, and rubbed my head. I didn't understand what he was trying to say and another boy and I looked at each other and giggled. When the old gentleman saw us laughing I thought he'd get mad, but he laughed, too, like he knew something I didn't. Now here I am an old man myself with a cane holding me up."

"But you are not defeated . . ."

"No, no, I am only a little worn out from victory after victory."

I try simply to enjoy folks, but sometimes in reflection I ask myself, What did I learn from him or her? From Louis I was certainly reminded that a Southerner can have a sense of humor about the Civil War as well as honor it. But more than anything I recalled the ancient lesson that whites, blacks, Jews, Methodists, Baptists, rich, poor, free, slaves, sane, or insane are all raised to the same level when Death takes us by the hand.

After I parted from Louis and was almost a block away I turned to see him under a giant cedar. His cane leaned against the tree and he held one of four brooms that I had noticed in the backseat of his car, next to boxes of newspaper stories about those buried at Memory Hill. He went from one grave to the next, sweeping away leaves.

Thunder rumbles in the night, lightning flashes yellow in the heavens, and wind blows as I approach Mara's Tara. Across the street on the second floor of the Flannery O'Connor home I see a bigger-than-life human shadow float across a room. But then the light goes out and the shadow vanishes; the wind picks up, howling through the trees like the voices of the Jewish mothers who once wailed at the brick wall over the loss of their sons.

The iron gate to Mara's Tara squeaks, as does the massive door when I tiptoe into the house. The grandfather clock is still ticktocking in the hallway at the foot of the stairs. I've become so comfortable in this home that when I pass General Hitchcock near my room I feel as though we had a cup of coffee together somewhere long ago and spoke of Rowena, how kind and generous she is.

I get undressed and crawl into bed to write in my journal, when I smell gardenias. They sit in a vase on the mantel with Road Rabbit propped against them and I can't swear that Rowena didn't hold the hand of her father when she placed them there this evening while my thoughts drifted in moonlight over tombstones.

My own father's presence I feel close every day in the staff he cut for me to make into a bow. It now leans in the corner of the room near the gardenias and atop it rests my hat, the tiny golden angel watching me from behind the crow feather. I cannot say if guardian angels are real and I don't pretend for a moment to claim that I understand the ways of the Great Goat, but I know now that this march to the sea seems blessed. The only fire I have encountered thus far has been at my campsites and in the passion of human hearts. If it proves in the end that the only true guardian angels are people, in their better moments, looking out for each other, then that's miracle enough for me.

Chapter Thirty-three

I've revealed so much about myself to you already that there's little sense in trying to hide a great deal at this late hour on the march to the sea. You recall, of course, that Sally gave me her phone number after I gave her the pea from the medicine pouch. I don't always have control of my thoughts—do you?—and more than once the picture of her almost naked in that leopard two-piece swimsuit has flashed through my mind.

In the middle of the night, after my stroll by Memory Hill, I awake from a dream about Sally. Why don't I just pick up the phone and call her? No, I'm not taking anything for granted, but neither am I blind to what I saw in her eyes when she suggested the picnic in the woods.

But then, again, I am not blind to my own psychology. I know myself pretty well. I am, in part, playing with this fantasy about Sally to help me deal with missing Debi and our relationship being at stake. No matter who or how many women or what positions I might ponder in the middle of the night, it is always Debi I return to because she is the one I love. Besides, she'll do anything with me that can be imagined for pleasure and all women aren't that passionate and free. I fall asleep once again with Debi in my arms.

I awake the following morning after seeing Daddy in the cornfield again. What in the name of creation is he trying to show or tell me? After the startling way I've come to connect with Rowena, I'm all the more convinced that the dream has a significant meaning. The Cherokee have a strong tradition of the Green Corn Dance. It's done each summer to give thanks to the Great Spirit for blessing them with the fruits of their labor, the corn. Is there something here I should perceive?

Bells ring from the direction of the church where Sherman's men filled the pipe organ with foraged molasses, and I open my eyes to behold Henry Hitchcock's diary on the nightstand, with the photo of General Hitchcock sticking from the pages.

Once dressed, I go downstairs to find Rowena making waffles. Her black maid, Mattie, is slicing plump red strawberries to spread on top of them.

"Mattie is more my friend than my maid," Rowena says. "We've known each other since I was seven years old."

"We played together at Glen Mary when we were little girls," Mattie says, her profile regal, her hair gray.

"Still do," Rowena says, pouring batter into the waffle iron. "When a wild hair gets us we hit the road just like you, but in a car."

"That's right," Mattie says, placing a strawberry to her lips. "Anytime the train leaves I'll be on it."

"She's a pill sometimes though," Rowena says.

"Only when you get carried away," Mattie says.

"I can't help myself," Rowena says. "I love fine china."

"Must be a cure for you somewhere," Mattie says.

"What are you talking about?" I ask, helping myself to one of the strawberries.

"I have a weakness for china cups," Rowena says as excess batter flows from the closed waffle iron. "I see one and I'm a goner. I have to buy it."

"Don't let her make you a promise," Mattie says.

"I won't deny it," Rowena says, "it's true. I swore to Mattie that I'd not buy any more china. Then, two weeks ago, she opened my car trunk looking for a wrench and found a whole box of china I had just bought and hid there from her. She marched into the house carrying it like it was state's evidence."

"How could you, Rowena?" Mattie says, the two little girls at Glen Mary still very much alive, playing house and sipping from those fine china cups that only years of friendship can fill.

After breakfast—the waffles were as tasty as yesterday's catfish—Rowena seems to have one of those wild hairs she spoke of, because we race down the rolling highway toward Glen Mary with such speed that we must be late for something I have yet to grasp. Our windows are down and her hair blows in the Georgia wind as her bare foot crowds the gas pedal.

Miles later Rowena stops the car on the side of the road to overlook Glen Mary. It sits over a hundred yards away and a single magnolia tree, clustered with big white blossoms, is all that stands between us and the massive mansion, its great manicured lawn as green as the chameleon in the grass at Mara's Tara.

"What do you see?" I ask with a tone that I hope doesn't scare away her vision.

"There on the steps is a little black girl, a slave, named Mary. She was assigned to sit there every night to announce when she spotted Sherman's men approaching. After the war, when General Hitchcock bought the plantation, she was part of it and slept on the floor at the foot of my great-aunt's bed. Mother later bought a bed for her and she died in it as an old woman. I always called her Aunt Mary. I see Mattie and me, too, skipping rope down at the edge of the woods with sugar biscuits wrapped up in a cloth for lunch. When Mother had part of the house remodeled, she found silver in the front wall that was hidden there from the Union soldiers. But what I see the most is a child upstairs in bed at night longing for her dad. Ever since I lost him I think I looked for a father figure. I thought my husband was it, but only three months after we married I realized that I was stronger than him, and that never changed all the many years we were married. A colonel in the Air Force, he finally retired and went hunting with our son-in-law in Colorado. Snow started to fall and they got inside his car to stay warm. My husband lit a cigar and they were talking about how peaceful it was there. Then halfway through his next sentence he dropped the cigar. He was gone. The day before he left on his trip, he told me his right hand was a little numb and that he was worried. I told him it was nothing because the day before that his doctor had examined him and said he was fine, that the tingling in his arm was just his nerves."

"You can't blame yourself," I say. "Think how fortunate he was to go quickly rather than suffer in a hospital."

"I don't think we ever really knew each other," she says, as if wishing that she could redo things. "I haven't seen our son in twelve years. He's a scriptwriter living in Los Angeles."

I'm so close to my mother that I can't imagine going for years without seeing or touching her. I fear much of me would harden if I had to do that, though through my father I learned the necessity of sometimes needing thick stones to build a wall.

"And don't you have a daughter?" I ask, recalling that when she mentioned her two days ago a light shined in her face.

"Oh, yes." Her tone warms a bit. "She lives in Florida and works for a vet. She has a way with animals. When I visited her last time, a tiger was in her home."

"In a cage."

"Oh, no, as free as the wind itself. It put its head in my lap while I sat on her couch watching *As the World Turns*."

"A baby tiger?"

"No, a full-grown one. Teeth this long."

"Rowena, you're a little nuts. But I think that's part of why I like you so much."

She offers a most discreet grin and we turn to Glen Mary, but I think it's clear to both of us that the mansion we now see isn't the one up there at the end of the great lawn, but the one we've built the past four days with the beams of conversation.

"You've let me in so far," Rowena says. "I think there's a little more light I'd like to shed on my life with you. If you'd care to hear?"

"Yes," I say, always ready to listen to this new and ever-fascinating friend.

She drives on down the road over the rolling countryside till we enter the tiny town of Sparta. It saddens me that some of the fine old homes are falling apart. Rowena stops the car in front of a house that is empty, a single white silky curtain dancing in the breeze blowing through a broken window.

"When I was a child," says Rowena, "I looked out the school window one day. I saw a boy on the playground throwing a ball overhead and catching it with his bare hands. When he turned and I saw his face and eyes he caught my heart just as surely as he caught that ball. I was in love with him from that moment on and he could've thrown me up or let me fall to the ground same as that ball. I was his. Fortunately, he became mine, too, and treated me with the gentleness I tried to show him. By the time we were teenagers all of the teachers knew how much we loved each other and they let us sit close to one another in the classrooms."

She pauses, peering into the house we're parked in front of as if the dancing silk curtain is a ghost she knows too well.

"What happened?" I ask.

"Our love got stronger by the month," she says, "and we planned to get married. This house is where he and his parents lived."

"But?" I say in almost a whisper.

"The evening he chose to tell his mother and father our dreams," she continues, "was the saddest of my life with the exception of having to part with my father."

"But what happened?"

"His parents had already arranged a marriage for him," says Rowena. "It tore my sweetheart apart, but his family was Jewish and he couldn't bring himself to break the tradition. It would've hurt his father too much if he'd done so, and he loved and honored him more than most can imagine."

"Did it make you bitter?" I say, feeling sympathetic.

"No, not bitter. But sad. My broken heart never fully healed. Sometimes I still feel the ball falling, hitting the ground."

She drives away from the house, the silky white curtain now calm as the breeze stops.

Chapter Thirty-four

The morning I'm to leave Milledgeville, I'm filled with conflicting emotions. I promised myself I'd make the march to Savannah in one month, the same amount of time it took Sherman and his men to hike it, and my time is running out. The open road—with new people, stories, and adventures—calls to me, but it also makes me a bit sad to leave Rowena and the luxury of Mara's Tara.

I stuff my clothes and Road Rabbit back into my pack, his floppy ears determined to hear one last ticktock of the downstairs grandfather clock. Before I head on, however, I phone Mother as I've been doing every few days to let her know I'm okay and see if she is too.

"I'm fine," she says, "and the garden's looking good. The corn is waist-high now and Nita and Clay are helping me keep it hoed. Logan's learned how to make frog houses with her little foot in the dirt while we work. Sandra phoned yesterday with good news. She has a lead part in an upcoming episode of *Unsolved Mysteries*. But Raymond was rushed to the emergency room last night."

"How is he?" I ask, recalling so well the last time I saw him on his front porch eating corn bread and milk and telling me he feared he'd die while I was away on my march.

"It was his heart," she says. "But he's pulled through and is back home now. He's got to stay out of this horrible heat though. I hope you won't push yourself too hard walking in the sun."

"If I get too tired," I say, "I'll just wad myself into a ball and roll on into Savannah."

"Yeah, well," says Mother, "watch those car tires."

Her voice always gives me a lift and I head downstairs with my pack and staff, more prepared to say good-bye to Rowena. However, when I see her face, eyes I've come to know so well, I feel a tug at my core to keep me here.

"I made you a couple of sandwiches," she says, holding up a brown paper bag.

"This isn't really good-bye," I tell her, placing the bag in my pack.

"No," she says. "The door is always open to you here."

We stand staring at each other, two people who have revealed so much in so little time. But as the Indian back near Conyers said a while ago, it's the distance the soul goes that matters, not the body. With that in mind, I feel that Rowena and I have been on a long, important, and fun cruise together. I put my arms around her just long enough to feel her take a deep breath, and then I'm out the door. I must hurry, for just down the road the city of Savannah is playing me a song.

Only a few blocks after leaving Rowena my emotions get jerked again. I enter the post office.

"Any general delivery for Jerry Ellis?" I ask.

"No," the clerk says when he returns from a back room.

I guess my face shows more than I sometimes realize, because . . .

"I'll double-check," says the clerk, his voice understanding.

My hope that Debi has sent me a letter Overnight Express builds again. But then . . .

"I'm sorry," the clerk says as he returns.

I leave the post office and walk on. Debi should have opened my letter two days ago. Did it not open her heart and mind to how much I love and need her? Is China more inviting? Can one man compete with an empire that rich in history and tradition? You're damned right I can, I tell myself. I have to believe that to push on. But am I just fooling myself?

Milledgeville fades into the distance as I cross the Oconee River, where a black man wades with his pants rolled to his knees. Only a hundred yards downstream and barely visible rests the remains of a toll bridge destroyed in the war, a floating log trapped against it. It's here that Sherman's men dumped wagon loads of Confederate weapons that they swiped from the state arsenal back in town.

"Looking for something?" I call out from the modern bridge high over his head.

"No," he shouts back. "Just feeling the mud between my toes."

I wave and he does the same, his face carefree and in bold contrast to any citizen of Milledgeville in November 1864, after the Yanks rolled from town. Georgia men, women, and children pawed Union campsites in search of grains of corn the horses had left behind. Others clawed dead animal skins for bits of meat while some squatted in fields to gnaw raw turnips, black smoke from charred buildings drifting into their cold nostrils as they chewed.

The Rebs in the area weren't taking the Union rampage lying down, and they shot or slit the throats of all stragglers they found, some two hundred after Atlanta was torched. But they were mere drops in a bucket compared to the 62,000 soldiers who moved seaward, the circus atmosphere growing stronger each day as more slaves followed to sing, dance, and rattle bones. Add to that the men's pet bear, owl, and Old Abe, the eagle, perched atop a cannon as the horses and wagons rattled forward, and it's a wonder tickets weren't sold. In the midst of it all one Yank killed a coral snake, pickled it in a jar of whiskey, and juggled it over his head as if it were the heart of the Confederacy itself.

I could do without the snake, but a glass of that whiskey would be welcomed right now to ease the pain in my once-again blistered feet. After walking four hours toward the town of Sandersville, my clothes are soaked with sweat, the thermometer pushing 100 degrees. My inner thighs have rubbed raw against my jeans and my whole body is starting to ache. My water is running low and I can't be sure when the next farmhouse or grocery store will appear, so I can fill my canteen. If Sherman could see me limping along now—and I can't

prove that he doesn't—he might have himself a hearty laugh
as he chewed on his cigar. When he and Henry Hitchcock
rode their horses here, his confidence was becoming so strong
that he could almost feel the Atlantic Ocean in the palm of his
hand, the capture of Savannah a ring on his finger.

To help ensure the success of his plan, Sherman ordered
Judson Kilpatrick's cavalry to charge Augusta. To lighten the
men's load, Kilpatrick had blankets thrown over the heads of
five hundred of their horses, which were then hit between the
eyes with axes. The massive animals were left to swell and rot
on the plantation where the men had camped, charging the
Southern air with yet more stink of "brother against brother."
The attack on Augusta, Sherman reasoned, would mislead the
Rebels and cause them to believe the capture of that city was
his goal, and it would pull Confederate Joe Wheeler and his
cavalry out of Sherman's way as well as clear of Millen, where
starving Union prisoners might be rescued.

Wheeler, born in Georgia, was a West Point graduate like
both Sherman and Hitchcock, and he had a habit of sometimes riding for hours with his eyes glued to trees as he
searched for bees' nests. He loved to suck honeycombs. He
stood only five feet, five inches tall and, according to one soldier, weighed all of 120 pounds if you put a rock in each
pocket and wet his hair.

During the Battle of Atlanta, Wheeler once beat Sherman's
cavalry and captured one of his generals and five hundred
men. It added insult to injury then when in Sandersville,
Wheeler and his men skirmished with the Yanks and drove
them out of town for the night. Sherman, upon learning that
almost a dozen of his soldiers had been captured in that fight
and shot at midnight by a mob, ordered the courthouse—used
as a fort, Hitchcock noted in his journal—burned to the
ground.

Only a few miles from Sandersville, as a cold wind howled
through the pines, a group of bummers, led by Captain
Charles Belknap, started a fire, too, but it was of a much different nature. The foragers busted into a rotting cabin and discovered two black girls hiding in the corner under blankets.

They wore thin, ragged dresses made of feed and flour sacks and shivered in the freezing shack. The men scrambled to get the fireplace ablaze to warm them.

"Wait a minute," one of the bummers said. "They're not Negroes, just dirty. We got to wash them."

"No," cried the first child, backing away. "I want Mama."

"Where is she?" the Yank asked.

"Mama gone," the second little girl said. "All gone."

The bummers cooked a meal. After the children ate they weren't so afraid, and the men bathed them. Then, true to their calling, they ransacked nearby houses and dressed the girls with such elegant and frilly clothes that they could've passed for children raised on a great plantation. Their beauty, however, did them little good when the men tried to find them a new home in the area.

"Open your eyes," said one Georgia mother. "I've already got more mouths to feed than I do pieces of bread."

That night, as they rode on mules eastward, a thunderstorm struck. The bummers hurried them into their arms and slept with them that way all night to keep them dry and warm. The next day they gave the girls to a regiment of soldiers who carried them piggyback, bouncing toward Savannah.

Sometimes I wonder why all men at all times don't treat each other with the dignity and respect those men showed the children of their enemy. I guess that's just asking far too much of grown folks who know it all.

A Southerner is born with more pride than is good for him—and I sure got a dose—but if a Yank offered me a ride on his back just now I'd be tempted to take it. My water is gone, as are two tuna sandwiches Rowena made for me this morning. I've walked almost fifteen miles and have another twenty to go before I hit Sandersville. Resting every few miles to avoid heatstroke, I doubt that I can make it to a cool motel shower before dark. I can't remember, in all my many treks, ever wanting a drink of water more than I do now. I'm not ashamed to lick my own sweat, salty and dripping to my lips.

This parched road seems to stretch forever and Mara's Tara must've been but some fantasy boiled in my brain by the

Georgia sun. Right now I couldn't agree more with the old saying that we never know just how good we've got it till the well runs dry. Yes, I'm obsessed with water. I wish a thunderstorm would explode in the heavens so I could rip my clothes off and stand naked in the pouring rain. But if there's a single cloud in sight it's for sharper eyes than mine.

Turning the next curve, however, hope appears in a small country church; it just might have an outside water faucet, or the doors might be left unlocked for a pilgrim like myself. As I get closer I see that someone with red spray paint has had divine guidance on the side of the wooden building: GOD IS NOT A BAPTIST. I'm certain that the inspired author could teach me all sorts of things about the meaning of life, but all my tired and heated brain can perceive just now is that *God is water*. And, amen, Brother, when I spot a faucet on the south side of the church. I turn the handle, and it not only works but is positioned upward to shoot water two feet into the burning air. I drop my pack, hat, and staff like hot potatoes and stick my face into the fountain and *glory be* I hereby baptize myself into the Church of Quenched Thirst. . . . *Hallelujah! Hallelujah!*

Filling the canteen, I remove my shoes and stick my feet into the holy water. I'm tempted to camp here and leave before sunrise while the day is still somewhat cool, but ever since I discovered in my research for this march that the 2nd Minnesota walked this route at dark with flaming pine knots to light their way I've been intrigued with my own night hike. I won't have to worry about one of my drummer boys, as did the 2nd Minnesota. Drummer William Bircher noticed his fellow musician, only fourteen years old, falling asleep as he walked through the smoke of flaming pine knots.

"You're exhausted," said Bircher. "Let me carry your drum and you can rest a little as we march."

"But I need to sleep for a while," said the boy, Simmers, as he handed his friend the drum.

"You'll get left behind and some Johnnie will cut your throat like a ripe melon."

Simmers stumbled sleepily and Bircher pulled him back

into the lines to keep moving on. But only minutes later he
dropped farther back and was never seen again, his short life
but a few fast drumbeats.

I haven't stumbled in sleep yet as I march on, but night fell
more than an hour ago and my canteen is empty again. My
body is shot, but I'm afraid to sit and rest because the numb-
ness would leave my feet and the pain and burning would be
pure hell to my new blisters if I started walking again. I
haven't seen a mileage sign for Sandersville in over three
hours and I'm not sure if it's three or six more miles into
town.

The headlights of a car or truck appear in the great distance
and race toward me. I begin to wave, not for a ride, but simply
to ask how far it is into town. The car slows, brightens its
lights, and then speeds on as if I'm nothing but a dirty thug
with a big stick in the night. I don't feel that anyone owes me
anything, but it hurts to be passed by, left behind in the darkness.

Another set of lights looms from around the curve and I
wave again, but the same thing happens and I walk on. Starting up a steep hill, I feel the pack getting heavier with each
step. Then my right arm begins to tingle and a tightness starts
in my chest as my legs become weak. I'm becoming afraid
now because I'm nauseous and have all the symptoms of a
heart attack. I've never experienced anything like this in my
life. Call it denial if you like, but I refuse to believe that my
body would fail me now. I've worked out faithfully for thirty
years and damned if I'll succumb to a little heat and exhaus-
tion on a Georgia roadside. Stopping and leaning on my staff,
however, I'm grateful that the symptoms pass.

I inch on up the steep hill. Now I just wish I could see the
WELCOME TO SANDERSVILLE sign, but all my eyes find are the
distant stars and occasional passing headlights as gnats, mosquitoes, and flying ants target my sunburned face.

Finally, after walking two more miles, I spot the lights of a
little grocery store. I fear, however, that it's already closed for
the day, but when I get there it's as open as a true friend's

arms. I stumble inside and the two clerks, one white and one black, eye me like something the rat drug in. I understand their suspicion and tell them what I'm doing.

"Can I sit for a while?" I ask after filling the biggest store cup with ice and Coke.

"Sure you can, honey," the huge black woman says. "But wait a second, what's that crawling on your face?"

I'm so tired that her enormous fingers seem like black snakes floating through the air to my cheek. Then she shows me the winged insect she finds there.

"Honey, you've been a taxi for this termite or whatever it is," she says, throwing it to the floor. "Here, sit on these milk cartons and put your money away. That cold drink is on us. Ain't that right, Missy?"

"Sure is," she says. "Make yourself at home."

"I'm a little put out by you coming in here though," says the black woman. "Now I'll worry till I know if you make it on to Savannah. My mama was the same way about everybody she took a liking to. A worrywart if ever there was one."

As I sit here on these plastic milk cartons sipping the ice-cold drink, I feel as though I have once again, at least for a moment, found the Holy Grail. A motel is just down the block where a shower and soft bed await me, and I've been taken in by total strangers where I can feel safe and let my thoughts drift about the store. Here, among canned goods, potato chips, and candy, is as important as any other place on earth.

I tell them more about my march to the sea and they listen as if they'd like to hit the open road too. The black woman's name is Seth and her face reminds me of "Mom," the black woman who made the shrimp and crabmeat salads at the Cajun restaurant where I waited tables for four long years on Bourbon Street in New Orleans. We were the busiest seafood joint in the entire City of the Saints and tourists from all over the world ate there. Customers had to pass the kitchen to get to the rest rooms and it would sometimes twist their minds a little to overhear me, a white man, calling out to the old black lady making salads . . .

"How's it coming, Mom?"

"Working hard, baby," she'd call back as if I were her son. "Making it pretty as sunrise so you'll get a great-day-in-the-morning tip."

"You're a sweet mom," I'd call back, because she liked for all the waiters, black or white, to cherish her that way.

It would be pushing it a bit to say all of us who worked in that Cajun restaurant were like one big family. But after four years there I got to know in great detail the joys and trials of my fellow workers, most of whom were black and, of course, descendants of slaves who had been sold just four blocks away at the slave exchange which is now The Original Pierre Maspero's Restaurant. Sometimes at work the beauty in their faces would astonish me so much that I'd have to be careful not to get caught staring. Those different shades of brown and black that border on a kind of majestic blue sent my mind to Africa, where I'd try to picture their ancestors among elephants and lions as they danced and sang in tribal tongues beneath the moon. You may rightfully wonder why I'm telling you this, but it's because of what "Mom" told me one night when I walked her down Bourbon Street to catch her bus home.

"See how the moon up there is black and white?" she said to me.

"Yes," I said. "I've always found it beautiful."

"Ain't made out of cheese," she told me. "The moon is made out of blacks and whites who have learned to love each other. When they die, their souls float up there to join together. The moon is up there to remind us of our capabilities down here on earth. A person has to look close at the moon to understand such things."

"Who told you that story?" I asked her.

"Ain't no story," she said. "It's the truth and when you get to be my age the truth comes to you whether you want it on your front porch or not."

"You've always made great salads, Mom," I told her as she started to board her bus. "But I didn't know till tonight just what you were putting in them."

*   *   *

Sitting on these plastic milk cartons and finishing my Coke, I'm watching Mom's bus disappear down New Orleans' Canal Street when from the Georgia night a young black man enters with a black girl.

"I'd like for you to meet my nephew, Alex," Seth tells me. "He has some interesting thoughts on black folks in the South."

"Don't get him started on that," says the black girl, who looks to be about the same age as him—twenty-two or twenty-three.

"And this is his sister, Roxie," Seth says.

Alex shakes my hand as his aunt Seth tells him what I'm doing. He removes his glasses, cleans them with his handkerchief, and puts them back on. Roxie hurries on between the aisles of canned goods as if she wants no part of me or him, her own brother.

"Alex is working on his master's degree in business at Emory University in Atlanta," Seth says, pride in her voice.

"Do you like it there?" I ask.

"I play the game," he says, "and tell the teachers what they want to hear. It makes them feel important to see their own words come back to them. I'll be glad to finish, though, and start making a few bucks. I'm going to open an import business."

"You sound pretty confident," I say.

"I am," he says. "You can do anything if you set your mind to it and don't give up."

"That at least helps the odds," I say.

"I've got cousins who don't even try to get ahead," he says, "because they think they don't have a chance, since they're black. They gave up before they started. They're still slaves and don't even know it."

"I knew it was coming," Roxie says, walking toward us with a bag of popcorn and two cans of Spam.

"What's worse," Alex continues, "is that they've made slaves of themselves because they think white people are against them."

"Some whites are against us," Roxie says, placing her items on the counter. "They want to hold us down."

"Yes," says Alex. "But that's simply another hurdle to jump in the business world. If you're fat or ugly, that can go against you as well. But you can't afford to give up."

"Listen at you," says Roxie. "Comparing fat and ugly to being black."

"I didn't say that," says Alex. "I said it's a tough world out there, where a lot of people have prejudices. You've got to be strong and inventive enough to overcome them."

"And that's why you think some African Americans were better off on a plantation before the Civil War?" Roxie says, her anger building.

"Those today who have no direction or motivation," Alex says, "and have children they don't support or have become drug addicts or alcoholics were better off as slaves. Like I said, there's many different kinds of slaves. The world today is filled with them—black and white."

"Guess you'd have been happy to have worked picking cotton from morning till night?" Roxie snaps.

"No," says Alex, "I would've hated it and run away or found a way to buy my freedom, as Frederick Douglass did. That's what we're all having to do today, find a way to buy our freedom while trying to make sure that our inevitable ball and chain is as light as possible."

"You make me sick with all your fancy college talk," Roxie says, paying Missy for the popcorn and two cans of Spam. "I think you want to be white."

"You know that's not true," says Alex. "I'm very proud of being black. But I don't see any reason for feeling ashamed of having a little vision in my life either. Do you, Aunt Seth?"

"I wouldn't get between you and Roxie right now if I had a big bulldog in each hand," says Seth.

When Alex and Roxie leave, I thank Seth and Missy for the Coke and place to rest for a while. Then I head on down the street toward the motel. I find myself replaying the conversation between Alex and Roxie, and it reminds me that the New South is a complex can of worms, crawling with a wide range of thoughts and feelings. After such a long day, it comforts me that I can now do something as simple as look up at the moon —and see "Mom" up there sprinkling that special something onto her salads.

Chapter Thirty-five

Sandersville is little more than a village, so I feel lucky that it has a new and comfortable motel. That shower I had dreamed of as I walked those thirty-five miles from Milledgeville hits the spot as well. My feet, even after a good night's rest, however, aren't doing any bragging about being tough guys. Their bottoms feel like I've walked thirty-five miles over the lit stogie tips Sherman flipped to the ground long ago.

I get my mind off the blistered flesh, though, when I phone seventy-year-old Lewis West. He jumps at the chance to escort me down into the basement of his drugstore, where those twelve Union soldiers were imprisoned the night the enraged mob dragged them out into a nearby field and filled them with lead. The next day, as we descend the wooden stairs a cool wave of moist earthy air greets us. The place is but a junk heap of old filing cabinets, desks, and medicine bottles resting in red powder, two inches thick in some spots, from the crumbling brick walls made of Georgia clay.

"When I was a boy," says Lewis, leading me from the basement, "I'd go stand in front of the Brown house, where Sherman slept the night he stayed in Sandersville. I wanted to go in there so bad I couldn't stand it, but Mrs. Brown wouldn't pay me any mind whatsoever. I might as well have been a tick on a hound's ear. Then, when I turned seven years old, an odd thing happened. It was my job to milk our two cows, Sally and Moo, so Daddy could use the cream in the malts he made at the soda fountain in the drugstore. Each morning I'd lead the cows from our barn to a pasture on the other side of town.

Each evening I'd go get them and milk them again. It so happened that I wasn't the worst marble player in these parts and one particular evening I had my pocket full of marbles. I was bored with those cows, but I loved tossing my marbles into the air to try to catch them as I led the animals to the barn. That got old, so I put my prized dillies on the ground and kicked them along. I was a better marble player than I was a kicker and those dillies rolled down into a ditch. A drainpipe met it and when I bent over to get the marbles I saw it sheltered Civil War–era sugar and cream holders. Sally and Moo never had to run so fast in their lives as when I gathered those silver pieces and ran home to show Mama. Now, she'd heard that somebody had just stolen some things from Mrs. Brown, and she called to see if she was missing what I had found. She had, and I got to take those sugar and cream holders to her myself. When I stepped inside that house where Sherman slept I felt like I had just made it to the top of a great mountain. Life wasn't as crazy then as it is now and everything had its special place in a home. When Mrs. Brown opened her china cabinet I saw right where the silver pieces went and I placed them there like I had been meant to all along. It turned out that four little black boys passing out fliers for the A & P grocery had taken the pieces and incriminated themselves by forgetting a whole stack of the ads inside the Brown house. A few years ago I got those very fliers from the Browns' attic and had them laminated. I'd like to give you one, if you want it."

I have little interest in carrying a grocery ad on to Savannah, but Lewis is so spellbound by getting, in his own way, this close to Sherman that I don't have the heart to say no. Sherman loved theatrics and often went to plays and circuses; if he could now see a Southerner this obsessed with a lamination of coffee and bread prices in Dixie he would be puffing away on a new cigar and blowing smoke rings toward the face of Robert E. Lee. For that matter, I see such fascination with Sherman everywhere I turn that it reminds me of how alleged pieces of Christ's cross and shawl were once sold like hotcakes to anyone desperate to get near immortality. But get a load of me, and a Rebel at that, doing more than my share to keep Sherman resurrected and marching across Georgia.

"I'd be honored to have one of those laminated ads," I say.

Lewis, a grinning possum, takes me down to his second drugstore near the hospital, where the ads are locked in his office. I'm right proud to get one, but I hadn't counted on the bonus. Lewis leads me to a door and unlocks it to reveal a big closet stacked with six wooden chairs.

"There they are," he says, as if I should know what he's talking about.

"I'm a little slow sometimes, Lewis. What are we really looking at here?"

"These are from the Browns' kitchen. Sherman sat in one of them."

A Southerner who doesn't respond to a Southerner with equal excitement, however outlandish it may seem at the time, shows another symptom of Dixie Denial. It's such misunderstood traits as this that have caused many outsiders in the South to scratch their heads over why they felt out of place. I step into the closet and shake a chair's leg just enough for Lewis to hear the rattle.

"Can I take this one with me?" I ask. "Then when I get tired on my march I can sit on something besides the ground and rest for a spell."

"Aaaaah . . ."

"Well, it never hurts to ask."

Marching on, I become curious as to what Henry Hitchcock had to say about leaving Sandersville. If Lewis hadn't been so stingy with his chairs, I'd have a better place to sit than on the earth right now. But since he gave me a pack of Doctor Johnson's Foot Powder—"has soothed millions of aching feet since 1870," says the fine print—I'm willing to let bygones be bygones. I dig into my pack and pull out Hitchcock's diary to read.

Ride from Sandersville here through pine forests over sandy road. Beautiful Sabbath morning; air delightful, a little bracing, sky and sunlight lovely as fog melted away; and the quiet of the woods is always soothing. Many thoughts rushed on me as we rode . . . on this sad and deadly errand. How can any man engage in a war unless he believes its prosecution a sacred duty! But for this, I could not stay in the service an hour: as it is, I cannot stay out of it. . . .

Slipping his journal back into the pack, I suspect Hitchcock spoke for many men—Northerners and Southerners—who felt torn about being in the war. As I walk on and see trees on either side of the road I think, too, of his writing about soothing woods. Anytime a man begins to hint at a sanctuary, whether it be a woman's arms, woods, or home, he's about ready for a break, though it might be difficult to admit.

The trees fade into the distance and it's again so hot that sheets of white dust, drifting in wind from various chalk quarries, almost make me believe that they're clouds of blowing snow. If they were, I'd scoop a snowball in my hand and rub it all over my face and neck before letting a chunk melt in my mouth.

I can't say that the constant calls of quail in the nearby fields cool me like snow, but for as long as I can remember I have found their whistles beautiful. Sometimes in the spring I sit in the woods at Tanager and imitate their calls. To have one answer and come running across the leaves to me is a kind of thrill that only nature can give. It empowers a man to feel that he is part of something that is still pure in a polluted land. A Southerner who doesn't whistle like a bird sometimes has one of the saddest ailments of Dixie Denial. He has forgotten that he can fly on the very breath that comes from his lips. Those who work in offices, however, might find it handy to limit their flights to lunch and coffee breaks.

I'm ready for a break myself from today's march because my left ankle, injured when I walked the Trail of Tears, is starting to swell. I'm limping and every few minutes I have to stop, leaning on my staff to take the weight off that foot. I'm still several miles west of Louisville on Highway 24 when a red pickup pulls up behind me. It's the third vehicle that has stopped today with people offering me lifts, and each time I chose to walk instead. They gave me funny looks, shook their heads, and drove away.

"Having trouble, neighbor?" says the driver of the pickup, in his late thirties.

"Just practicing my limp," I say, and explain my mission.

"I live nearby," he says. "Why don't you spend the night and my wife will fix us a good dinner. In the morning you can join the Civil War again."

He introduces himself as Gary Cobb, and I'm not certain that I want to go with him. I can't put my finger on just why I feel this way, but my instincts are nudging me.

"If you don't want to spend the night," says Gary, "I'll bring you back to the road after we've had dinner. You're burning up out here and it'll cool off when the sun goes down."

I place my pack and staff in the back of the truck. *Keep a close lookout, Road Rabbit. Two heads are better than one.* But I begin to relax as I become more acquainted with Gary. He grew up in this area and works for a kaolin (chalk or white clay) mine. His heart, however, is more involved with Broken Shackles Ranch, a 275-acre retreat for teenagers who have had scrapes with the law, which he owns and manages.

"We get boys in from all over Georgia," says Gary. "None of them have histories of violence; they are mostly in need of some love and discipline to get their self-esteem up. My wife and I cleared the road to the ranch with chain saws and built the home ourselves. We named it what we did because a lot of the kids were brought to us with their wrists and ankles shackled."

Gary stops at the ranch and we go inside so he can see how things are going with his staff and the teenagers before we head on to his home just down the road. The five kids—two blacks and three whites—gather around Gary and he places his arms around their shoulders as if they were his own children. I don't doubt that he founded the ranch to give from his heart, but it also seems apparent he may welcome their attention and love as much as they do his. I don't have any trouble with the hard truth that most of us give to get; strong commitments stem from deep personal needs. In regard to Sherman, I've never for a heartbeat bought the notion that he gave so much of himself during the Civil War for the sole aim of preserving the Union. Fame, the challenge, and hunger for excitement and adventure as well as wanting to feel needed and in control just might have been a little of the salt he sprinkled on that food we all eat in the secret midnight hours. If I sound judgmental here, guess again; it makes Sherman all the more real and fascinating to me.

Gary and I leave the ranch for his home two miles away. His two sons are at a Boy Scout Camp in North Carolina and I'll get their bedroom, complete with aquarium rippling with perch the boys caught in the nearby creek. Gary's red-haired mom, Evelyn, lives in the garage apartment adjoining the house. She suffers from lupus and it sometimes affects her memory. During dinner—the fried green tomatoes aren't bad at all—she repeats what she says.

"I'm so sorry," she says, her face melting my heart. "Did I say pass the pepper already?"

Gary's wife, Kathy, is equally humble. When she led us in saying grace before dinner, I saw Evelyn with her eyes open looking at me. We both smiled like we were children getting away with something.

"I have to go to Denver in the morning on business," Gary says after dinner. "I don't relish the trip but I have to work to keep the ranch going. Honey, did you pack my bag already?"

"Sure did," says Kathy.

"You put in my novel by Louis L'Amour and my Bible too? That's good. Are you a religious man, Alabama?"

"I have a spiritual side," I say, wanting to avoid Bible Belt boxing and thinking the South, for all my deep and committed love for it, bugs me as far as some of its dogmatic religions. Some of the same folks who were preaching love and kindness before the Civil War were also racists. Then, too, all this dogma has created a very repressed society when it comes to sex. Many Southerners—or Yanks for that matter—are so afraid of their own bodies that I wonder if they even look at their own reflections in mirrors when they're naked. It isn't simply that I think being afraid of sex is a mistake—we should certainly be careful in this diseased day and age—but anytime a man is scared of his own flesh and his desires you can bet he's also frightened by any thoughts or concepts foreign to him. Such a fixed position serves only to enslave man. In the same breath here, I don't feel it wise for me to be so rigid when it comes to pigeonholing others either. "Each to his own," I add.

"Won't matter much longer anyway," says Gary. "Same sexes sleeping together, people killing babies, drugs, violence . . . the world is soon coming to an end. At least we'll all be called home."

"Amen," says his mother. "Did I say that already?"

"No, Mama, and it never hurts to say it again."

"Amen," she says.

"If the world is about to end," I say, "why are you doing so much to try to help it with the ranch?"

"Can't give up just because the fire's coming," says Gary.

Well, what with Armageddon just around the bend and hell and brimstone heating up inside, when Gary turns the TV to Pat Robertson I decide to take him up on an earlier invitation and hop into the backyard Jacuzzi under the big pecan tree. It's dark when I crawl into the massaging water and the Georgia stars are magnificent. Ten gourds, dangling from a nearby pole at the edge of a field, hung there for purple martins, rattle in the evening breeze while an electronic bug zapper, fastened to a telephone pole and radiating a blue light, offers a loud, crisp snap from time to time when an insect flies in and gets fried to bug heaven.

"How's the water?" Gary calls, his head sticking out the back door.

"Perfect."

He disappears into the house, back to Pat Robertson, and I close my eyes to sink into the Jacuzzi. It relaxes me, even as I'm surrounded by hard-core fundamentalists. Besides, I have been treated with nothing but warmth and generosity here tonight. And we in the Church of Quenched Thirst believe that the Great Goat baaas for one and all. *Splish-splash.*

Chapter Thirty-six

Parting with Gary's family and one of the best Jacuzzis in the Bible Belt, I push on across the Ogeechee River and into the tiny town of Louisville. I hurry into the post office.

"Any general delivery for Ellis?"

"No," says the woman. "No such animal for anybody today."

My heart sinks and I exit to the street. In the center of Louisville stand massive beams that once supported the roof of a slave market. It both fascinates and repulses me that here men and women were stripped bare to be examined by would-be buyers.

Hey, look at this one. He's got a strong back.

Yeah, but his teeth are bad and he's got a boil on his right leg.

Now, over here's some sweet brown sugar.

She's young too. Feel how firm.

Make a good house nigger. She could cook upstairs as well as down.

Yeah, bet she could poke week-old ashes into fire.

A block from the site of the slave market I enter a small café and order breakfast. While the two eggs fry I sip coffee and tend to my journal, which has in its own way—like my map, staff, and Road Rabbit—become my friend on this Dixie odyssey. It's no secret that a man's feelings are often seen not only in what he writes, but in his handwriting itself, and when I scribble thoughts of Debi just now I note that my hand slows down as if even my fingers are trying to tell me something. If I could hold her just now I'd let my fingers become as tender as the glow of a lightning bug shining over her entire body, inch by inch, as I admire all I've been missing.

The waitress brings eggs and grits, but my appetite is for Debi. I tell the server I'll be right back and go outside to the pay phone. I call the Sandersville post office.

"Ellis?" says the postal clerk.

"Yes, I was in there yesterday."

"Oh, yeah, the Stick Man. No, still nothing for you."

"Thanks—"

"Wait a second. Yeah, you got something here from Tacoma, Washington."

"Can you forward it?" I ask, a mixture of hope and fear rising within me.

He says he can, and since I'm only days away from Savannah now, I ask him to send it there. The very city that was a crowning glory for Sherman will also hold my destiny. Then I can dance there in the ocean with love itself, or be swept out to sea by its loss and curse China as I sink, my fist shaking as it vanishes beneath the water.

Thoughts of Debi stay with me as I continue on down Highway 17 into Millen and hike several miles north of town to the site of a Civil War stockade where up to ten thousand Union soldiers were imprisoned. When Kilpatrick's cavalry charged this way, following an Augusta skirmish with Wheeler's horsemen, they arrived too late to rescue any prisoners. The last few men were loaded onto a Rebel train and carried down the tracks while Kilpatrick and his men, on the opposite side of the Ogeechee, could only swear and wave their swords against the Georgia sky, thick with Spanish moss hanging from the trees.

The Yanks crossed the river to find seven prisoners so fresh with death that they had not yet been buried. They placed them in a trench with their comrades where a rough-sawed pine board stated 650 BURIED HERE.

John Potter of the 101st Illinois scouted the prison grounds for trinkets to add to his war memorabilia. He wrote:

It was the barest spot I ever saw. The trees and stumps and roots to the smallest fiber had been dug out for fuel, not a rag or a button or even a chip could be found.

Today the prison site is Magnolia Springs State Park and the place is jumping with busloads of black children and adults cooking hamburgers and hot dogs. As I walk among them under the towering pines by the swimming pool some stare at my pack and staff.

"Say, man, what are you, Moses?" says a boy about nine or ten years old.

"I'm walking the route of Sherman's March to the Sea."

"Sherman?" says another boy, stepping closer. "That what my uncle call his mangy old dog."

The two boys laugh, but their eyes have such gleams that I'm drawn to them. Two girls now join us and I feel like I'm becoming a spectacle. A woman about my age, turning beef patties on the nearby grill, looks on with caution.

"Don't mind these boys," one of the girls says. "They ignorant."

"And you ugly as that alligator down there in that water," the first boy says, referring to the great spring where, indeed, a big gator's head and eyes stick from the surface.

"Sherman was a general," the same girl says. "He helped free black people in the Civil War."

"That's right," I say. "Where we stand now was once a prison for Union soldiers."

"They sure had a good swimming pool," the first boy says, his palm slapping that of the second.

The woman cooking the hamburgers rolls her eyes and shakes her head as I walk on, the kids hurrying to the picnic table where she sets a plate of patties and buns.

I hike some two hundred yards into the woods and up a hill overlooking the park. I'm amazed that the foundation of the Confederate fort that was headquarters for the prison is still intact. Circular, with a ditch around its base some six feet deep, it's about fifty feet in diameter. I climb atop it, imagining the great watchtower from which one could see the prisoners as well as approaching troops. Though none of the fort's walls remain, I feel or imagine the presence of the Rebs who were stationed here. I think, however, that it's one of the last spots I would've wanted to be. I've seen photographs of some Civil War prisoners and they looked as much like living skeletons as Jews in German concentration camps.

Highway 17 stretches from Millen to Savannah along the east side of the Ogeechee. The sun and humidity are pure hell to a man carrying a heavy pack and the road is so remote that farmhouses are few and far between, a small grocery store as rare as cool shade. Don't even think about a motel and its refreshing shower.

But I'm thrilled to be within fifty miles of Savannah and still in one piece, though my left ankle puts up a pretty cocky argument. The sun is as brutal here as anywhere else on the trek, but the rolling hills vanished days ago and level ground makes for easier walking. I find joy in all the Spanish moss too. My family and I used to go to Daytona, Florida, each summer for four days of vacation, and traveling at night to avoid most traffic, my sisters and I would raise our heads from our pillows from time to time to see if moss yet loomed from trees in the moonlight. Once it appeared, hanging from branches like grandfathers' long gray beards, we could sleep no more, for we had at last, once again, crossed that magical line into a world so exotic that anything could happen. It wasn't till I got older that I grasped that our vacations were wonderful not only because of playing in the ocean itself, but because my parents and sisters and I were together and as carefree as the wind coming off the waves at night when we walked the beach and pretended that it was all ours. It was the one time of the year, too, that I saw my mother and father touch each other the most, and to this day I still think such moments are what make people with deep feelings love to live. So now as I hike along this swampy road where seabirds drift overhead and moss hangs thick, the very smell of the ocean in the air, I not only near my Civil War destination but walk once again with my family along the waves of our private beach, safe and secure from the world's musket fire.

Chapter Thirty-seven

Still some thirty miles from Savannah, I come across an enormous cornfield and enter it as if Daddy will step forward to greet me. But all I find is tonight's dinner, three ears of corn that I stuff into my pack.

Pitching my tent overlooking the Ogeechee, I build a fire. Once I've wrapped the corn in aluminum foil I place it near the flames and cover it with sandy soil.

By the time the first Union infantrymen arrived here, the foraging feasts were over. The advancing cavalrymen had swiped what food they could find from the few plantations and the marshland's chief crop of rice required tedious hulling before it could be cooked and eaten. The tasty yams, plump turkeys, and cured hams of central Georgia were as absent as the thousands of buildings that had been burned along the way. Supply wagons followed, as did that massive herd of bellowing cattle, but they were days away and the party had been too good to just all at once turn to a monk's diet. One group of foragers killed a mule, sliced and roasted it.

"Best beefsteak I ever ate," wrote a lip-smacking soldier.

If some had grown impatient for better food, others became totally disgusted with the freed slaves that swarmed to their columns like bees to honey. On Ebenezer Creek, only a few miles from where I'm camping, some five hundred blacks—mostly children and women—followed Union soldiers led by General Jefferson C. Davis, a proslavery sympathizer. The 58th Indiana Regiment had labored all night to lay a pontoon bridge after the Rebs had burned the original crossing. Once the fourteen thousand soldiers, horses, wagons, and guns reached the other side, the blacks scrambled that way as well only to find that Davis had ordered the bridge cut and pulled from them. Panic struck and Indiana chaplain John Hight observed:

> There went up from that multitude a cry of agony. . . . They made a wild rush . . . some plunged into the water, and swam across. Others ran wildly up and down the bank, shaking with terror.

The screams of women and children softened the hearts of some of the Yanks, however, and they threw logs and branches into the creek for black men to build a raft. Blankets were frantically cut into strips to make a rope to pull the raft back and forth over the creek, each trip carrying only six slaves and sinking many times. Mothers with babies in their arms were caught in the swift current and washed downstream to drown; their yells for help later reached Washington and haunted Sherman in a way he had not dreamed. Yet others, on the verge of climbing aboard the raft, were grabbed by Wheeler's men and returned to their owners. This thing called emancipation had become a monster in the swamp.

No one can say for certain what Sherman himself would've done if he'd been at Ebenezer Creek, but he was only miles away with troubles of his own. The 1st Alabama Cavalry, moving in front of the general as his bodyguard, stepped on Confederate land mines, which blasted horses and riders to kingdom come. Both the general and Henry Hitchcock, upon seeing the dead—and one boyish soldier crawling across the ground with a trail of blood where a foot had been—were not pleased.

"Bring up those Rebel prisoners," Sherman shouted. "Put them on their hands and knees and let them scratch for their lives."

"We'll get blown up," a Rebel yelled as his trembling fingers searched the dirt for more weapons.

"To hell with you," said Sherman, watching the boy who

lost his foot be carried into a farmhouse where surgeons would
amputate his leg.

After adding more wood to the flames to make sure the corn
keeps cooking, I unzip my pack and remove Hitchcock's diary
to see what he wrote about the fireworks:

> The Rebel prisoners . . . very carefully—and without inci-
> dent—soon uncovered seven more torpedoes . . . just under
> the surface, and so arranged as to explode when the friction
> tube was trod on even by a man's ordinary step. Four of these
> were simply 12 lb. shells, with a sort of nipple projecting from
> the fuse-hole; the other three were large copper cylinders,
> rounded at each end.

The only thing I see sticking from the earth where I'm
camped is a plastic holder for a six-pack of beer. Just whether
or not that proved to be a weapon if the consumer got behind
the wheel of a car I can't say. But I wouldn't mind having a
cold one myself right now to drink before I dig into the corn.

I put Hitchcock's diary in the pack and get my tiny box of
Morton's salt with a picture of a little girl holding an umbrella.
I take the foil from the glowing coals and open it to find the
three ears steaming hot. I wish I had some butter to smear on
them, but when they finally cool the salt seasons them just
fine. It's been over six hours since I've eaten and the corn is as
sweet and juicy as any I can remember. It sticks to my teeth,
and I eat so hurriedly that I'm almost certain a stranger happening upon me by boat or foot would see a pig sitting by a
fire. Frankly, I don't care. One of the great beauties of camping alone is that you can pretty well do whatever you damned
well please and not have to worry about a pointed finger, cold
eye, or strained small talk. You're free to oink to your heart's
content all the while knowing—forget what the world sees—
that you're the rarest of nightingales. Yes, I'm getting a bit
goofy, because I've been on the march for a month and I'm
becoming ecstatic that I'm almost close enough to Savannah to
smell the perfume there. Still, even in the very midst of my

approaching celebration, I also feel a tug at my shirttail. Every journey has its own spirit and all those I've met and experienced feed it. It will not release me till it so chooses, for the very thing that sometimes sets a man free also owns him. Some call it fate or destiny.

It doesn't matter what anyone calls the river only ten feet from me; it flows toward the Atlantic as it has done for thousands of years and probably will for thousands more. I like such consistency and have more than once turned to a river to help me find my own peace. With that in mind, I take a hook, line, and sinker from my pack. It would suit me just fine to awake at dawn to find that I'd caught a big catfish. I don't have cornmeal or oil to fry it in, but I can reuse the foil that worked so well baking the corn.

Needing bait, I turn over a couple of logs in hope of finding a worm. I'm out of luck. If I had a handsaw, I'd fiddle for some earthworms. Some might think I'm kidding, but fiddling for worms is as Southern as playing baseball is American.

To fiddle for worms you find a moist area in the woods by a tree, often a dogwood, no bigger around than a man's wrist. Saw the tree off some eight or ten inches from the ground, then saw straight through the middle of the stump, taking your time to send the vibrations through the roots deep into the earth. In a matter of minutes, as surely as if you were a great fiddle player, the ground will come alive with worms squirming all around you. The first time I saw my father do this I was amazed, for I was too young to comprehend the earthquake song. He possessed special powers.

While I have no saw I do find where someone has cut a pole, perhaps for fishing, and it strikes me that a rock rubbed against its stump might send vibrations into the ground almost as well as a toothed tool. Locating a big enough rock is no small chore, but once I do I soon have the roots of the cut sapling toe-tapping to my tune. The soil here is more sandy than rich and I'm not overly hopeful about guests looming from the ground. But in a few minutes one—no, two worms wiggle among the fallen leaves as if to show me they can do the Twist as well as the Watusi and have even learned a few moves from the movie *Dirty Dancing.*

Well, cute as the couple are, I escort them to my hook and throw them into the Ogeechee, where they sink to the bottom. I don't use a fishing pole, but simply tie my line to a bush as twilight falls over the swamp. Oh, yeah, don't forget to spit on bait for good luck.

When I hear a loud splash upriver, it dawns on me that alligators swim these currents, as well as water moccasins. But any fear soon subsides as a loon begins to call out somewhere among the Spanish moss. Then a gentle bat dips and darts over the treetops, its wings as thin and soft as the cloth coat of Road Rabbit.

I gathered an armload of driftwood earlier and now place a few sticks onto the fire. It blazes as I crawl into my tent and snuggle up against my pack. An owl begins to hoot as I fall asleep, only to awake sometime in the night to a dream that lingers as if it needs to talk to me. My father led me behind his "old home place," where in reality there once stood an enormous grove of walnut trees. But during the Great Depression Daddy's father, desperate for food money for his twelve children, sold them for rare lumber. Even the roots themselves were dug from the earth to be used as gun stocks. But in this dream I just awoke from, I saw Daddy sitting on the same spot and all the trees had returned. They were loaded with walnuts and my father was cracking them on a rock with a hammer just as I had seen him do many times in private as he made up little songs he sang only to himself. He looked so happy that I cannot recall ever having a dream that gave me such peace. I have no doubt, in my heart, that Daddy came from the other world to say hello and let me know that he's doing just fine, that there's plenty of walnuts to go around when I get there too. Oh, if only I could now feel such a sense of completion with the dream about Daddy in the cornfield.

Morning sunlight filters through the cypress, gum, and pines, and I crawl from the tent to see the bush shaking where I tied my fishing line. Judging by the force of the jerks, my dancing worms have hooked a big catfish, bass, or carp. I slip into my hiking shoes and hurry that way. Pulling in the line, I'm careful because whatever I've caught weighs several pounds and I don't want to break the nylon. I'm hoping for a catfish, but when the surface of the water finally splashes I see that it's a big turtle. It must've just gotten hooked or its powerful jaws would've snapped my line. I ease it onto the bank and it opens its mouth as if to invite me to stick my finger there. I'm not a squeamish person; I used to hunt and fish a lot and have skinned animals to tan their hides. But it bothers me to see the hook in the turtle's mouth just now, its wrinkled face and eyes seeming filled with feelings and thoughts. Using my pocketknife and a stick I try to remove the hook, but it's a waste of time, for the barbs are too deep in his flesh.

I finally just cut the line and stroke the turtle's head once with my finger before lowering him into the Ogeechee, his webbed claws splashing as he disappears in the muddy water. Chances are that he'll be just fine. He is, after all, one of Dixie's creatures, and though us Rebels may have a history of sometimes biting off more than we can chew, it has never stopped us from trying to bite off just a little bit more.

Chapter Thirty-eight

Only a month had passed since the great arson circus departed the charred remains of Atlanta. The 62,000 Union soldiers had swept across Georgia like a mighty hand, five columns strong, to cover a path sixty miles wide and three hundred miles long. No one before that mighty palm went untouched. Southern pantries had been cleaned out, buildings burned, animals butchered, and railroads wrecked, leaving a trail of Sherman's Neckties where Confederate trains once rolled. Thousands of Georgia citizens were now not only hungry and cold, but they trembled in the aftershock of seeing their homeland trampled by total strangers. As Sherman had planned, their very spirits were breaking and the beloved Confederacy was in grave danger of losing the war as well as the faith of its followers.

"Pierce the shell of the Confederacy," Sherman was fond of saying, "and you'll find it empty inside."

On the outskirts of Savannah, those five columns of Union soldiers now began to close around the city like fingers making a fist around a cherished and long-sought prize. General William Hardee, born in Georgia, and now in charge of the nine thousand Rebels defending the city, thought it wise not to be caught in that squeeze. He planned for his men to escape and fight another time rather than see the beautiful city burned to the ground. His men worked around the clock to build a pontoon bridge over the Savannah River for their evacuation. It suited General Hardee just fine that the Union soldiers were too far away to see its construction.

Within days of arriving at the outskirts of Savannah, Sherman ordered an attack on Fort McAllister to the south, where the Rebs controlled access to the Atlantic by way of the Ogeechee. The Yanks, running low on food, needed to reach their supply ships that awaited them off-shore. Standing on the nearby roof of a rice mill, he watched his men storm and overtake the fort, the Rebels inside resorting to hand-to-hand combat and refusing to make a formal surrender. The Union soldiers ran a U.S. flag atop the fort, broke into the wine cellar, and toasted their victory.

"Take a good, big drink," Sherman said, "a long breath, and then *yell like the devil.*"

The general took a nap in the fort and then braved torpedo-infested water in a rowboat to meet with General John Foster. He had only recently landed with soldiers on nearby Hilton Head Island, South Carolina, and they were just what Sherman needed to close in on the Rebels from the north side of the city along the Savannah River.

Before Sherman or those soldiers reached Savannah, however, General Hardee ordered his guns to blast the Yankees throughout the night to help hide the Rebel exodus across the river. The bridge was made of giant beams from the docks and anchored by train wheels. Rice straw was spread over loose boards to muffle the sounds of hooves and marching men, many of whom had fought in the hellish Battle of Griswold-ville. Some preferred to go barefoot rather than wear shoes donated by Savannah citizens; they were all made for women and the awkward high heels made loud, clanking sounds beneath the soldiers who wore them.

It was so foggy the night of the evacuation that the moon often vanished in the darkness while teamsters cracked whips and cursed their animals; some slipped from the makeshift bridge and splashed into the river as the heavy wagons pulled them to the bottom. A band played "Dixie."

On December 21, 1864, after the Confederate troops had fled, Savannah's mayor—Dr. Richard Arnold—surrendered the city at four-thirty in the morning. At last the arson circus could, at least for a while, put away the fire and roll into the elegant port city to dance in the streets with the pet bear, the owl, Old Abe—the eagle—and thousands of slaves, some dressed in fancy clothes and feathered hats foraged from plantations. While they clapped and sang, that one Yank juggled the coral snake pickled in a jar of whiskey.

"I feel like one who had walked a narrow plank," said Sherman on returning to Savannah after the month's historic march. "I look back and wonder if I really did it."

When I arrive in Savannah on a Saturday afternoon, I don't wonder if I really did it. But I wonder what will happen now that I'm entering the next phase of the odyssey. The trek has filled me with so much of life and its magic through the people I've met and the thoughts I've had that it seems something must be awaiting me here as if to help me level off from the electrifying surge. You, however, may already know what I'm really thinking and feeling in the very center of my core. Yes, that letter from Debi. The post office is closed already for today and now I won't be able to get the news till Monday morning.

I've heard it said many times that the true body of love has no room for fear. And while I feel this journey has in some ways transformed me—allowed me new insights, more freedom, and added strength—I won't claim that my love is without fear that Debi has decided to move to China. Yes, I can pretend that I now walk this trail of love between now and Monday with total grace. But of all my humble prayers to the Great Goat, my most fervent is that Debi has reached out once again from love's ledge so that we both might be spared the fall. If she has reached out, I'll be one of the happiest men in the whole of Dixie. But if she has chosen to follow her own Oriental path solo, a part of me—after finding such rich life in my odyssey across Georgia—will die. You may say that that's a small price to pay to honor my heritage and the Confederacy compared to those who died on the battlefield—and you'd be right. I cannot argue with logic. My mind is a reasonable sort of fellow. But my heart . . . my heart has never been able to understand loss.

Ever since the Civil War, the Southern heart has been trying to process its hurt. The South has a tradition of doing this with song, and I think that is the greatest Southern tradition of all. It's been honored by the slaves who lost their freedom and homelands and the Native Americans who were pushed to Oklahoma. The South is a song, from gospel to country to rock, calling out to all of America. Me, I don't even sound good when I sing in the shower, but the great need to sing is with me day and night. My heart is forever crying out, sometimes with joy, sometimes with sadness. Right now it is crying out with a song to reach Debi. But all I have are my words on paper. That, and my fingers, my whole body. I have always felt that I can sing my deepest feelings when I hold a woman naked in my arms. I have no fear then, only celebration and joy. I cannot hide from you how much—oh, how much—I wish I could hold Debi right now and sing my song.

As I hike down Bull Street into the historic section of Savannah, the very street Sherman traveled on entering town, I smell the ocean and feel a bit like I'm floating among the palm trees overhead. I'm limping because of the strained muscle in my left foot, and I'm sunburned. Heat rash covers my inner thighs and chiggers gnaw near them on more tender flesh. I'm once again soaked with sweat and my clothes are dirty.

I splurge and get a balcony room in one of Savannah's best bed-and-breakfasts. On the third floor, my window overlooks a courtyard where vines, flowers, and fountains flourish. Other guests here are from all over America and Europe and I feel like I've reached the promised land. The abundant Spanish moss in the trees is no less exotic than when I was a child en route to Florida with my family.

After treating my body and its vacationing chiggers to a long shower, I slip into clean jeans and T-shirt and start walking toward the Savannah River where the nine thousand Rebels escaped the Union soldiers. It's a bit odd to be without my staff, its tip tapping a tune. But the heavy pack? Man, oh, man, what a treat to be free of that.

A horse-drawn carriage rolls past loaded with eight Girl Scouts and the clippidy-clop of hooves on the cobbled street blends with the whimsical sound of a harmonica. It's being played by a man with a big white beard as he pedals by on a bicycle. He has such a radiant complexion with light-filled blue eyes that I'd love to know what he's thinking.

"Nice tune," I call out, hoping to hook a conversation.

He lowers the harmonica from his mouth and circles back to me. A red cardboard sign, the size of my hand, is penned to his white shirt. On it is written HI, MY NAME'S ARTHUR. IT'S MY BIRTHDAY.

"You like my music?" he asks.

"Sure do."

"Oh, then you should one day hear me *sing*. That is, if you're not afraid to fly among the stars. Are you?"

"Not as long as my feet are on the ground," I say, both amused and intrigued.

"Never know till you try," he says, pedaling on. "But then, others never try till they know and then they've thought about it so much that it's too *laaaaate*."

As the last word lingers in his mouth he turns the corner and disappears behind a Victorian house, the harmonica music starting again as if it had waited on him there while he paused to tinker with my mind. Then, as surely as if I never saw him at all, the music fades into the Georgia breeze.

Arriving at the river, I spot a boat made of car tires stuffed with thousands of plastic containers like those that hold Coke and Pepsi and all those other drinks Americans guzzle. On the boat's blue-and-yellow mast are the symbol for ying and yang and the words CREATE ECO-RAFT. Green canvas covers what appears to be the cabin and a two-eyed gas burner for cooking sets near it on the deck. The whole boat reminds me of an old hippie bus looking for a happening.

"What's with the boat?" I ask a woman wearing shades and a red hat.

"Somebody said it arrived this morning from central Florida and is headed to New York to save the world," she says. "I work there in that candy store and just came over to get a closer look. The crew was gone when I got here."

"Out to save the world?"

"Something like that, somebody told me."

"I guess the crew needed a break. Saving the world probably gets tiring at times."

"It's all I can do to sell candy," she says, eyeing her watch. "I better get back to it, too, or I won't have a job to save myself."

Thunder rumbles as the woman, fat as a butterball, wobbles back toward the store. I leave as well and by the time I reach the B&B the wind is wild, lightning flashing yellow as rain begins to pour.

I climb the stairs to my room, remove my shirt, and stand on the balcony to let the howling wind blow water all over me. This is the first rain I've encountered since I left Eatonton and many times on the hot, dry march I wished I could do exactly what I'm doing now. I open my mouth and catch the rain running down my face as well as that blowing in sheets from the sky. If I look like a man possessed to those watching from the protection of their windows, so be it. I didn't realize till now that rain is Debi and I want every drop of her before she vanishes into the clouds, thunder, and lightning.

Chapter Thirty-nine

It's Sunday morning and church bells ring across Savannah as I step from my room onto the wrought-iron balcony. Last night's rainstorm cleared the air and today, despite a little fog, the sky is as blue as the eyes of yesterday's white-bearded harmonica player on the bicycle. Seagulls drift overhead and a mockingbird in a nearby tree sings with such beauty and joy that I wish I could whistle half as well.

The bird begins a new tune as I descend the stairs and cross the courtyard on a coffee expedition. Inside the B&B dining room, I pour myself a cup and am looking for cream when a rather tall, slender man enters and points to the door behind me. I open it and find a refrigerator filled with fruit, cheese, and a pitcher of milk. I pour some into my coffee.

"You a guest or do you work here?" I ask.

"Neither one," he says, pouring himself a cup of coffee. "I live down the block and pop in some mornings when I'm too lazy to brew my own."

When I went to bed last night I supposed I would awake this morning to find that my excitement at arriving in Savannah had toned down some. But on the contrary, this town—reminding me a great deal of festive New Orleans—seems so filled with spontaneous characters such as this gentlemanly cup-of-coffee thief that I may have to put the pack back on to keep me down-to-earth.

"I just got into town yesterday," I say, sipping my coffee as the stranger studies me.

"A crow feather, poisonous rattler, and a little angel," he says, craning his neck as if looking to find something more on my hat. "What are you, a religious snake handler?"

"Worse than that. I'm a writer. I've been walking the route of Sherman's March to the Sea to gather stories along the way."

"You've got to contact Arthur Gordon. His family knew Sherman. His aunt Daisy founded the Girl Scouts and sat on the general's knee when he occupied the city. Besides that, Arthur's a ball of fire himself. Some years ago he was editor in chief of *Cosmopolitan* magazine and wrote a bestseller about World War Two that sold almost a million copies."

His information takes me back to the Juliette Gordon Low Highway only a few miles from my home and how I drove down it to get to Atlanta with thoughts of contacting the very family I'm now being told about. This coincidence excites me so much that a part of me wants to tell this total stranger about how I came to stay with Rowena and what a rare discovery we made. But I decide to simply thank him for the advice and sip my coffee with increased knowledge that the odyssey is still alive and well. The Great Goat has baaed once again.

"Can I pour you more coffee?" I ask, holding the pot.

"I've got to go," he says. "Yes, I'll take it with me."

After coffee, I go back to my room and phone Arthur Gordon. Road Rabbit, sitting atop my pack next to the staff, seems to bend his long ears toward me.

"I don't have time to meet with you," says Mr. Gordon. "I'm packing today and leaving tomorrow for New England. Contact my sister, Mary, and maybe she'll invite you over to chew the fat."

Disappointed, I hang up. But when I phone his sister, Mary Gordon Platt, who is eighty-six years old, I get a voice that I like better than his. She invites me to her home this afternoon around five.

With several hours before I'm to see Mary I bounce from the B&B toward the river in hope of meeting the crew on that boat out to save the world; fellow travelers often have kindred spirits.

But before I get to the water I spot the Colonial Cemetery, where morning fog still floats among the graves. A spiderweb as big as an umbrella stretches between two limbs and quivers in the breeze. If the spider in its dew-covered center had been here when Sherman's men arrived, it would've seen Union soldiers use hammers and chisels to change dates on tombstones; one reads 127 YEARS OLD instead of 27 YEARS OLD. They also removed Southern bodies from the crypts to turn the tombs into housing. Most of the Yanks, however, lived in a shantytown they built next to the graveyard. Burning garbage and an open sewer put a stink in the makeshift paradise.

"It is rather a vile place to come a thousand miles to camp," said Chaplain Hight of the 58th Indiana.

But while in Savannah the soldiers were paid for the first time in months and turned the stay into a party. If blacks rattling bones and singing and dancing in the streets at night didn't win a man's fancy he could slide into one of many bordellos that thrived on the city's new cash flow. Dice and poker were as close as the nose on a man's face, and if that was too slow for a soldier's taste he could bet on races where his comrades rode champion horses stolen from Georgia plantations. Then, if he blew all of his pay, he could swim for free in the Savannah River and hope he wasn't so drunk as to mistake a Rebel torpedo for a friendly log.

Arriving at the water, I discover eight others have gathered to gawk at the hippie boat, its yin and yang sail flapping in the wind. On the deck is the crew of two. One is a muscular black man and the other, white, is slender and in his forties with a long beard decorated with red, blue, and yellow beads. Barefoot, he wears a gold ring on his big toe. I half expect a near-naked belly dancer to pop from the cabin jingling bells. The bearded man pours tobacco from a pouch of Bugle Boy to roll a cigarette, and just beneath him, on the side of the boat, is a sign that reads:

WISH LIST

Solar Panel
Wind Generator

"The boat is made from stuff society discards," says the white man. "It contains four hundred fifty car tires and twelve thousand plastic liter bottles. The whole idea of the journey is to make people aware of how wasteful we are in today's world. That and to have as much fun as possible along the way."

"Hear, hear," comes a voice from the back of the crowd, and I turn to behold the white-bearded harmonica player on his bicycle. "Nothing is more wasted in our society than the opportunity to enjoy life. Please, no applause, I want to remain a modest man."

He bows as if he's just finished directing the world's greatest orchestra, and his little red sign saying HI, MY NAME'S ARTHUR. IT'S MY BIRTHDAY dangles from the pin on his shirt. On his handlebars is a five-gallon plastic bucket with a golf club sticking from it along with a plastic bag stuffed with notebooks and a fishing net.

"From here we sail to New York," says the black man to the crowd, "where MTV will be interviewing us before we try to make it all the way to Europe."

I'm not certain their boat will endure the Atlantic, but I find it curious that right here where the black and white comrades follow their dream is the very spot where the first slaves were docked and sold in Savannah. (Did you know that the song "Amazing Grace" was written by a slave trader after his ship wrecked, and he started to drown but was saved by one of the captured Africans?) In fact, the cobblestones I'm standing on were used as the ballast in the slave ships. Then, in the Civil War, the Rebs used it to build fortifications in the river like this dock.

Arthur rolls his bicycle over the cobblestones and through the onlookers to get a better look at the wish list on the side of the boat. Studying it for several seconds, he pulls a pen from his pocket, writes on the back of his birthday sign, and turns it over so all can see.

ARTHUR'S WISH LIST

A new rowboat
A place to live
A pretty woman to love me
A free lunch
ANYTHING YOU'LL GIVE ME

I'm so taken with his exuberant, carefree manner that I can't resist walking over to him. He turns the wish list toward me, a light in his blue eyes.

"I have a magnifying glass in my bag if you have trouble seeing," he says.

His clothes are not only clean, but have been ironed. He strikes me as a mixture of Walt Whitman and Mark Twain. Yet, he is distinctly himself.

"If you took a speed-reading class," he says, still holding the wish list toward me, "you should get a refund."

He appears to be in his late sixties or early seventies and I've never seen such a rare combination of strength and vulnerability glued together with impishness.

"Can I borrow your pen?" I ask.

He hands it to me and I put a check mark by *A free lunch*.

"You mean it?" he says, humility in his voice.

"Yeah, don't you?" I say, pointing to the wish list.

"I mean everything I say," he sings, and then hurries the harmonica from his shirt pocket to his lips for a few quick notes before sticking it back in his pocket to sing again. "I say everything I mean that's why I stay so lean. People don't want to hear what isn't so very dear and tips are like lips, they only fall on those who makes others feel just fine. And with this lunch you're about to buy, could I have a glass of wine?"

The crowd at the save-the-world boat studies Arthur and I

as if he's a bit flipped and I'm suspect myself for talking with him. Well, some are called to save the world while others are simply called to lunch.

"Where would you like to eat?" I ask.

Chapter Forty

Arthur and I take a table at a sidewalk café. Since he asked for that glass of wine it crosses my mind that he may be a boozer. But he looks too healthy for that and after one glass of burgundy he refuses more.

"No," he says. "I allow myself one beer or wine per day and that's all. I have to stay in shape for my performances as well as my autumn trips."

"You look like you're on a constant trip," I say.

He cocks his head just so and raises an eyebrow as if its slightest movement could tie me in knots before I knew what happened. But then, in the same breath, his blue eyes offer such warmth that they promise to free me.

"I guess you'd better understand me if you saw one of my billboards," he says.

He reaches into his wallet, removes a business card, and hands it to me. I stick my spoon in the bowl of clam chowder and examine the card. It is as full of life as Arthur is. A smiling stick figure rows a boat surrounded by jumping fish, hearts, singing flowers, musical palm trees, and a winking sun. In the center of the card is ARTHUR C. BRANANON, BORN JUNE 27, 1921.

Arthur jerks a comb from his pocket and runs it through his big white bushy beard.

"A beard is like a woman," he sings. "It needs to be touched every day, otherwise a man must pay."

Our waitress brings more bread and he sticks the comb back into his pocket.

"My dear," he says, "if I were a young man, I'd write you a

love letter you would never forget. But since I'm an old man
I've forgotten what to write. I hope you will forgive me this
small shortcoming and love me just the same?"

The waitress, in her early twenties and blessed with great
beauty, giggles and walks away.

"Do you think I won her over?" says Arthur, his face as
vulnerable as his voice.

"She won't be able to sleep tonight," I say, turning back to
his card. "What does the *C* stand for in your name?"

"Cowboy," he says. "I also go by Wizard, Mayor of Johnson
Square, and Torch."

"I see the cowboy and the wizard. What's with Mayor and
Torch?"

"I've performed for over twenty years at Johnson Square,
and Torch because I carried a flamethrower in World War Two.
Didn't want to use the damned thing, but my sergeant made
me. I didn't want to be in the Marines, either, but I did four
years and two tours of Guadalcanal. Only good thing that came
of it is my monthly veteran's check and I got to see *Gone With
the Wind* twenty-one times on a sheet stretched between two
palm trees. I wouldn't have joined the Marines, but I grew up
in an orphanage here in Savannah and when I turned eighteen
I had some trouble with the law. The judge told me I could go
to jail or to war. I could never stand being locked up. I have to
be free or I'll go crazy. Some think I am anyway, but I always
get the last laugh. See the rowboat on my card?"

"And on your wish list too."

"I've had three stolen from me the past ten years. Each
September I row from here to Florida down the Intracoastal
Waterway."

"That's several hundred miles," I say, a bit impressed and
feeling a touch of brotherhood with this fellow wanderer.

"I live in a tent and fish for my food. When I was a child an
old man taught me how to make nets and I do that now to sell
or trade them. A lot of the time people I meet in boats give me
shrimp or fish for nothing."

He hurries from his chair to his bicycle and returns with the
plastic bag from the handlebars. He pulls out a map and

spreads it on the table, holding down the corners with forks and knives.

"All those *X*'s are my secret camping spots between here and Florida," he says.

"You live in a tent now?"

"No, but I may have to in a few days. I worked for a friend of mine for twenty years, doing wiring, and he owned the apartment building where I've lived all this time. He never charged me a penny, but he died last week of a heart attack and his daughter inherited the place. I don't know if she's going to kick me out or not."

"That's why you put *A place to live* on your wish list."

"Would you buy me a house? Okay, how about a rowboat?"

"Why do you keep getting them swiped?"

"People see them where I camp and just take them. I can't stand there all day like a guard at Buckingham Palace."

"You don't seem very angry at the thieves."

"Oh, sometimes I boil. Never do that to coffee; it makes it taste horrible. But being angry isn't going to row me from here to Florida. I've got to get another boat. Would you like to take my picture? I'll only charge *you* a dollar. Of course, if you want to tip on top of that it's up to you."

"You know what, Arthur-Cowboy-Wizard-Torch-Mayor-of-Johnson-Square?"

"Oh, you have a memory."

"I get the feeling you're pulling my leg from here to Atlanta."

"That'll be a dollar more. Whoa, look what time it is."

"But you're not wearing a watch."

"I go by table time. All the food's gone."

The waitress brings the check. While I dig into my wallet he offers to read her palm. She giggles and lets him hold her hand.

"I see cash coming your way very shortly," he says.

I hand the young woman my credit card.

"Okay," says Arthur, releasing her hand. "Sometimes I confuse money with plastic. But it's not as bad as people who confuse living with working. Which reminds me, I've got a performance to do at two on Johnson Square or I'll never get a new rowboat. Since you're cheap, perhaps you could at least buy me the oars. Don't look so serious. I enjoyed the lunch. Thank you. Maybe next time you'll take us to a place with some atmosphere."

He stuffs his map back into his plastic bag and hurries to his bicycle. He slings his leg over the seat and starts to pedal away, but circles back.

"You have my card," he sings, "and you know where I live. Come by sometime and we'll swap some lies. If you get hungry I'll cook you some fries. We can eat them in Hong Kong with pickled flies."

He disappears around the corner and I hear the harmonica music begin to play. The waitress returns with my credit card.

"Who was that masked man?" she asks.

Long after the harmonica music fades into the wind I'm still tingling from meeting Arthur. Old Southern fox that he is, I find myself starting to care about him. I have at least a little understanding of such a Rebel and realize his deep need to touch others as well as have his life stirred by them. As I leave the café I'm tempted to swing over to Johnson Square to watch him perform. But I plan on staying several days in Savannah and will catch his daily two o'clock show another time. Right now, thinking of meeting with Mary at five, I walk to the Girl Scouts' headquarters, a beautiful Victorian house, where Juliette Gordon Low—Mary's aunt Daisy—lived when she founded the famed organization. The sidewalk is lined with many Brownies and Girl Scouts waiting to tour their heroine's home.

"Why do you like the Girl Scouts?" I ask one of the girls in line as I recall that Debi was a Girl Scout for eleven years.

"You get to do fun stuff," she says, "and it makes you more confident."

"You make new friends, too," says a second girl, who's black.

"My mother was a Girl Scout," says a third girl, "and she makes me do whatever she did."

"Don't you like it?" I ask.

"I like my mother too," says the girl. "But I don't want to be her. Madonna's cool though."

I was a Cub Scout and certainly have nothing against the Girl Scouts or Brownies, but standing in line is the last thing I want to do right now. I head on down the street to Madison Square and the elegant Green house. This was where Sherman stayed while in Savannah, and that may be appropriate because it was the first home in Savannah to have gaslights. Sherman's eyes could see flames wherever he looked, tiny echoes of the fires his men had set between here and Atlanta. The general was most definitely in the limelight as the newest and greatest Federal hero. His military success across Georgia had not blurred his good business sense either. Following the advice of a U.S. Treasury agent, A. G. Browne, Sherman telegraphed President Lincoln:

> *I beg to present to you as a Christmas gift the city of Savannah, with one hundred fifty heavy guns and plenty of ammunition, also about 25,000 bales of cotton.*

Sherman's gesture not only pleased Lincoln, it thrilled the entire Union as the news spread like confetti in wind among Northern papers. But for a gift that grandiose it's not totally unexpected that a rotten apple would be found among the rubies and diamonds, and for Sherman it came in the wrapping of Secretary of War Edwin Stanton.

Stanton, upon learning of the cruel treatment of blacks at Ebenezer Creek, was disgusted and traveled to Savannah to see Sherman about the incident. It was common knowledge that the general had a dislike of blacks and Stanton was determined to make him squirm. Nor was this the first time he and Stanton had bumped shoulders over African Americans. The general had opposed letting them enlist as soldiers.

Sherman defended General Davis, who was in charge during the incident at Ebenezer Creek, but Stanton wasn't satisfied. He instructed Sherman to assemble twenty of Savannah's black leaders and preachers to further explore racial problems. They met at Sherman's headquarters in the Green house and

when Stanton asked the general to leave the room, Sherman
was angered.

> It certainly was a strange fact that the great War Secretary
> should have catechized Negroes concerning the character of a
> general who had commanded a hundred thousand men in bat-
> tle, had captured cities, conducted sixty-five thousand men
> successfully across four hundred miles of hostile territory, and
> had just brought tens of thousands of freedmen to a place of
> security.

This morning over coffee, thinking I would later visit the
Green house, I dug into Henry Hitchcock's journal to see
what he had to say about the blacks in Savannah. He wrote
while sitting in Sherman's bedroom:

> After we came to this house they soon began to find out that
> he [Sherman] would see them, and for several days there was
> a constant stream of them, old and young, men, women, and
> children, black, yellow and cream-colored, uncouth and well-
> bred, bashful and talkative—but always respectful and well-
> behaved. . . . Almost all of them who have talked at all have
> spoken of our success and their deliverance with an appar-
> ently religious feeling.—"Been prayin' for you all long time,
> Sir, prayin' day and night for you, and now, bless God, you is
> come. . . ."

While Sherman puffed on his cigar in the hallway, behind
closed doors the black leaders and preachers had only praise
for him. But even after Stanton left Savannah the general wondered, in a letter written to General Henry Halleck:

> But the Nigger? Why, in God's name, can't sensible men let
> him alone?

I'm not at all surprised that Sherman was a chameleon about
race. I have yet to meet a man who is totally without fear,
ignorance, or an undetermined dose of cultural brainwashing,

and the one who claims he is makes me almost as uncomfortable as the one who brags of his prejudice. When, though, in the name of humanity—if not plain old common sense itself—will men, women, and children gather at the river to wash themselves free of the dirt created by racism? Isn't it long overdue that we let the stream of life take away that dirt, which grows only thorns?

But I'm certainly no squeaky-clean Rebel myself. I confess modest annoyance with people who speak so softly that I can't understand them. This is true now as I tour the Green house and enter Sherman's bedroom. The guide, a little old lady with a sweet face, speaks as if she is deep in the bottom of a well and refuses to apply volume for fear that the earthen walls will tumble down atop her. To hear what she says, I must stand close to her and bend toward her mouth; I may look like a masher trying to smell the perfume on her neck. When she turns toward me each time, I straighten back up like a Southern gentleman, her words becoming once again so faint that I want to drop a rope down into the well and pull her up into the light of day. But when she leads the group from the general's bedroom, I linger to place my hand on the marble mantel where Sherman himself must've placed his many times as he puffed his cigars. I can see smoke rings filling the room like the general's newly acquired fame. His constantly nervous foot, however, reveals his thoughts about Stanton's racial confrontation. The hero is not without his slings and arrows.

Chapter Forty-one

It's a few minutes till five o'clock when I arrive at Mary's modest but charming house. My knock on the door is so brisk that a woodpecker like Clyde himself might turn a beak, if only to consider pecking my sometimes wooden head.

The door opens to a very slender lady in a well-tailored dress who brings Katharine Hepburn to mind. That she's twice my age hasn't dulled her beauty, and her eyes have the light and joy any young woman with a lick of sense would admire and perhaps envy. Her mother and Daisy were sisters, and the Gordons were among the principal founders of Savannah. Mary's great-grandfather, William Gordon, not only started the city's cotton exchange but owned the Central Railroad of Georgia, which the Union soldiers destroyed as they marched to the sea. As I returned to the B&B after seeing the Green house, I strolled over a few blocks to behold a monument honoring the Gordons' contribution to Savannah. Now, here before me, Mary is a living tribute to her family and, I hope, a good storyteller concerning Sherman's visits to the Gordon home in 1864.

"Please come in, Mr. Ellis," she says as we shake hands. Her wrinkled skin is warm.

"It is very kind of you to let a total stranger into your home," I say, taking a chair with a view of a life-size oil painting of Daisy.

"Oh," she begins with a musical laugh, "two Southerners are never really strangers."

"That's true," I say, thinking that Southern hospitality is

very much alive and well in the New South. "But why, do you suppose, is that the case?"

"Well"—more of her inspiring laughter—"you feel comfortable with what you see and experience the most. Most Southerners know their traditions like the face of a friend. And just like that friend, we may not prosper from all he or she is, but we still know what we can count on. Can I now count on you letting me make you a drink, sir?"

She disappears into the kitchen to pour us bourbon and water and soon returns with the drinks on a silver tray. Her movements, though fragile, reflect her sophisticated upbringing; they're smooth and graceful. That her hand trembles just a bit when she gives me the glass makes her all the more human. I try to get to that part of myself and put her at ease by telling her a few things about myself and what I've experienced on my journey. She seems especially interested in how close I am to my mother and two sisters.

"I've been playing a game with myself on this march to help me feel that my family is safe," I say.

"Oh?"

"When I lived in New Orleans for many years," I say, "I learned to cook Cajun food. I guess I got it from Mother, but I've always felt that cooking and giving people your best dish is one way of letting them know you care. So sometimes at night on this walk when I've had a fire to cook on I've envisioned my whole family there with me. I've served them some mighty tasty Cajun feasts out of a pot not much bigger than a coffee cup. Not only did it make me feel close to them, but their dishes were pretty easy to clean too."

There goes her enchanting laughter again.

"Family's crucial," she says. "I've always been crazy about my brother, Arthur—a Rhodes scholar, by the way. He's in his eighties, like myself, and we're the only ones left in the family who knew Daisy. When we pass on, that personal link will bon voyage with us."

"I see you inherited a painting of her."

"I'd like to say that's true. But we cut cards to see who would get it and I was lucky with an ace."

She once again breaks into her gentle, musical laughter and I'm more taken with it, and her eyes and face, than I am with the historic painting.

"Daisy was a high card herself long before she founded the Girl Scouts," Mary says. "I was eighteen when she died, so I knew her quite well. The year she died she threw me a wild party. Fortunately she remembered this one, but she had a habit of inviting people over and then forgetting it till they showed up at her door. Anyway, my party was complete with a big band and little favors from Europe for all the guests. She loved to dress like a Gypsy and went about the party telling fortunes. I remember [that wonderful carefree laughter again] right before the bash she was disappointed that her camellias hadn't bloomed, so she took a pair of scissors next door to her neighbor's house and cut their flowers. Then she sneaked back home and taped them to her bushes. She reminded me a bit of my father. I was born on April Fools' Day and he was always up to something. He was in the cotton business, and one birthday he presented me with a cake made all of cotton.

"Oh, but listen at *me* talk about myself. Here, let's back up a piece and look at Daisy. She was four years old when General Sherman arrived in Savannah. He was close friends with the Kinzie family, Daisy's grandparents back in Chicago. In fact, Daisy's grandfather was the Union paymaster. Well, Sherman had brought letters from the Kinzies to Granny and showed up one day at the Gordon home to deliver them. She was said to be warm to him, but she had had a rough time in Savannah because some thought she was a Yankee spy, since she was from Chicago. More than once people dumped garbage on her lawn. Granny had a real bite, though, and once called on a Savannah socialite. The butler said she wasn't in and Granny told him that the next time the woman left the house she should take her head with her. Granny had seen her peek from the upstairs window. She met Grandpa when she was eighteen and touring the Yale library with a group of girls. She had wandered off on her own and was sliding down the railing of the stairs when she crashed into Grandpa and crushed his hat. I'm pretty sure Daisy got part of her spirit from her.

"Sherman came to the Gordon home several times, and all the while Grandpa was a Confederate captain under Wheeler, away in South Carolina. One of his letters to Granny expressed concern that she was being friendly to the enemy, but he sure didn't have to worry about Daisy or her sister, Eleanor, being anything but Rebels through and through. Daisy liked the general a great deal, but when he came that first time and sat her on his knee she put her fingers in his hair, searching for the horns the devil himself was supposed to wear. Sherman was good-humored about it and told General Howard how delightful the Gordon girls were. Howard had children of his own and missed them terribly. He visited the Gordon home then himself and Daisy was intrigued with the loss of his arm.

" 'Do you feel sorry for me?' he asked.

" 'Yes,' said Daisy. 'What happened to it?'

" 'I lost it in battle,' he said.

" 'A Yankee got it?'

" 'No,' he said, 'a Rebel blew it off.'

" 'I bet it was my papa,' Daisy said. 'He has shot lots of Yankees.' "

Mary's laughter fills the room once again and maybe it's the single bourbon that does it to me, but I think I see new life in the painting of Daisy on the wall. I certainly feel more life in me as I watch Mary waltz with such strong family memories.

"Sherman gave Daisy and her sister the first sugar candy they ever tasted," Mary says. "But his gestures of kindness went much further than that. He arranged a white flag of truce so Granny could be escorted to South Carolina to meet Grandpa. Then, when orders came that the families of Rebel officers in Savannah had to leave the city, Sherman arranged passage on a steamer to New York for Granny and her daughters. From there they took a train to Chicago. On the way Daisy and Eleanor heard a group of people in their car singing Union songs such as 'John Brown's Body' and 'We'll Hang Jeff Davis to a Sour Apple Tree.' It was more than the Georgia girls could bear and they began to shout:

Jeff Davis rides a milk-white horse
And Lincoln rides a mule—
Jeff Davis is a gentleman,
And Lincoln is a fool!

"Granny tried to make them shut up, but the passengers started to laugh.

" 'They shouldn't hang Jeff Davis on a *sour* apple tree,' Daisy said, 'because he's Papa's friend. I wouldn't care if they hung him on a *sweet* apple tree, but not a *sour* one.'

"Later on in Chicago," Mary says, "when the war was over, a group of people gathered on Michigan Avenue in front of where Daisy lived and began to sing in celebration. Daisy thought the Rebels had won and climbed atop her gate to sing 'Dixie' at the top of her lungs. An onlooker finally set her straight.

" 'The Confederacy is gone,' he told her.

"Daisy was heartbroken.

" 'But where did it go?' she asked."

Mary raises the glass to her lips and drinks the last of her bourbon and water. As I do the same I find myself turning yet again to the painting of Daisy.

"Well," I say, "she may have wondered what became of the Confederacy, but sounds like she found herself by organizing the Girl Scouts."

"Oh, she never lost her spark, that's for sure. The day she presented the newly designed shoes for the girls, she wore a pair and stood on her head so those around her could get a better look. I don't know if the Girl Scouts would've been so successful at another time in history, but with it being organized to help with World War One it fit in perfectly. The Scouts sold Liberty Bonds, worked at Red Cross centers, and planted thousands of gardens. Daisy couldn't have been prouder of her girls and she often dressed in her Girl Scout uniform just to show that pride. Her belt carried a knife, a whistle, and a tin drinking cup. She became a very popular speaker and at one gathering, when a friend was speaking, she was disappointed that the audience wasn't applauding. Daisy was sitting way in back of the speaker and couldn't hear well enough to know what she was saying, but every time she paused Daisy filled in the silence by clapping like mad. It wasn't till the end of the speech that she learned that the whole talk had been about her. Oh, my, she was a card."

"Sounds like you were very close."

"Yes, it was difficult for anybody not to like her. She was very tender and generous. The year she threw that big party for me she already knew she was dying of cancer but kept it secret."

"I empathize with you," I say. "It reaches me in a very personal way."

"Does it?"

"My father kept it a secret that he had heart trouble," I say. "The last two years of his life he had become rather gentle and more at peace. I often saw something new and profound in his eyes when he looked at me and especially when we worked together in the garden or walked up to the cabin we built together in the woods. I thought I was seeing the wisdom of age in his eyes. But it was even more than that. He was already telling me good-bye."

"You honor an old lady by letting her in this way," she says.

Then, as with Rowena, I find myself enjoying the silence with Mary—as if we don't always have to rely upon the sound of words to hear the song.

"I've held only one thing against Daisy," Mary says.

"Yeah?"

Mary points to the wall behind me and I turn to study the oil painting of a very pretty child in a Girl Scout uniform.

"That's you?" I ask.

"When Daisy told me she had arranged for me to sit for a painting I was very excited. That is, till I discovered I had to wear that outfit."

She breaks yet again into some of the most beautiful and uplifting laughter I've ever heard. I look back at the child in the painting and then to Mary, seeing her aunt Daisy still sitting atop that Chicago gate singing "Dixie" at the top of her lungs.

Chapter Forty-two

The two hours I spend with Mary do more than entertain me with stories about the Civil War. The more she talks the more I begin to see her and how those in the past live on in her soul and personality. At my request she gets out the family photo album and I sit beside her as we crawl into the time machine to behold her as a child with hair as red as Sherman's when he was a boy. Then, as I see her grow into womanhood, marry, raise a family, and bury a husband, it takes me closer to her and those I love.

"You must miss your mother," Mary says. "I'm sure, and especially after your father's death, she misses you."

"Yes," I say, "I've phoned her every few days to let her know I'm okay, but it's not the same as looking into her eyes. I miss my girlfriend as well. We've had some trouble over my taking this trip and there's a letter from her now waiting for me in the Savannah post office. I'm both excited and afraid to pick it up. We may go our separate ways."

"There are so many roads," she says. "We're blessed when we can travel on one with the person we love."

The road from the palms of Savannah to the oaks of Tanager begin to call me now, but I don't want to leave town without seeing Mary again, and I ask her if I can come back.

"I feel very talkative around you," she says. "You listen as if what I say matters, and I fear I've said too much already. But if you really care to return, you'd make an old lady happy."

I go back to the B&B and watch the sunset from the wrought-iron balcony outside my room. Funny, but the same ball of fire in the sky that scorched me for weeks as I marched, cursing, beneath it is again becoming that miraculous star a man beholds once his mission has made it to the shade. When I was a child Daddy showed me how I could press the tips of my thumb and index finger almost together and peek through them so that it looked like I was holding the moon. I do that now with the setting sun as if it were no bigger than a BB, the star yet another gift from the Great Goat that I might drop into my pocket and carry with the Yankee bullet from the Battle of Griswoldville and the medicine pouch I've carried across Georgia.

I'm sure the rest of the world, however, is grateful on the following morning that I've left the sun in the sky where it belongs.

It's only six o'clock when I wake, and with over two hours before the post office opens I decide to call on Arthur-Cow-boy-Torch-Wizard-Mayor-of-Johnson-Square. He told me yesterday at lunch that he has breakfast every morning at seven in a place called Larry's, and I head that way.

I spot Arthur's bicycle parked by the entrance to the café and today he must be feeling patriotic; an American flag sticks from the handlebars and waves in glory in the early morning breeze.

Entering the restaurant, I discover Arthur seated in a booth all alone and writing in a notebook. I walk over to him; his birthday sign is once again pinned to his shirt.

"Mind if I join you?" I ask.

"Oh, it's you. Have a seat. You're just in time to buy me breakfast. See how I note each day in my journal?"

He points to a circle he has drawn—and eat your heart out, Henry Hitchcock, Arthur has also filled that particular page with tiny drawings of people's faces.

"It's through each circle I step into a new day," Arthur says. "That line there was written about meeting you yesterday. Don't bother to look too closely. I didn't have a lot to say about you," he adds with impish eyes and then looks about for the waitress. "I ordered a scrambled egg, but when I saw it there was too much slime around it. I finally told the waitress

to just fry the damned thing. I could've done it myself if I'd
had the old flamethrower I used to carry."

"You would've made a good Union soldier on the March to
the Sea with that thing shooting fire."

"Bite your tongue, sir. I was Dixie born and will Dixie die.
Besides, to my knowledge, I'm the only living man who can
still kick his heels to do the Sherman Shuffle."

"Sherman Shuffle?"

"That's the dance the citizens of Savannah did when Sherman finally left the city. They were so happy that they danced
in the streets."

"I've never heard of it."

"Of course you've never heard of it. You haven't yet learned
to be that good of a listener. I could teach you to listen that
well, but I don't turn walkers into wise men for nothing. How
much cash are you carrying? Can you get an advance on your
credit card?"

The waitress brings his breakfast.

"Is that better, Arthur?" she asks, winking at me.

"The egg's okay," he says. "But your wink could pick up a
little speed if you don't want me to see it."

She takes my order. When she walks away I discover Arthur
is raising his spoon over his head. He lowers it in slow motion
toward his plate, makes the sound of a mule, and scoops up
some grits, creating a tiny line through them.

"See what a fine row I just plowed?" he says. "Now, in
fertile Southern soil like that you can plant corn that'll grow
ten feet tall. Taller if you put some Miracle-Gro on it. Most
people just don't know how to enjoy breakfast. They gobble
down their grits like they were something ordinary when they
could be having the time of their lives."

I thought I had done pretty fair in my life by learning a little
something from Mustard 101. But next to Professor Arthur, I
see I have a long way to go. Is it possible that my accusing,
Dixie Denial finger should now point to myself? I have, after
all, never plowed my grits with a spoon, and for all my claims
at being a free spirit and a Rebel maybe I've really just begun
to pull the wool from my eyes.

"Oh, hell," Arthur says. "She forgot to bring jelly."

His hand shoots straight over his head as if daring a bolt of lightning to crash through the ceiling and knock him dead. The café is packed and more than a dozen folks start gawking, grinning, pointing, and nudging others to look at Arthur.

"Sometimes two hands are better than one," Arthur says.

He then raises his other hand and looks like Superman trying to fly away from breakfast to rescue a damsel in distress, but running short on aerial power.

"Jelly, jelly, jelly," he begins to sing. "Jelly in my belly is all I ask of you. Then I'll eat my breakfast and I will be through."

The waitress bring his jelly and my breakfast.

"Thank you," he says. "My arms were getting tired."

"Waiting tables is hard work," he says after she leaves, "so I tip fifty cents every time I eat."

"That's not much."

"Yeah, but I'm having to save for my rowboat. Besides, these are rough times. The new landlord left a note on my door last night saying she wants to meet with me this evening. I'm afraid she'll tell me to leave. If she does, I think I know a place I can pitch my tent over on the river. Want to go with me to check on it?"

"What will it cost me?"

"Not a penny."

On one hand Arthur is right, for after breakfast we start for the river and he doesn't ask for one red cent. But it's me who must pedal his bicycle while he rides on back waving at people as if he were grand marshal of a great parade.

"When I tap you on the left shoulder turn left," he says. "Same for the right shoulder. If I tap you on the head once, stop. If I tap twice, go."

He taps me on the back seven times.

"What does that mean?" I ask.

"You're doing a good job. Don't you want a little recognition?"

I sometimes wonder how I get myself into people's lives so quickly, and this is one of those times. I have no desire to be elsewhere right now, but I wish he wouldn't sing quite so loudly, since my ears are close to his mouth.

"Down the road we go, hoo, hoo," he sings. "Down the road the road we go, hee, hee."

When we arrive at a massive cemetery on the river, Arthur taps my right shoulder and I guide the bike through the gates to coast among hundreds of ancient and new graves beneath trees covered with moss. A life-size marble angel appears and Arthur taps that I should stop beside her.

"I come to her almost every day," he says, sliding from the bike. "I'm a photographer as well as a performer and I've caught her beauty in sunrise fog, where she floats among the clouds of heaven itself."

I park the bike and step closer to the stone angel.

"She does look almost alive," I say, daring to touch her wing.

"More so than him," Arthur says, pointing to a new grave some fifty feet away. "It's where they buried my friend, the landlord I worked for all those years."

I follow Arthur to the grave and he kneels to wipe a leaf from it.

"I don't have that many more years left to live either," he says. "Now, don't stand there with a long face. You didn't know him at all and by the time I'm through with you you'll wish you hadn't met me."

He motions for me to follow him and leave the bike in care of the angel. We then walk through a field to a tree overlooking the water, where a small fish leaps into the air and lands with a splash. A crab crawls over a wet rock.

"If I get kicked out of my room," he says, "I'll pitch my tent here. There's a water faucet near the gates to the cemetery and just look at this view of the river and all those birds wading around. I can toss one of my nets at just the right tide and pull in dinner."

"It's a beautiful spot," I say, "but these sand flies are biting the shit out of us."

"Yeah," he says as we slap the insects, "it's not the perfect postcard. If I get kicked out of my room, I don't know what I'll do. How much space do you have where you live in Alabama?"

Chapter Forty-three

Arthur, tapping away as I pedal, directs his bicycle some two miles from the river to the building where he lives on Bull Street, only five blocks from Mary's home. I'm pleased when he invites me into his quarters, which were originally designed to be a giant office. The place has no shower or tub, so Arthur bathes in a child's plastic wading pool. Still, the cozy place is clean and dozens of photos hang on the walls. One is of Bette Davis and another is of Albert Einstein with a quote below it: IMAGINATION IS MORE IMPORTANT THAN KNOWLEDGE. The biggest picture, however, is of Arthur himself playing the harmonica.

"That's a huge picture of yourself there," I tease him. "What happened to the modest man you said you wanted to be down by the docks when I first met you?"

"That's in public," he says. "What I do at home is my own business."

A fishing net that he's repairing is stretched between a chair and the window and the nearby wall is stacked to the ceiling with books.

"You're well-read," I say.

"No, I just collect books for when I get too old to do anything else but read. Here, I want you to read this."

He hands me his Marine discharge papers.

"You weren't fooling," I say. "You did two tours of Guadalcanal and spent four years in the service. Says you were a sharpshooter."

"I wanted to prove it to you."

"Arthur, you don't have anything to prove to me. I like you just fine as you are, not for anything you did."

"Yeah?"

I nod and he digs deeper into the plastic bag where he got the Marine papers. He pulls out his birth certificate and the tip of his index finger shows me where his father was a photographer like himself.

"You were lucky to know your father," he says. "I never knew mine at all. But one day at the orphanage a man showed up and told me my father had just died. He asked if I'd like to see him before he was buried. I said yes and went with him. He'd been living in Savannah all that time and I didn't even know it. When I saw my father lying there I didn't know what I was feeling exactly. He was a total stranger, but I came from him and a woman I never met. Sometimes when I take pictures I think of him."

As I walk from Arthur's place toward the post office I think not only about the experience Arthur had with his father but about what he said about mine: *You were lucky to know your father*. Indeed, I feel exceptionally lucky, especially since my march to the sea was done in part to honor my father and it has turned out to be so filled with wonder and unique experiences and people. And the staff that Daddy had cut for me to make a bow has, in a way, turned out to be one after all. The arrow is made of all that has happened along the way. And just where it will land as it now shoots through time and space is not yet fully known. But part of its destination may depend on what's in the letter from Debi.

When I spot the post office two blocks away my heart quickens. I go inside and the clerk gives me a thick envelope. I step outside and tear it open only to find an audiotape with *Better this way* written on it. I don't have a good feeling and I won't be able to hear the tape till I get back to the B&B. I have a small cassette player in my pack because I sometimes listened to Civil War songs when I camped at night.

Recalling that the save-the-world boat was to leave this morning, I walk to the river to tell the crew good-bye. But when I get there I'm too late. The boat is so far down the river it looks no bigger than a bottle with a note in it, bobbing up and down as it floats to the sea.

As I lean on the railing along the historic dock and gaze across the river into South Carolina—the first state to secede from the Union and often blamed by the Yanks as the evil inspiration for the war—I can almost see Sherman and his 62,000 soldiers marching that way as they leave Savannah, the arson circus fueled to blaze like hell itself once again.

"This march across South Carolina will be one of the most horrible things in the history of the world," said Sherman. "The Devil himself couldn't restrain my men."

Before Henry Hitchcock left Savannah with Sherman to march into South Carolina and help deliver the blows that would end the Civil War, he mailed his diary to his wife in St. Louis as a means of sharing his journey across Georgia with her.

I wonder if I did the right thing by sending Debi photo-copied pages of my journal to share my march with her. Did my recent letter to her get past her most guarded doorways? With her tape in my hand, I walk back to the B&B and place it in my player. Road Rabbit doesn't smile when I click it on to her voice:

It's almost midnight and I'm sitting on the little dock behind Huck Farm, the summer camp where I started cooking for the children here a few days ago. Taco Bell is now a feather in my hat, but I'm not certain where I'd chose to wear it—perhaps south of the border. Here I cook almost anything I want and the kids have nicknamed me Cookie. Can you hear my foot splash the water? How about the rim of my wineglass against the microphone? The moon is bright enough for me to see ripples in the Puget Sound and earlier today a heron waded nearby. I thought of you and your love of cranes and all birds for that matter. You're something of a bird yourself. I'm never cer-tain when you'll want to fly or where you'll go or land. This spring and summer is turning out to be a journey of my own, exploring who I am in this crazy world and who you are and do we fit?

My parents arrived in Washington two weeks ago from teaching in China and they're already busy working on their new house for when

*they retire here in another five years. Watching them pour their hearts
and souls into that dream house has made me think of Tanager and
the addition we've started there. I keep seeing that big hole in the wall
where you removed the window and part of the wall to make a door.
The blue tarp you nailed over it to hold out the rain flaps in my
mind when the wind blows the trees over Huck Farm. That hole in
the cabin is also a hole in my heart, torn there when you insisted on
going on your march without me. I've asked myself, if you truly love
me, how you could be that selfish? The answer has not jumped into
my arms. But seeing my father the past two weeks has reminded me
how powerful the love can be between a father and a child. I know
you almost worshipped your dad and his loss took the breath from
your soul for a while. I hope your journey has allowed you to once
again breathe with him, or that part of him that is you.*

*I've never had the allegiance to the Northwest, where I grew up, as
you have to the South. But your journal is helping me better grasp
what those mountains there mean to you. I have much yet to learn
about the Dixie you find so dear, so thick in your bones and blood.
Your bond with the earth and trees there, however, begins to give me a
little hope because in my daydreams I sometimes walk the trails
we've made together at Tanager and it stirs something within. In
these fantasies I also walk that special trail to the Courting Tree
where we have carved our names inside the heart. I see you sitting
there on its crooked trunk with your feet dangling and sometimes it
does my heart a world of good to push you over backwards with your
feet flying up toward the sky.*

*I always catch you, however, just before you hit the ground. I want
this hole in my heart to heal just as I want that hole in the side of the
cabin to become a door to the addition we started. But it is more
than a door to a new room. Isn't it a passage to who we might
become together? If I could hold you just now I think the feeling itself
could begin to build and heal wood and stone and heart. Yes, I've
chosen you—and us—over China, my darling. Does this mean that I
can accept it the next time you're compelled to march off alone? I'm
not sure and I rather doubt it. But I'm willing to chance it. Besides,
who can say the time won't come when I'll need to follow my own
star solo across some ocean within where my streams have yet to lead
me. Then, my dear, will you be able to handle the route I'm having to*

now walk as I wait and sometimes worry more than I would dare show to beauty or beast?

As for my being a goat woman and traveling across America in a wagon pulled by a herd, I think you've been in the Georgia sun a bit too long. I wish just now I could cool you in the shade of this great Washington moon as we splash our feet in the water. Yes, as when we met in Denver, I would once again rub your sore feet, if you could once again show the same tenderness you did that night. But don't hold back too long, for it's your fire I'm now needing as much as your gentleness. I want to be wrapped in your heat and feel your lips wherever passion leads you. And, wanderer that you are, I haven't a trace of doubt that it would lead you to all the right spots. Oh, baby, to hear one of your reaching-the-end-of-the-trail moans just now would make my foot kick enough water from the Sound to splash all of Seattle with a good, hard rain.

Call me as soon as you can and let me know my Rebel is safe. This very moment I'm holding the moon between my thumb and index finger like you showed me. I think I'll drop it into my glass, pour it full once more, and toast us, knowing that we both behold the same light of the moon as well as what I trust to be that greater light, the love of each other.

As the tape ends I'm overwhelmed with emotion and leap to my feet to swing my right fist high overhead as I give a Rebel yell at the top of my lungs. Lost in ecstasy, I begin to rewind the tape to hear it again as footsteps thunder up the iron stairway to my room. A knock pounds my door. I open it to the B&B manager. His face is urgent and perplexed.

"Is something wrong, sir?" he asks.

"No. I'm just in love."

"I'm glad to hear it," he says as his eyes scan the room and bed as though he might find a wild woman there. "But could you keep it a little more to yourself?"

"I'll try," I say. But I'm not too big on promises today when it comes to controlling my passion.

I lift the tape player and tell him what's just happened. He seems relieved and happy for me as he descends the stairs. I click the tape on to Debi's voice to begin her letter anew, and it's as if, like in some love story come true, a man and woman together are the greatest adventure on earth. Where shall we go now? What shall we do?

Chapter Forty-four

The March to the Sea made Sherman a national hero and one of the greatest generals in American history. But that which gave him such honor and glory also began to haunt him in his later life.

To escape some of the pressure of being so famous, he often attended the theater, preferring Shakespeare, and usually alone because his wife refused to go; she feared being trapped in a burning building. But even in a place of entertainment Sherman was not free. When he entered, the audience usually recognized him and gave a standing ovation. He was such a restless spirit—and who wouldn't be after a life of grand excitement—that he would leave each performance during the intermission to return the next night to see the play's climax.

At almost every function he attended a band felt compelled to play "Marching Through Georgia," which his soldiers had sung over and over again on the March to the Sea. In his final years Sherman grew sick of the song.

"These army meetings," he said, "are becoming to me most oppressive and distasteful, because in spite of my wishes they advertise me and exhibit me as a prominent animal in Barnum's show. I can expect little rest till I reach the cemetery."

Sherman, an asthmatic, died of pneumonia on Valentine's Day in 1891 at the age of seventy-one, in his New York home located at 75 West Seventy-first Street near Central Park. In his last gasp for air, he placed his left hand over his heart as if it were a salute. That night sculptors covered his face with plaster, bringing him one step closer to immortality.

News of the general's death jarred the nation and telegrams and letters poured in to his family. One came from Mark Twain, as did one from Buffalo Bill [Cody]. President Benjamin Harrison, a commander under Sherman during the Atlanta campaign, sent his condolences. Even the newspaper of the city Sherman burned to the ground, the *Atlanta Constitution*, had a few kind words:

> . . . the fact looms up that this man was one of the greatest soldiers of the age. . . . But when the business of war was over—when he had accomplished his mission—he showed a softer side, and men and women, even among his former foes, found him a very lovable man.

Sherman had asked for a simple funeral, but a nation is often as deaf to its heroes as it is to its prophets. In the drawing room of his home his casket was left open and for two whole days people from all walks of life eased along the line to finally behold the face of the giant. On Sherman's face flickered the lights of six nearby candles while an American flag draped the casket along with the general's sword, spurs, hat, and scabbard. He was dressed in full uniform and the Legion of Honor sash.

A special train with military guards carried Sherman from New York to St. Louis. On the front of the engine was a picture of the general and all along the route people gathered in droves to behold his last journey. His old friend Henry Hitchcock, who had made arrangements for him to be buried next to his wife and children in the Calvary Cemetery, met the train.

Confederate General Joseph E. Johnston was honored to be one of Sherman's pallbearers. It was a chilly, windy day and a friend advised Johnston to put his hat back on to avoid catching a cold.

"If I were in his place and he standing in mine," said the old Rebel, "he would not put on his hat."

Five weeks later Johnston died of pneumonia.

As Sherman was lowered into his grave, soldiers from his 13th Infantry fired three shots, followed by the echo of cannons in the distance. A lone musician, standing over the final resting place, played taps.

In the weeks to come, as Sherman had requested on the day he died, a monument was placed over him to read:

FAITHFUL AND HONORABLE

I leave the B&B and walk several blocks toward the river before I spot the monument that towers over Johnson Square, the first of twenty-four squares created in designing the streets of Savannah. I'm headed that way now because it's almost two o'clock and I want to see Arthur perform today.

There's no sign of Arthur when I arrive at the square and I hope nothing has happened to him. For that matter, I feel so good about what Debi said on her tape that I hope no ill fortune has fallen on anyone today. I phoned her as soon as I listened to her tape the second time. I didn't give a Rebel yell when she answered the phone, but I was tempted.

"I've made plane reservations to arrive in Seattle in three days," I told her. "Is that good for you?"

"Yes," came her seductive voice. "That'll give me just enough time to . . ."

"To what?"

"Just hold your horses, Reb," she said. "You'll see when you get here."

Ever since we hung up I've been picking my brain to try to figure out what she's up to. With her great romantic imagination there's just no telling. I don't mind though; the very anticipation arouses me.

I take a seat on a park bench by an old man feeding popcorn to the pigeons. He wears a Masonic ring.

"You from Savannah?" I ask.

"My whole life."

"Have you ever seen a gentleman with a bushy beard perform here?"

"Arthur?" he chuckles. "Everybody in the city knows Arthur."

"A little strange, huh?" I say, seeking an opinion besides my own.

"Some think he is. But we wear our lives by the cloth we've been cut from. Myself, I come here once or twice a week to watch Arthur just so I don't start taking myself too seriously. My wife died last year and a man of my age can let the world close in on him, if he's not careful. Arthur's my medicine. A spoonful at a time usually does the trick. Here comes the old coot now."

"Why are you feeding that popcorn to the birds?" Arthur shouts as his bicycle rolls into the square. "*I* eat popcorn."

Arthur sticks his hand into the bag of popcorn and stuffs it into his mouth. Two pieces fall to the ground and six pigeons peck them.

"Not enough salt on it," Arthur says, leaning his bike against a tree. "And it's messed up my mouth for playing."

The old man sitting beside me shakes his head and throws more popcorn to the birds. Arthur, after placing his five-gallon plastic bucket in my lap for safekeeping, pulls a toothbrush from the bag on his handlebars and begins brushing his teeth. Tourists gawk.

"I treat my harmonica with respect," Arthur says, his birthday sign still pinned to his shirt. "Last thing on earth I want to do is insult it by blowing pieces of bad popcorn into its soul. Most people don't even realize a musical instrument is alive, but it is."

He takes a swig of water from a canteen fastened to his bike's back fender and spits it on the brush. When he puts the water container away, he begins to exercise his mouth, twisting it up and down and sideways.

"Me, me, me, me," he sings. "You, you, you, you."

"What's the name of that song, Arthur?" I ask.

"Can't you see I don't have time to be interviewed right now, that I'm about to go onstage?"

"Sorry, Arthur. Do you do the Sherman Shuffle this show?"

He grabs the plastic bucket from my lap and raises the open end to my ear, where he sticks his mouth as if we're having a very private and urgent meeting.

"Don't ever let anyone hear you say I can do the Sherman Shuffle," he whispers. "I would be hounded to death by the press and I want to remain a modest man. Is that clear?"

"Yes," I whisper into the plastic bucket.

Arthur then takes that bucket and places it upside down in the center of the square. Resting his right foot atop it, he begins to play his harmonica, sounding like a freight train roaring across Georgia. The more onlookers who gather, the more Arthur gives of himself through his music. Every now and then he spins around on one foot and lifts the bucket to his mouth to create an echo as he sings, sounding a bit like Bob Dylan:

> I loved Mary Lou, but now she's gone.
> I have no boat, I have no home.
> I'm a bicycle sailor with rubber galoshes on.
> If you get into trouble just sing this song.

Then he places his right foot atop the bucket again and returns to playing the harmonica as if he had never stopped. For the first time it dawns on me that one of the things I like about Arthur is that he reminds me a little of my father.

> Birds can't fly to the moon
> Rabbits don't sing to loons
> Fish don't bite at noon
> People don't really need spoons

"When Arthur came home from World War Two," says the old man next to me on the bench, "he bought a white suit, hat, and cane and left for fame and fortune in Hollywood. He ended up hitchhiking and hopping trains to get there. Then he wandered around the streets playing his harmonica hoping somebody would discover him and put him in the movies. Well, you see what the Mayor of Johnson Square does today."

A historical marker on the square says that where Arthur now stands is also where Chekilli, principal chief of the Creek Nation, once retold the myth of the origin of his people.

Henry Clay, Daniel Webster, and John Wesley also spoke on the same spot. My, oh, my, how men throughout the centuries try to make their marks in history.

> I loved Mary Lou, but now she's gone.
> I have no boat, I have no home.
> I'm a bicycle sailor with rubber galoshes on.
> If you get into trouble just sing this song.

Those that gathered around Arthur leave when he offers his plastic bucket as a fine home for tips. Even the old man by me on the bench walks away without dropping a penny into the container. It's easy to see in Arthur's blue eyes that he has felt better. Maybe I flatter myself, but I suspect, judging by how he looks my way, that he's a bit embarrassed because he had hoped to show me how much money he could earn with his talent. I thought his performance was great and I understand how some days strangers are glued to their pocket change. But then a small boy, holding his father's hand, walks to the bucket and drops a dollar into it. Arthur's face lights up with new hope and it looks too good to see it fade. I walk over and place a five-dollar bill in the bucket.

"It took you long enough," says Arthur, the gleam in his eyes still singing a song.

Chapter Forty-five

The day I'm to leave Savannah I load my pack one final time on this odyssey; Road Rabbit's long ears are the last to go in. I pay my B&B bill and put the pack in the trunk of the one-way rented car that will take me back to the mountains of north Alabama.

The past few days I've divided my time between Arthur and Mary, and I don't think the Great Goat could've picked two more diverse Southerners for me to grow close to as I end the journey. Mary, on the one hand, comes from a privileged family in Savannah. Her great-grandfather was mayor of the city several times. On the other hand, Arthur, the humble Mayor of Johnson Square, didn't know his family at all and grew up poor. Still, each is rich in his own special way and makes growing older a more inviting path. I ache a bit, however, at thoughts of telling them good-bye.

I drive over to Mary's house and when I enter I no longer wait in the living room to receive a drink. I go into the kitchen and help her. Today we skip the bourbon and sip cranberry juice as we sit on the couch together below the painting of Daisy. It warms me that Mary now trusts me enough to reveal intimate little things about herself.

"I went for a drive with a friend of mine this morning," she says, once again offering her musical laughter. "I stopped the car in a spot overlooking the park. My friend is my age and we could see ourselves when we were children playing there together. Then we lit two cigarettes and smoked like we were getting away with something that would shake the world if it only knew. I told her she should start using her cane and she told me I should use mine."

Mary begins to laugh so hard that she can hardly stop.

"Then we each got out of the car and with the cigarettes still in our hands," she continues, "we began to have this foot race across the park. Of course, it was all we could do to barely walk, but it was the race of the century for us, smoke rising from our old hands like Olympic torches."

When I prepare to leave, she walks me to the door. I want to ease my arms around her and give a gentle squeeze, but she is so fragile I fear I might hurt her. She grasps my need, however, and gives me the most beautiful wink I've ever gotten from a woman of any age.

I crawl into the car and drive to Larry's, where I find Arthur eating lunch in a booth by the wall. I sit across from him and give him a paper bag with Kmart printed on it.

"Happy birthday," I say. "Sorry I didn't get a chance to wrap it."

"Me too."

He opens the bag and finds a photo album.

"I might even put one of your pictures in it," he says. "Thank you. You've been bringing me good luck too. My new landlord not only told me I could stay in the room as long as I wanted, but she gave me twenty shirts her father left behind when he died. I'm going to sell half of them and put the money toward my rowboat. I found one for sale that belongs to a college kid and he's giving me a good deal. I want you to pedal us down to the docks so I can show it to you."

"We can go in my car."

"Car?"

"I rented one. Remember, I said I was leaving today."

"*Leaving?*"

As I drive away from the café Arthur taps me on the right shoulder.

"We're not on the bike," I say. "Why don't you just tell me when to turn?"

"You need to stay in practice."

We arrive at the docks on the Intracoastal Waterway and I

park the car. Getting out, I find Arthur still seated. I go to his rolled-down window.

"What's wrong?" I ask. "I thought we were getting out here to see the boat you want."

"I want you to see it," he says. "But can't you show a little respect to an elder and open the door for me?"

"You're pretty demanding, Arthur," I say as I open the door.

"You just wait till I tell you what I've got for you," he says, leading the way down the docks to a rowboat ten feet off the ground on a storage rack. "She's a beauty, ain't she?"

"All aluminum. Looks pretty solid."

"Plenty big enough for two people."

"Don't see why not."

"Then you'll row to Florida with me?"

"I can't," I say, more than just a little touched. "My girlfriend's waiting for me."

"I could show you things you've never seen before. I have camping spots that are free of flies. We won't get bitten there. I know people along the way you'll find fascinating. Not as fascinating as me, maybe, but not sticks in the mud either."

"I'm honored, Arthur. I know what a loner you are."

"But you won't go?" he asks, his blue eyes sad.

"I'm never sure when the road will call. Could I have a rain check?"

"Will you give me a blank check?"

He tells me I can join him at anytime on his autumn trek and I drive, complete with tapped shoulders, back to his bicycle parked at the café. I leave the car and walk him to his bike for a formal good-bye.

"Hey," he calls out as I'm about to get back into the car.

Then, there in the café parking lot next to his bicycle with the American flag sticking from the handlebars, he does a military march headed straight my way, pulls a cigarette lighter from his pocket, snaps on the flame, and spins in a circle as the fire seems to chase its own tail.

"In case something were to happen to me," he sings, "I've chosen you to carry on the tradition of the Sherman Shuffle, so get it right."

All the while now his shoulders are going up and down as his hips gyrate Elvis Presley style. Then, without missing a beat, he reverses the spin as he turns up the flame on the lighter. He finally holds the fire stretched out in front of him in his left hand, wiggles his hips yet again, then shuffles his feet back and forth while his right hand shoots to his forehead to salute the great Georgia sky and send me on my merry way.

As I drive across Georgia toward Alabama I feel both the Old South and the New South stir within my heart. If I had any fears when I began my march that the best of the Old had been swallowed by the New, most of them have now been put to rest. I now know that Southern hospitality is still alive and well. I have seen grace, warmth, strength, humor, imagination, and pride in the people I met along my path. As long as those character traits are honored and respected, the South I so love will never fall. Indeed, it will only rise higher.

When I arrive back in Fort Payne that evening Lookout and Sand mountains never looked better or more inviting. I park the car outside Mother's house and kneel to kiss the ground beneath the towering oaks and pines. Mother hurries out to greet me. She has never looked more beautiful, nor been more welcome in my life. How thankful I am to see the joy and warmth in her eyes. How relieved I am that she will now be able to sleep at night without worrying about me marching to the sea. I wrap my arms around her and hold her as if we've been apart for years.

"I've got dinner cooked for you," she says. "Are you hungry?"

There's no better feeling in the world to a Southerner than sitting at a table with his family after being away for a while and eating what they've raised in their garden. Corn bread, beans, tomatoes, squash, and corn are not merely foods; they're proof again that the earth, where we have laid to rest so many ancestors, gives as well as takes. And for a people so historically bound to the soil, for which the Civil War was rightly or wrongly fought, this is not only crucial but holy. We base our lives upon the lessons we get from the very dirt on which we walk. Our roots go into it as deeply as those of a giant oak. It's in our blood and under our nails; no form of Dixie Denial will get it out. It shows us from childhood on how we, too, erode; freeze; become mud; harden; crack open; get pushed around, spit on, and dug into, as well as offer clear springs, mighty rivers, welcome seeds, blossom with fruits of all kinds and rise up from lowly depths to create mountains as high as the greatest dreams.

When night falls and Mother washes the dishes, I walk with my staff to the garden as I did within minutes of arriving home today. In the moonlight, the corn which was only ankle-high when I began my march to the sea is now over my head. An owl begins to hoot from a tree up on the hill at Tanager as I stroll between the rows of corn and let the long green leaves brush against my face and bare arms like fingers of someone I love. They remind me how Daddy and I once planted corn together and how our Cherokee ancestors praised the earth in the Green Corn Dance, giving thanks for the nourishment of their bodies and souls. Then, as I move on between the moon-lit rows I feel overcome with emotion. And maybe that's all it is, just old-fashioned Southern emotion needing to be released like a song calling out from deep within my heart, but I see Daddy in the corn just like I have several times in my dreams. I step closer to him, to put my arms around him one last time. But before I reach him he raises his hand and points. This time, at last, I see that he is pointing at his chair with the two pipes beneath the pear tree where he so often sat. There sitting in that chair now is myself. I am seeing myself. I am seeing that Daddy lives on in me.

I walk to the chair beneath the pear tree and sit with the staff stretched across my legs in the moonlight. Lightning bugs flicker yellow all across the garden and I still see Daddy there. He looks happy, at peace, and so am I. I am he and he is the corn. We are the South. We are one and the same. The arrow has landed and brought my heart home.

Chapter Forty-six

I awake at dawn the first morning back home from my march to the sea to the coos of doves in the garden. I'm grateful I don't have to hike across Georgia today, but as the journey turned out I wouldn't trade that experience for the whole state. Well, okay, so I might. But I did hesitate there for a moment.

I don't, however, have to hesitate about flying to Seattle to see Debi. Did I tell you her middle name is Anne and that when I feel the most intimate with her I sometimes call her Debi Anne?

Still thinking of Debi, I get out of bed, get dressed, pour a cup of coffee, and hike up the hill to Tanager. Halfway there Clyde calls out, his red head a ball of fire shooting through the green leaves. He's a most welcome friend to see, but so is the tanager up there in the oak over the addition to the cabin. I slice an apple for the bird and place it on the bird feeder I nailed into the oak last year. The tanager is too bashful to fly down and eat the fruit till I leave. That may not seem very brave compared to what some humans risk, but how many of us have flapped our wings from Dixie to the jungles of Guatemala? We all have our callings, don't we?

I enter the cabin and set my empty coffee cup on the mantel where pictures of Grandpa Croft and Grandpa Ellis sit. I'm proud to see that they can at least sit on the same log together, though Grandpa Croft does keep looking out the corner of his Rebel eye at that Alabama Yank, Grandpa Ellis. Road Rabbit sits in the window sill near where I placed my staff when I came up here last night. My old faded trail hat rests atop it. Hitchcock's journal with its photo of General Hitchcock, the gift from Rowena, waits on a nearby shelf along with my journal for anytime I care to explore my march to the sea. The bullet Bud gave me from the Battle of Griswoldville is a souvenir between the legs of Road Rabbit, as if he will gladly tell anyone about it, if he's in the right mood to make music. The autograph of Goat Man on my hat has faded from the Georgia sun, but it's still there. You just have to look closely to see it, like my New Orleans "Mom" said about understanding the moon.

I have to get back down the hill so I won't be late for breakfast. Nita and Logan are joining Mother and me this morning to celebrate my return.

Walking down the hill, I view the great Lookout Mountain to the east. I remember how, on the day I drove toward Atlanta to begin my trek, it reminded me of Martin Luther King, Jr., because he referred to it in his "I Have a Dream" speech.

I have a dream too. I dream that the South that has always nurtured me and brought me back home into its arms will always thrive with Rebels. Indeed, let Rebels all yell with fighting passion against ignorance, hatred, racism, greed, selfishness, self-righteousness, and fear of those we don't easily understand. Let us honor our ancestors by having the courage and dignity to open our doors with grace and kindness through Southern hospitality to all who come to us with warm hearts and open minds. For those who come with icy spirits and narrow thoughts, let's reach out to them with the strength our forefathers showed in battle. But for those who would continue to judge us in a complex world, let us Southerners join hands to kick their asses out of Dixie and all the way to the Gulf of Mexico. No, wait a second. I just heard the Great Goat baa in the distance. I guess he wants us to show more patience than that. Then we can go to kicking.

When I enter home, Nita and Logan are already at the breakfast table. Mother is placing the biscuits there.

"I want the ho-cake," says Logan, who's only three.

"No, it's Jerry's," Nita says. "Because he just got back home."

"No," I say, placing the ho-cake on her plate. "It's time for the next generation to feel special."

"What do you say, Logan?" Nita says.

"It's hot," says Logan, touching the ho-cake.

Nita shakes her head.

"Thank you, Uncle Jerry," Logan says. "Now let's make the circle, Mama."

We hold hands and Logan gives thanks for the food and our being together, as she did on the morning I left for my walk to the sea. Holding my mother's hand, and that of Nita, now I feel that the circle has once again been completed. Life is not only rich, but full—almost. I have only to hold Debi to own the world.

As I soar across America on the jet headed to Seattle I try to guess what Debi hinted at having up her sleeve when I phoned her from Savannah. But that walnut in my skull takes a backseat to my heart and all my senses, aching to wrap around the lover and friend I've longed for for the past six weeks, at times with such passion and urgency I even began, in my most private moments, to wonder if she was but someone I had dreamed up. Have you ever felt such closeness with another? Will you allow me to tell you now that in some ways I've started to feel a bond with you that's so strong it isn't easy for me to let go? You have, after all, marched with me to the sea, and how often do people do a thing like that together? It's hard to tell you good-bye, you know how much trouble I have with that from all I told you about Daddy. So, if it suits you, I'll just say I hope to see you later, somewhere on down that next inevitable road.

When the plane lands and I exit I don't see Debi. I become a bit alarmed that fate might at the last moment play a dirty trick and take her from me. But then I spot her and a thrill rushes through me as if the Great Goat has saved his rarest baa for this very moment. Debi Anne is wearing a lacy dress like one Scarlett wore in *Gone With the Wind*. Wrapping our arms around each other, I feel like if I died right now I'd have the perfect departure. I made it across Georgia, over the abyss of lost love, and back into the life of the person whose very touch makes me feel whole.

"You like the dress?" she says. "I made it for this evening."

"It looks fantastic," I say. "But it's missing one thing."

"What?"

I reach into my pocket, remove Hat Angel, and pin her on the lacy dress over Debi's chest.

"That she may protect your heart and our love just as she looked over me as I marched to the sea," I say.

"I have something for you too," says Debi. "Shall we go see?"

She drives us to downtown Seattle, where she escorts me into one of the city's finest hotels. She then holds up a key and I follow her onto the elevator. It takes us to the top, to the penthouse. She leads me out to the patio overlooking the Puget Sound, where gulls fly and two great ships are arriving. There's a bottle of champagne in ice near the patio ledge.

"I'm dumbfounded," I say. "Shall I open the champagne?"

"In a moment," she says. "First I want to do something I've been dreaming of since I got the early parts of your journal."

"What's that?"

"The way you snuggled with your pack some nights in the tent and imagined we were slow dancing," she says. "I want to do that now."

We ease our arms around each other and begin to dance across the patio over the top of the world. With our bodies so close together, I feel I can sing my song now. My fingers inch down her back to her hips.

"You're not wearing any panties," I say, becoming all the more aroused.

"I'm not?" she says, her moist lips barely brushing mine. "I wonder how I forgot that?"

Her grin is as faint as my fingertips are gentle as they now begin to roll her dress up her thighs.

"No," she whispers. "Not just yet. Let the dance go on just a little longer."

Epilogue

The year after my walk across the great state of Georgia, Rowena threw a party for Debi and me in her Milledgeville mansion. Members of the local historic society came along with other colorful characters, including Flannery O'Connor's niece—in a tizzy over what I had written about her famous aunt's house being in need of repair. Please know that the grand home has since been renovated to its former splendor.

In the years that followed the party, Rowena's childhood boyfriend came courting after the passing of his wife. Rowena overflowed with youthful joy as she told me by phone that they were talking about getting married. Before the wedding could take place, she died of cancer. Her daughter sold the mansion, its memory forever a part of my soul.

The Goat Man died the year before Rowena, and so did my Sand Mountain cousin, Raymond. Bud Merritt has retired and plays bluegrass with his wife, when he isn't searching for Civil War artifacts. The whimsical songwriting Arthur continues to have his bicycles stolen. Little Joe, who climbed a magnolia tree to gather a blossom for me when I spent the night with his family in Eatonton's Brer Rabbit country, graduated from high school this year.

Just as I was once compelled to walk across Georgia, Debi had a calling in 1994 to spend forty days and nights alone in the Great Salt Lake Desert in the heart of winter. She almost died her second night there when a freak blizzard hit. Her book about the ordeal won her a featured guest spot on *Oprah*. We are now married and have traveled to Asia and Europe, where we live six months each year. I continue to write, and we are currently building a three-story chalet on the Alabama land where I grew up. It is the first major step toward building a writer's colony, which will open in 2003.

Don't be a stranger. I welcome your e-letters (tanager@tds.net).

Bibliography

Davis, Burke, *Sherman's March.* New York, Vintage Books, 1980.

Gragg, Rod, *Civil War Quiz and Fact Book.* New York, Harper & Row, 1985.

————, *The Illustrated Confederate Reader.* New York, Harper & Row, 1989.

Howe, M. A. DeWolfe, ed., *Marching with Sherman: The Diaries of Henry Hitchcock.* New Haven, CT, Yale University Press, 1927.

Lawrence, Daisy Gordon, and Shultz, Gladys Denny, *Lady from Savannah: The Life of Juliette Low.* New York, The Girl Scouts of the United States of America, 1988.

Lunt, Dolly Summer, *A Woman's War-Time Journal.* Macon, GA, The J. W. Burke Co., 1927.

Marszalek, John F., *Sherman, a Soldier's Passion for Order.* New York, The Free Press, 1993.

Robertson, James I., *Soldiers Blue & Gray.* Columbia, SC, University of South Carolina Press, 1988.

Articles

Long, Susan, "What Ever Happened to the Goat Man?" *Middle Georgia Magazine, The Peach State Quarterly.* Macon, GA, Vol. 3 (1993), pp. 12–15.

Video Documentary

Southern Creations, *"GOAT MAN": THE LIFE & TIMES OF CHES McCARTNEY.* Zebulon, GA, 1993.